'80629'

A Mengele Experiment

Gene Church

'80629' A Mengele Experiment

International Standard Book Number 0-9644293-2-2
Copyright 1986 Gene Church
Cover Copyright 1996 Route 66 Publishing Ltd.

Printed in participation with the Dallas Memorial Center for Holocaust Studies. Special thanks to Janos Nanasi, assistant to the Executive Director.

Library of Congress CIP Card Number 96-6247 CIP
Church, Gene.
   '80629': a Mengel experiment / Gene Church.
     p.   cm.
   Originally published: Richardson, Tex.: S.K. Damon Pub. Co.,
c 1986.
     ISBN 0-9644293-2-2 (pbk.)
     1. Auchswitz (Poland : Concentration camp) 2. Oran, Jack.
3. Holocaust, Jewish (1939-1945) 4. Human experimentation in
medicine--Poland. 5. Holocaust survivors--Biography. I. Title.
D805.P7C46   1944
940.53' 18' 094386--dc20

Route 66
Publishing, Ltd.

P. O. Box 25222 Albuquerque, New Mexico 87125
800-687-0912   505-268-4478

For...

Pesach, Shaina, Shifra, Miram, Moishe, Henia, Mania Skurnik: innocent victims and loved family members who will never be forgotten.

Also...

Felicity and Katy Church and all the other children of the world who need to know the horrific truth of the Holocaust. With awareness may they grow up in peace and understanding, possessing the strength and wisdom to prevent its ever happening again.

Chapter 1

Yakoff's dark brown eyes were wide open, just as they had been throughout most of the three day ordeal. He laid very still, rocking only slightly as the passenger car leaned one way and then the other. Back and forth, back and forth, for three full days and two sleepless nights. Filled with questioning, wondering, anticipation. Fear was a way of life by now, after what he'd already been through.

The only real noticeable sound was the constant clackety-clack of the wheels directly below him. That, and the subtle murmurings coming from Miriam, his infant niece, as she suckled his older sister's breast. The child's lucky, Yakoff thought. All the food the rest of the family brought with them had been gone for a full day and a half. They tried to conserve the few morsels they were able to grab up as the evacuation began and ration it out to the children, but now it was all gone. And no one aboard had any idea when they might be fed.

Actually no one on board had any idea about anything. Where they were, where they were going, what they'd possibly done to deserve or warrant such inhumane treatment, no ideas at all. There was speculation of course, lots of that. Mostly from the older men as they tried to maintain some degree of order amid the pandemonium and the stark and terrified eyes of the children. It was mostly a calming device to keep minds busy, active, away from the hardships and suffering every passenger on the train had already endured.

Sometimes the women would raise their voices, offering opinions. These were usually ceased with a harsh or stern look. This was neither the time nor place for a woman's viewpoint.

Relocation or resettlement were the phrases most often used; to another ghetto, further away from the front. But the only two things Yakoff and the others knew for sure was that the twenty-car passenger train was heading southwest, away from Warsaw, deeper into the bowels of occupied Poland. And, that the babies were the only ones eating.

1

Exhaustion had overcome nearly everyone and this night the train was quiet. Only the constant clacking of the wheels. It was a droning, rhythmic, metronome effect which couldn't have been less soothing. Each turn of the wheel and each sway of the antiquated cars carried the passengers further away from their homes, further away from loved ones they'd been forced to leave behind. And going where? Towards what final or eventual destination? No one knew. They just rolled blindly into the night.

A low, painfilled guttural scream eased its way under the door of their compartment. Yakoff raised up his head and looked towards the door but it was impossible to tell from where the sound was coming. Perhaps another compartment, perhaps someone sitting outside the door in the aisle. The train was jammed with bodies. There were people everywhere. It was packed, one solid mass of humanity, so packed that movement was impossible.

The restrooms at the end of each car were stuffed with people clinging desperately to what few belongings they could carry with them in rolled up blankets or satchels. But that mattered little; the bodies were crammed so tightly in the aisles it was impossible to get to the restrooms anyway. Any mobility was completely out of the question. So the people, the passengers, all of them, had to relieve themselves wherever they could. Mostly it was in their own clothing, where they sat trapped by an immovable wall of human flesh.

The stench that grew by the hour in its intensity created an involuntary gag-like effect in peoples' throats. People threw up on the floors and on each other. There was no place to remove the dried remains; the passengers had been clearly warned against opening any of the windows. They would be shot they were told, in no uncertain terms, if they even tried.

Eyes that before had only been sullen, deep and mournful, were now also red and swollen from the tears; tears from the filth, stench and tireless persecution. And the wondering, the wondering of where they were being taken ... and why.

When they boarded the train in Mlava, three days ago, Yakoff, being the eldest son, followed his father's example and helped keep the family together so at least they could ride in the same compartment. For a fleeting second it was theirs alone. Then others were shoved without compassion or regard for humanity into the small sitting room until the bodies were mashed and pressed tightly against each other.

2

Unbearable was more appropriate than uncomfortable. But Yakoff and his family, along with the other passengers, had long since learned from the cold and hungry experiences of their recent lives, much could be endured in the pursuit of their very survival. Unpleasantries were commonplace. Humiliation was accepted. Ridicule had become the norm.

When the train jerked away from the station that cold, bleak December morning in 1942, those standing were thrown into the laps of others fortunate enough to have found some small degree of solace in the eight worn velvet seats; four on each side facing each other. The leg room between the seats was filled with a frightened contingency of strangers.

When the slow lurching motion evened out and the train was finally moving smoothly, rearrangements took place in the overly cramped room. The elderly and the women were politely offered seats that had been occupied by some of the earlier arrivals. Yakoff and his younger brother, Moishe climbed up and assumed prone positions in the two overhead luggage racks, one on each side of the compartment. This provided just enough space for the others to sit on the floor. There wasn't enough room to move about, but at least they were sitting.

The scream that had startled Yakoff segued into an uncontrolled series of gut wrenching sobs, one after the other. And no one in the room had any idea what the cause or creation of those sobs might have been. His heart ached, wishing he could help the poor agonized and unseen soul in the distance. But movement was impossible. Perhaps someone nearer could do something.

His eyes moved to the left of the door and settled on his niece, Miriam, while she continued to eat. It wasn't jealousy that consumed Yakoff as he studied the innocent child. Rather, it was concern for what would become of her, a helpless infant. What possibly will become of her?

Shifra, Yakoff's older sister, cradled the child to her breast and noticed the head peeking over the edge of the luggage rack. When their eyes met, Shifra's seemed strangely lost, void, somehow hollow and empty. Hope seemed to have disappeared, as it had in the eyes of so many of the others.

Yakoff forced a small smile at his sister, to comfort, console, tell her with his eyes that everything was going to be all right. But her face remained blank, expressionless. She patted her child gently on the back and lowered her empty eyes toward the floor. Yakoff's heart reached out for her. It had only been a short time ago that her husband was killed at the Russian front while trying to escape to freedom. Now Shifra was a twenty-year-old widow with an infant. But the country was in turmoil and the young lady with the empty eyes was far from alone.

To her left sat Pesach, Yakoff's father, and Shaina, his mother. The boy held a deep respect and affection for his parents. They were decent, caring, hard working people who had struggled to raise six children in an atmosphere and a time that was incredibly trying, even for the strongest willed.

There was unity in their family, a harmony created by standards, morals, and a lifetime of religious ethics, embellished with the simplicity of the basic desire to exist. Yakoff enjoyed and even loved their closeness. The family unit was the central and focal point of life itself, just as it had been for generations. And without the family and the continuation of it, what would there be?

He pondered that thought as he looked at his parents. Time and circumstance had taken its toll on their appearance and they each looked considerably older than their actual age. But the spark was still there and sometimes the youthfulness would surface, even during the hardest of hardships. They appeared to be asleep but Yakoff had always felt that his father slept with one eye open, watching out for and protecting his family.

Beside them sat his grandparents on his mother's side, Yzchak and Beena. Eight mouths to feed had been burden enough, adding two more when his grandparents were forced to move in with them made the task nearly impossible. But family was family and sacrifices were made. The soup just got a little thinner and the floor a little more crowded and they survived as a family, with love, concern, and respect, each for the other.

Miriam, Yakoff's younger sister, sat on the floor with her head resting on her mother's knee. He watched as the pretty young face turned slowly from side to side, as if she were shaking her head "no." In the darkness it almost appeared she was moving her mouth. Perhaps a prayer. Perhaps a wish. Perhaps another in an endless series of nightmares.

It seemed fortunate, Yakoff considered, that his two older sisters had firmly decided and then somehow miraculously managed to remain in Warsaw. As bad as it was back then, it was never close to the squalor and degradation the rest of the family was experiencing this night.

In addition to the eight family members, nine counting the infant, there were twelve other people in the compartment. Not all strangers either. Most of them were casual acquaintances from the ghetto. There were twenty-one people crammed inside a compartment designed for eight. Crammed and packed to the point that none of them were able to move. The only occasional exception was when all the bodies would shift, giving one person barely enough room to stand and stretch legs and backs riddled with constant aches, pains and cramps.

Even this minor luxury wasn't afforded to Yakoff and his younger brother Moishe. They remained in the luggage racks for the entire trip. Three days and two nights. Their skin worn raw from the swaying of the car. Painful bleeding sores were opening on their bodies.

Yakoff's ears perked up. He heard something. Something different. At first he couldn't quite put his finger on it but then it came to him. It was the wheels of the train directly below him. They were slowing. In the distance he could also hear the engine as its rhythmic chugging pattern diminished in both volume and speed.

The blackness of the night carefully disguised the river Przemsza they'd just crossed as well as the small wooden sign at the train station announcing the sleepy little town they were passing through.

Yakoff leaned cautiously over the rail. "Father," he whispered.

The man didn't open his eyes. "I know son," he said. Then he nodded twice and squeezed his wife closer to his side. He looked at the boy in the luggage rack..."It's just another stop. That's all ."

The boy looked out the soot-covered window. The darkness and nothingness spread into infinity. He'd felt this same burning anxiety on each prior occasion when the train stopped to take on water for the engine. Each time his anticipation magnified. Each time the fear of the unknown deepened. It was past logical and conscious thought, past the festering sores on his bones as he shifted unsuccessfully, trying to find a comfortable position. This time the anxiety and fear bore deep into his soul.

As the slowing became more obvious and noticeable, other passengers in the compartment started to stir. There was a low, hushed murmuring that began to encompass the entire room. Yakoff's anticipation was shared. It permeated their co-habitated enclosure, their prison; the one with the velvet covered seats and intricately carved oak paneling on the walls.

People twisted, craning their necks to see out the window but there was nothing to see. Only vast, empty blackness. The murmuring became a babble. Its intensity grew in volume in diametric proportion to the train's decreasing speed. The baby started to cry.

5

Slower, slower, the train jerked to a violent stop, sliding people across the floor. Shifra held her daughter closer to her body, rocking slightly. The baby stopped. Then all noise stopped. The compartment was silent. Deadly silent. So was the entire train. But just for a second.

"Raus!! Raus!!"

The silence was shattered by deep-throated Germans screaming in their native tongue for the passengers to get off the train.

There was a moment of disbelief which completely erased the three long days filled with concern and anticipation. This feeling was instantly followed by a sense of relief, a heavy sigh. They were finally going to get off the train.

"Raus!! Raus!!"

Yakoff looked out the window and still couldn't see anything, only some indistinguishable shadows moving about in the darkness. The car began to rock to and fro from the sudden surge of people, all moving, trying to exit the train at once. The screaming outside continued as the passengers in Yakoff's compartment struggled to get to their feet. Bundles of what few precious belongings they'd been able to bring with them were clutched tightly to their sides. All order was lost.

The aisle outside the sliding door was jammed as more than a hundred people tried to inch their way forward. They were pressed, body to body. It was a fight for freedom, fresh air, movement of any kind. And certainly there must be food and water waiting. Certainly. The fact that no one still had any idea of where they might be had little import at this moment. Release from this damnable moving prison was the only concern. Nothing outside could possibly be worse than the filth, stench, and hunger of this hellhole.

Voices in the night continued to scream for the passengers to move faster, faster. There was a slight break in the moving human chain and several people from Yakoff's compartment slipped into the aisle and were swept out of sight. People were trying to keep families together in the mad rush for the doors. Children were crying as they were pushed and pulled along by the mass. Mothers and older sisters tried unsuccessfully to comfort or console. Older people fell down and were helped back up by the younger strong ones.

Yakoff could still hear the sobbing that had begun earlier and now seemed like an eternity ago. It was getting louder, coming closer. Then he understood the grief and agony creating the sobbing. An elderly man with a long grey beard was carried down the aisle by two boys about Yakoff's age. The man had died during the night. He was murdered, strangled by the lethal hands of the train and the trip. The sobbing widow followed behind, clutching his hat to her breast.

Yakoff and Moishe climbed down from the luggage racks as their father tried to shield and cover Shifra's eyes from the corpse. There was an unspoken yet understood communication among the family as they grabbed up their few belongings and stood, waiting for a chance to exit the compartment. Yakoff helped his grandparents to their feet and gave both a brave smile which was unreturned. Perhaps they knew differently.

The screaming outside the train increased in its pace and intensity as the family moved into the aisle and among the sea of people. They were all huddled together as if for some slight degree of protection, shuffling towards the fresh, cool, night air, slowly filtering its way in their direction. There were voices in the crowd and others from outside. The talk was of food and of water. There were voices down the aisle, behind him and out of sight, whispering about people who died during the trip. There were muffled cries of "What will become of us?" but it didn't register as a question. It was an unanswered statement of resolution. A resolve from the elderly, those who had lived through the persecution the longest, that their fate would be no better than the existence they'd known since the unholy ghettos were formed and the walls of imprisonment constructed.

Now they reached the door of the train and a huge bank of floodlights flashed in their eyes. The lights were blinding and everyone instinctively tried to cover their eyes while still desperately clinging to a loved one. The screaming in German continued until the last person was herded off the train with violent pushes and shoves. Yakoff's eyes slowly adjusted to the light. He looked around. The screaming voices belonged to uniformed SS men carrying carbines which were trained on them.

They were everywhere. They formed a solid line facing all the departing passengers. They stood on the roof of the train looking down. They were in the doorways of the railcars to prevent anyone from reentering. Several of them had vicious German Shepherds at their sides, growling incessantly, foam drooling from their mouths, snapping their sharp, dirty, yellow teeth at any passenger who dared venture either too near them or too far away from the area they were ordered to occupy.

It seemed that the train had stopped in the middle of nowhere. It wasn't a rail-siding, they were standing on dirt which was pressed hard and flat by countless others before them. No one noticed that the dirt had more of a dark red hue than the expected murky brown. Their thoughts and primary concerns were centered on staying in their designated place, behind a two-inch white line painted on the ground, and away from the eager, snarling dogs.

Yakoff looked down the long line of railcars. Thousands of people were huddled together, fearful of what the night would bring. They were individually alone even though surrounded by a swelling mass of their peers, their friends, their families; and all breathing fresh air for the first time in three full days.

But there was something different and unusual about the night air filtering its way through Yakoff's nostrils and into his lungs. An aroma he'd never before experienced. He whispered to others around him but no one else could define it either. The night was cold and Yakoff tugged at his collar to protect himself from the chill. Then he put his arm around his younger sister to help shield her from the biting December wind. But the wind carried that odd aroma, a pungent smell hanging in the air all around them. It wouldn't go away. Although the smell was tolerable it carried a psychological sickness, an unexplainable feeling that settled hard in his throat, stomach and heart.

The throng milled about anxiously. They were mostly quiet. Every eye was wide open, watching, wondering. A few pushed their way through the crowd, looking for family members who were lost during the rush and chaos. Names were desperately whispered in hushed tones, assistance was provided whenever possible. For the most part however, the majority of the three-thousand-plus people remained remarkably calm. It was a passive resistance, honed and fine-tuned for more than 2,000 years. To some it was a dull acceptance of their fate. To the Nazis it was amusing.

The SS troops, brandishing rifles, began to move toward the sea of frightened people, screaming, "All men between the ages of 18 and 40 step to the left side of the line. All others move to the right."

Many in the crowd who didn't understand German shuffled aimlessly, wondering what the command meant. Others who did, hesitated. Yakoff, his arm still around his sister's shoulder, reached out and took his mother's hand. He was familiar with the SS. He'd lived under their rule for more than three years in various controlled and grief-stricken ghettos.

Now, for the first time, the SS troops were joined by several members of Hitler's feared Gestapo. Their ominous and ruthless presence was instantly recognizable by the long, black leather coats they always seemed to be wearing. Compared to the Gestapo and their history of grotesque brutality, the snarling, growling German Shepherds seemed like harmless, docile puppies. When these men spoke, the sounds rolled from their lips in evil hisses. Their rank and status within Hitler's war machine gave them the unquestioned and unchallenged power of life and death over anyone.

The command for separation was repeated; this time louder, more forceful, more violent. People were hesitant and held on dearly to loved ones. The overriding thought and feeling was togetherness. That's all any of them wanted, to stay together. A few started slowly to cross the line to their newly assigned positions. Most held back, huddled closely with family members, silently praying for some miracle of God they'd be overlooked.

But the Germans were experienced in what they were doing. They were thorough and explicit in movement and mentality, no one would be overlooked. No one was ever overlooked. They were careful about that.

Soldiers moved swiftly into the crowd and forcefully pulled clinging couples apart, violently pushing the women to the other side of the line. The children and infants were pulled along. The elderly, sensing the futility of resistance, lowered their eyes to the ground and slowly followed, occasionally with the unnecessary assistance of a rifle butt in the small of their backs.

Crying and sobbing filled the night as families were separated by the starched, polished soldiers. People were viciously and callously ripped away from a last embrace with loved ones. It was an agonizing wail from the mouths and hearts of innocent victims, a cry that had sounded throughout all human history, reaching to the clouds above and hanging there for the world to hear. But no one heard.

Down the row a woman was pulled away from her husband and pushed to the other side. The man's eyes widened and his nostrils flared. He took two quick steps to retrieve his wife and was met in the face by the butt of an SS rifle. Yakoff was close enough to see. Blood splattered everywhere. The man's knees buckled and he crumpled like a rag doll to the dirt below. The wife let out a horrible scream and tried to reach him but was restrained by soldiers who enjoyed inflicting the pain.

The man's nose was split across his face and blood flowed freely. His eyes were open. He made no movement, other than a slight twitching in his legs. Two children, obviously the man's, gasped and cried in horror. Instinctively they tried to get to the lifeless form but two smiling soldiers grabbed the children and lifted them off the ground by their hair. Several in the crowd took a step forward but were held at bay as twenty cocked rifles were trained on them. The people returned to their assigned positions and watched hopelessly, in disbelief, as two members of the SS dragged the man's body to the women's side of the line and dropped it into a heap. The man's wife and children flung themselves on the body and wept uncontrollably. Through their tears and agony soft prayers were recited by those nearby. But all in vain.

The floodgates of violence had been opened and the Nazis moved more rapidly. Orders were screamed directly into faces which didn't comprehend. Lack of instant adherence to their unquestionable command was met with strict and obscene brutality. There was no favoritism shown. The women, children, and elderly were mistreated with the same hostility as the able-bodied men. People were knocked to the ground, stomped and kicked for moving too slowly. It all seemed mindless, senseless, a living nightmare. And for what possible reason? What had they done? What crimes had they committed?

Seeing the pandemonium and violence moving closer to where they were standing, Shaina, Yakoff's mother, quickly kissed her husband on the lips and started to move the majority of the family forward. Yakoff's hand still tightly held his mother's. He had an unexplained but clear sense of foreboding. He didn't want to let go. And yet he knew he must.

She turned and looked toward her eldest son and their eyes met for a brief and fleeting instant. They were surrounded by a cacophony of sound: screaming, crying, wailing, bustling activity and movement. Still, for this one brief second, the look they shared expressed the love they felt for each other. It was a timeless look, a timeless feeling.

Yakoff slowly let his mother's hand slip from his own. He stood beside his father and watched as his family moved to the other side of the line...his mother, his older and younger sisters, his grandfather and grandmother, his infant niece, and his younger brother, Moishe, who was too small to pass for eighteen.

Yakoff felt his father's hand on his shoulder. There was a gentle squeeze, transmitting the message, "Be strong." He looked into his father's learned and experienced eyes and for the first time in his life saw tears.

The separation process was completed quickly and efficiently. The uniformed SS with their rifles, dogs, and Gestapo, had meticulously seen to that. The passengers were ordered to leave everything they were carrying on the ground. There was no explanation as to when or how their few belongings would be returned. And there was still no explanation as to where they were.

The mid-December chill returned to Yakoff's bones. It was a damp, clammy cold which cut through his thin wool jacket and stayed there. His eyes adjusted to the glaring floodlights trained down on the new arrivals and for the first time, if he squinted, he could see beyond them. What he saw, running in either direction into the darkness, was a high, barbed wire fence. The sighting had little effect. Recent times had given him cause to grow familiar with high barbed wire fences. He was also used to living within them.

The line of men began to move down the train, shuffling slowly, little talk or conversation, only eyes riveted towards the women, children, and elderly who waited and in return watched helplessly as their men were marched away.

Yakoff heard a rumbling in the night air. Far off at first, then growing in volume, coming towards them from their right. Lights accompanied the rumbling which now shook the very ground on which they stood. He saw headlights. A huge convoy of black German transport trucks. The hated red swastikas were boldly displayed on both doors of each vehicle.

The trucks roared to a deafening halt directly across from the train and the lights and engines were left running. SS men, positioned every ten feet between the arrivals, began to shout crudely for the women to move toward the trucks. Movement was slow at first as the women tried to help the elderly and frail but the pace was quickened as the soldiers pressed forward, pushing, shoving, hitting, striking no one in particular. Just a race in general.

The rear gates of the trucks were slammed open and more SS men appeared. They violently herded the women and others into the trucks until they were packed as tightly as they were on the train. There was no humanity shown or assistance offered. Only brutality and incessant abuse. The men were forced to watch helplessly as their wives, children, and parents were denigrated and abused before their very eyes.

Finally one man screamed "Stop it!" and started to cross the line. A machine gun burst into the air halting him in his tracks. People ducked and cowered. Now it was very quiet, only the crying and the moaning.

A boy, no older than Yakoff, seeing his mother slapped in the face and pushed to the ground, began to run toward her. An SS man turned and holding the barrel of his rifle like a baseball bat, swung with all his might. The stock of the weapon hit the boy squarely in the knees and instantly broke them both. An agonizing scream filled the air but the noise subsided as several SS men, with the heels of their highly polished black boots, stomped the boy's face and head until they were flat with the ground. Those standing nearby heard the boy's skull as it cracked: an egg pulverized by a pile driver.

Yakoff watched as his mother and family were forcibly pushed into the rear of one of the huge black beasts. There was no good-bye wave, no shouts proclaiming "Long live Poland", only a last, hurting, painfilled glimpse of the woman who meant so much to him. When would he see her again, or be with her? There were no answers or explanations, only questions.

The powerful engines were revved up and the grinding of gears followed. Then the coarse and ugly military vehicles slowly pulled forward, away from the remaining men, and toward a destination known only by the smiling SS troops.

Yakoff watched, blinking back tears, until the trucks were out of sight. His heart pounded with grief and frustration. Adrenaline surged through his body as if a giant unseen faucet had been opened. There was disgust, and a hate that permeated his soul, a rage burning inside that Yakoff's had never before experienced. But the grief, hate and rage had to be muffled, contained, controlled. It had to be held inside and never shown. He had seen firsthand that the slightest display of resistance was instantly translated into suicide, death, extermination.

The line of men continued to shuffle along, constantly aware and forcefully reminded of the ever present, armed SS guards. There were two tables at the front of the line with more uniformed soldiers sitting behind them filling out forms. The questions were the same for everyone. "Age?" and "Occupation?"

Yakoff's father leaned forward and whispered, "Say you're a gardener".

"Age!" the SS officer blurted.

"Eighteen."

Yakoff tried to disguise the emotion which filled and tugged at his vocal cords. The SS man raised his eyes and shot the boy an evil smile. Then he looked back down, making a notation on his form.

"Occupation!"

"Gardener."

"Pass."

Yakoff walked away from the table and joined the line ahead as it marched away from the train, into the darkness. He could hear his father's voice behind him..."Forty... gardener..." and then Pesach caught up. They walked without speaking, each trying silently to console the other.

12

There were five, maybe six hundred men in the silent march, bordered on each side by heavily armed SS troops who jeered and taunted. The soldiers laughed, ridiculed, and made fun of their prisoners, hurling insults and slurs, one after the other, over the entire mile and a half they walked that freezing night. The bestial bullies with guns and clubs never tired of their fun.

The wondering didn't cease. The uncertainty about everything now thrust upon them only served to magnify it a hundredfold. Where had the women and their families been taken? Where were they being taken? Where were they? And what would become of them?

No one knew.

Yakoff had chronologically become a man five years ago through the teachings and laws of the Jewish religion. He'd been through and experienced much since the Germans invaded his native Poland in September of '39. Even so, he remained a youngster in his parents' eyes. But tonight, this cold and dreary December night that was never to be forgotten, an eighteen year old boy got off a train and was forced to become a man; a man in body, mind, spirit and heart.

He raised his eyes along with the others and looked straight ahead. They were moving toward a two-story, red brick structure with a large opening on the ground floor. The opening was sealed with a swinging gate made from thick mesh wire.

As the column of men drew nearer, more armed SS troops came out of the structure and slowly pushed the heavy wire gates open. It was impossible for Yakoff and the others to know or even begin to comprehend that as they walked through the red brick archway they were actually entering the gates of hell.

Chapter II

Again Yakoff noticed the strange aroma in the air. It wasn't that the smell had gone away or even temporarily subsided. He'd just managed to put it out of his mind for a moment or two. Now it was back, just as before. A sickly, fatty smell. Cooking. He looked well ahead and a little to his right. Perhaps a thousand yards away, he could see a flickering reddish glow, dancing against the black sky. His thoughts understandably returned to food. It'd been a long time since he'd eaten anything. But who, he asked himself, would be roasting great quantities of meat at this hour? It must have been near midnight.

The road they silently walked was unpaved. The temperature was flirting with the freezing mark but hadn't quite arrived. So they walked through mud, a quagmire which viciously grabbed hold of your foot each time you put it down. Each step became more difficult than the last. The thick slimy goo engulfed and consumed every single threadbare shoe. Toes became numb. Calves and thighs ached from the strain. Just ahead, a man's shoe became stuck and came off his foot. He stopped, bent down to pick it up and was instantly hit in the back by the barrels of two SS rifles. Then the Nazis laughed as they ground his gasping, choking face into the mud with their boots. After awhile the man slowly stood up and continued the walk with one bare foot.

There were barbed wire fences on either side of the road, eight feet high and supported by thick steel posts every ten feet. It was impossible for Yakoff to be sure, but it sounded like the wires were emitting a low dull hum of some sort. Again, no explanation, just the tireless and constant struggle with the mud below.

Covered lights flickering from the tops of every fourth pole illuminated countless drab buildings as far as the eye could see. Even with the illumination, the surroundings and the place seemed to be without color. A low grey mist hung in the air, covering everything, distorting perspective.

14

It's another ghetto, was Yakoff's first thought as his eyes began slowly to readjust to his new surroundings. Increased and massive security to be sure, but another ghetto nonetheless. Then a secondary thought. It's a forced labor camp. He'd heard rumors about those in hushed conversations on the street but he had never talked with anyone who'd actually been to one.

Surprisingly enough, both thoughts carried with them a degree of hope. If in fact they had been transported to a different ghetto or a labor camp, there remained the glimmer of a possibility that the families would somehow be reunited. That was the unspoken but overriding thought, wish, and prayer as they plodded through the mud, step by agonizing step.

The SS man in the lead stopped and pointed to the right with his rifle. The weary and beleaguered column obediently followed his directions and turned off the main road, onto one much smaller. Its condition was much worse than the last. Now the sticky mud came up to and sometimes even over their nearly frozen ankles.

Movement became increasingly difficult as they walked through another gate, this one steel and twelve feet high. Again Yakoff was aware of the low humming sound in the air. Hungry, bone-tired, afraid, concerned for his family. Little if any conscious thought had been given to the size or immensity of the enclosure they'd just entered. No one had paid any attention to the fact they'd just walked nearly five hundred yards down the main road before turning to their left and onto the smaller one.

Once again the barbed wire fences rose up on both sides and buildings faded into the far reaching distance. They walked another grueling hundred yards, struggling every step of the way, fighting to keep moving and avoid the inevitable blows which rained down unmercifully on those who fell behind.

A turn to the right, through another tall steel gate, toward a one-story red brick building. Shelter at last, warmth, a place to finally sleep.

The SS remained outside as the men filed into the long narrow building with whitewashed walls. Once inside there was no sight of any uniformed soldiers and the new arrivals felt they could finally relax.

They were wrong.

The room was filled with men whose faces exhibited the same hardened look as their own, a direct, painful result of the rigors of a war being fought in their own backyard. But these men were noticeably different. Their hair was cut abnormally short and they wore uniforms, coats with black and dark blue stripes and matching pants. Several were remarkably thin and their eyes overflowed with rage and anger.

One of the men in Yakoff's group stepped timidly forward and opened his mouth as if to ask a question. Before a sound was heard he was struck full in the face with a whip. The impact knocked him to his knees, took his breath away and opened several instant, bleeding welts. Stricken with terror he looked up at the uniformed tormentor and wisely chose to keep the question to himself. The others in the group stared in disbelief. Those across from them, wearing the tattered, misfitting uniforms, smiled sadistically.

"Been here two minutes and already you want to ask questions." The man with the whip was large, burly. He had a scar, an evil looking and unhealed gash running the entire width of his forehead. The man kneeling was pleading with his eyes for mercy but the larger one kicked him in the chest knocking him over backwards and into a limp, unconscious heap.

"Any more questions?!"

There weren't. Only more stunned silence.

The rest of the uniformed men quickly joined their apparent leader in screaming at the new arrivals at the top of their voices. First they were ordered to strip naked. Those who hesitated in the slightest were savagely beaten by those doing the yelling. There was chaos, pandemonium as five or six-hundred men tried to rip off their clothing at the same time. People tangled and fell to the floor as they tried to hurry.

"Faster!! Faster!!"

Some wearing stripes carried sticks or clubs three feet long, one inch in diameter, made from wood and used to smash innocent, unsuspecting victims across their backs as they tried to untie mud-caked shoes.

In moments the task was completed. Hundreds of men stood naked, bruises and welts beginning to raise on winter- white skin. Several were bleeding from fresh, newly opened wounds. Fear overrode any semblance of embarrassment.

Clothing and shoes were collected and thrown into large vats for decontamination. Then they were forced under ice- cold showers which did little to take the sting from their chilled-to-the-marrow bones. The momentary dousing could have been refreshing after the ordeal of the train; but the continued yelling, screaming and hitting placed that concept well beyond reach.

As they exited the shower area the men were individually dipped into a foul smelling bluish-green fluid. Its purpose was to eliminate any lice or other crawling insects which may have been lingering or festering on their tired and exhausted bodies.

Then, while they stood dripping and shivering following the delousing, the barbers took over. Yakoff watched helplessly as his long black hair fell quickly to the cold dirt floor. Each man in turn was shorn to grotesqueness. Resistance was instantly met with ruthless, savage cruelty.

Long lines were formed and the men filed past tables where new clothing was issued: uniforms with blue and black stripes. With no regard to shape or size, they each received a shirt, a pair of trousers, a garment referred to as an overcoat, actually nothing more than another threadbare knee length shirt, a woolen cap and a pair of wooden clogs. No socks, no underwear. The new clothing emitted a musty, foul smell and had a well-worn feeling. One of the men's shirts had a bullet hole with accompanying powder burns in the center of its back. He quickly put it on without complaining or calling its attention to the men with the sticks.

Up ahead, Yakoff noticed a group of tables holding several sewing machines. The men moved forward, quickly, silently. Speech or talk for any reason was forbidden. Only their tormentors were allowed the luxury of conversation. And how they reveled in that privilege. Yakoff overheard bits and smatterings while the line shuffled forward, gleaning that they had been taken to a forced labor camp. One of the men with brown teeth and sunken eyes mentioned to another, "These newcomers got it easy compared to what it was like when I got here."

This information, whether real or imagined, caused little comfort, only more concern and questioning.

Labor camp, Yakoff thought. Labor camp. Hard, grueling work for the duration but at least they'll all be alive when the war's over, no matter who wins. At this moment, that was the very least of his concerns. He wanted to keep his mind busy, occupied, off of and away from the horribleness of his surroundings and all he'd just witnessed.

Thoughts drifted to his mother and the rest of the family and how they'd all be together again soon. He sensed the difficulty they'd face but they'd made it this far, hadn't they? He tried to force the train ride from his mind. They'd survived that, hadn't they?

More people were screaming for the line to move faster. New arrivals were struck with the sticks without rhyme or reason. Strangely and sickly enough, the tormentors enjoyed it. They took pride in their elevated status as well as absolute position of authority.

But aren't they the same as us, Yakoff asked himself. They're wearing the same uniforms, we all have the same hideous haircuts. He pursed his lips and shook his head slightly so as to not draw attention. When he lifted his questioning eyes to the heavens, he noticed the rafters of the building. There were slogans, block lettered in German, on nearly every one of the wooden beams

The youngster had been blessed with a good ear and the innate ability to pick up languages quickly and easily. He was already fluent in Hebrew, Yiddish, Polish and German. The last, being learned out of necessity in the ghetto.

The slogans were short, quick, to the point. His eyes passed from beam to beam...

"Respect your superiors..."

"Be clean..."

"One louse-your death..."

"Be hard-working and obedient..."

"The block is your home."

He scarcely had time to offer any conscious thought to the bearing or significance that these words would have on his life when he heard a painfilled scream up ahead.

A body slumped backwards to the floor and several clogged feet were fiercely and liberally applied to his stomach and sides. The poor man tried to protect himself but it was a hopeless endeavor. No one standing nearby offered any resistance. They watched, relieved for the most part it wasn't themselves on the floor. Slowly, spitting blood, he returned to his feet and whatever they were doing up there went on like nothing had happened.

The line moved forward until Yakoff, with his father still behind him, reached a row of desks. Men, wearing stripes and seated, were asking questions, filling out forms.

"Name? Age? Occupation? Last address? Birthplace?"

"Sierpc, Poland," Yakoff answered.

The man looked up cautiously, slowly shifting his eyes from side to side, checking silently to see if they were being watched.

"I'm from just outside Sierpc," the man whispered. "How many others are there?" The questioning voice was unlike the rest with their incessant screaming. It quietly and subtly offered a degree of concern, perhaps even compassion.

"We all came from Stregova," Yakoff whispered back. "The ghetto..."

"I know," he said, returning to his form.

Yakoff leaned closer across the desk, being careful not to touch it. He followed the stranger's lead and also glanced cautiously from side to side. He swallowed hard before he could get out the question. "Where are the women? Our families?"

The man straightened up and then twisted uncomfortably. His eyes avoided Yakoff's and his face contorted to a blank, empty stare. It had a void, a hollowness the boy had never seen before. He nodded his head slightly, two times, in a direction which seemed to indicate outside, towards the northwest.

Yakoff blinked, not understanding the man's subtle signal. The only reflection or remembrance from that direction was the flickering reddish glow dancing in the night sky.

"Move!! Move!!"

A bear-like paw grabbed his shoulder, pushing him toward the next station. He'd seen what was coming out of the comer of his eye and shifted quickly, trying to avoid it, thinking for a second he might magically become invisible and avoid the inevitable.

The needles were long and awesome, lying in a pile on the table, unsterilized and wielded by gruesome, brutal looking men with filthy hands and dirt caked beneath their fingernails. And God, it was strange how they too enjoyed what they were doing.

"Left arm. Sleeve up."

It was a command, not a request, and certainly not a question.

Yakoff raised his left sleeve, the man snatched him by the wrist. Then he turned around and picked at random one of the needles from the pile, dipped its tip into a black stagnant liquid, and with no expression jammed the instrument deep into Yakoff's forearm.

The pain burned, a blanketing sensation that covered his body and shot to the brain. It was an uncontrollable response, certainly not pre-meditated, as he jerked his arm away from the man's harsh grasp.

He didn't see the clenched fist as it hurtled toward his face. Only the shock from the impact as the knuckles squarely met his mouth, cutting open the insides of both lips, loosening his teeth, driving him backwards to the floor. Wooden shoes found their way to his sides and chest. He shook his head, removing the cobwebs of confusion and quickly jumped to his feet.

"Left arm. Sleeve up."

The command was exactly the same as before. The man with the needle felt nothing for Yakoff's position or pain. He was doing his job. That's all.

As Yakoff faced his tormentor, he could feel blood trickling down the inside of his throat. The warm sensation when he swallowed actually felt good. With his tongue he could feel his four front teeth, barely there, hanging by sensitive and exposed nerves. He fought back tears of pain and offered his left arm to the prisoner holding the needle. The process was agonizing but there was no alternative. Time after time after time the needle was dipped into the ink and brutally jabbed into his arm. Dip, jab. Dip, jab. Dip, jab. Slowly, methodically, over and over until it was done; excruciating minutes, seeming like hours. There were twenty others simultaneously experiencing the same ordeal.

When finished there was blood dripping from his arm. The pain that lingered wasn't nearly as bad as the pain during. What sort of animals would do this to another human being, Yakoff silently questioned. Still no answers. Still no explanations. He was herded with the others toward the next station, the one with the humming sewing machines.

He looked at the raw, bleeding skin for the first time. Marked, branded, tattooed with a permanent identification number that would never come off, never go away. Yakoff's left forearm now read "80629". His father, the next in line, was similarly marked with 80630. They were also branded with a triangle underneath the number, the point facing downward, a sign for the world to see that they were Jews, now and forever.

Shirts were handed to the men at the sewing machines and the numbers on their arms were duplicated above each left breast pocket.

A whispering murmur, slow, steady, began to spread among the new arrivals. Yakoff didn't understand what they were talking about but it had something to do with gas, or a gas chamber, or burning of some sort.

"Achtung!! Achtung!!"

The door suddenly burst open and a man was screaming at the top of his voice. People in the room snapped to attention and the others, the ones with fresh tattoos, confused and disoriented, tried to follow their example. Those not immediately conforming to the unusual standards of this bizarre society were hurried along with blows from the heavy-handed, well-used whips and sticks.

An SS man, tall, erect, impeccably outfitted, marched confidently into the barrack. "Caps off," the men wielding the sticks shouted. Those within striking distance who didn't instantly respond learned a painful lesson, one which would long be remembered. Caps were always removed in the presence of an SS man.

The Nazi eyed the fresh arrivals like so much meat, creating an unusual but absolute feeling of insignificance. A cowering sensation filled the room and hung there, an impending dark cloud, ominous. His tone was strong, forceful. The words were short, finite, clipped off at the ends like tails from unsuspecting dogs.

"This is Birkenau," he said. As if he were speaking to no one, like the room was empty except for himself. "You are prisoners in a concentration camp. Escape is impossible. Death is inevitable. Every SS recruit that you see is your commander."

Yakoff had heard the harsh, vile words before but truly didn't understand them. He was confused, frightened, tired, emotionally racked with pain, misery, frustration. There are so many of us wearing striped uniforms and only one of him. How is this possible? Why are the other prisoners on his side, treating us this way? Aren't they with us, one of us, condemned just as we are?

The SS man approached the new arrivals being cautious and careful against coming too close. "You. You. You," he said, pointing at different men. He selected twenty and ordered them to follow him. Pesach, Yakoff's father was among the selectees as well as an uncle. The youngster moved unobtrusively through the shell-shocked crowd until he reached his cousin Leon's side. Together they watched, silently, helplessly, as both of their fathers followed the Nazi.

The two boys, Leon's younger brother Nathan, and Shaya, another cousin, were positioned near the rear of the group. Yakoff checked again for safety's sake and leaned towards a man seated behind a sewing machine. "Where are they taking them?" he whispered.

The man, deep in concentration, didn't look up. "Sonderkommando", he said quietly.

"What's that?"

And now he did raise his head. The eyes were hollow pits, sunken deeply into his face. Every bone in his skull was glaring, pronounced. "You'll learn soon enough," was all he said. "Soon enough."

Shouts and screams penetrated the quiet of the room. More shoving, pushing and hitting occurred as the men were quickly grouped into lines, five abreast, then marched back outside.

"Silence!! There will be no talking outside the barrack!" The order came from somewhere but it didn't really matter. Commands were hurled from every direction. There were indiscriminate blows from all sides as the men shuffled through the door. A man was knocked to his knees, causing a jam. Others behind helped him up, as they too felt the sharp biting sting of the sticks.

The column was marching west and this time was worse than before. The mud kept gripping the wooden clogs and each step became a struggle. It oozed beneath their feet, between their toes, it was two degrees away from freezing, creating an icy sting that worsened with each strained movement.

The strange aroma lingered in the air, the reddish glow remained in the sky. Hushed murmurs and guarded whispers passed from row to row. Yakoff heard it from a man behind him, but didn't turn to see who it was. "The glow," the man whispered, "in the sky... the Nazis are burning our families." There was a stunned silence. "And the smell," he continued, gagging as he spoke. "The smell is their flesh burning...."

They continued their plodding through the freezing mud. Its stinging sensation, from only a second ago, stopped abruptly. Feelings were twisted instantly, grotesquely into a total numbness of body, mind and spirit. It was a numbness that ripped Yakoff's heart to shreds. Physical pain went away. His feet, back, arm, teeth, nothing. This was a pain of the heart.

At first it was unbelievable, truly impossible to comprehend. No one could do this, Yakoff's logic screamed. No one, not even the Nazis, would ever do such a thing ... no one.

A man beside Yakoff whispered the horrible information to others walking in front. And they trudged through the night and the mud. He tried desperately to disbelieve but within a few steps the reality settled with alarming finality. They were all dead. A sickness squeezed at his stomach and he wanted to throw up. But he knew that he couldn't. He caught the vile, foul liquid as it rose into his mouth and re-swallowed.

Nearly all of the men, including Yakoff's, had just spent nearly a year in a Jewish ghetto in Stregova. None of them were privileged enough to be aware that only two weeks earlier the "Palestine Post" in Jerusalem had carried a front page article condemning the atrocities of the Nazis as they mindlessly carried out Hitler's master plan. "Mass butchery of Poland's Jews" was the headline.

The most ruthless methods are being used in Poland to give effect to the order made by Himmler himself that the whole Jewish population must be exterminated by the end of the year.

Special battalions commanded by SS men seize the victims, including old people and cripples who are taken to cemeteries and shot.

The remainder are loaded into cattle trucks (railroad boxcars) at the rate of 150 to a truck intended for 40. The floor is covered with a thick layer of lime sprinkled with water and the doors of the truck are sealed. Wherever the trains pull up, half the people are dead.

Those surviving are sent to special camps. Once there, the so called 'settlers' are mass murdered. Only the young and relatively strong are left alive, for they provide valuable slave labor for the Germans.

Yakoff thought of his cousins for support or comfort but quickly realized their loss this night had been the same as his own. Complete, total. Then came the equally awesome thought; the same loss was being tragically felt by virtually every single man in the column.

By now the barbaric information had reached the front of the line and the men became still, quiet, only the sloshing of the five-hundred pairs of clogs in the mud could be heard. There was sobbing behind him, to his left, all around. A woman's name was mournfully whispered over and over. More soft anguish could be heard, then the prayers.

Yakoff stared straight ahead for a few steps then looked up into the sky as the flickering red ashes ascended into the low hanging clouds. "On their way to heaven," he whispered quietly. Tears streamed down both cheeks but he refused to allow himself to cry out with agony like so many of the others around him.

This is a time for strength, he mentally repeated. The immense hurt and sorrow had to be pushed down deep inside and kept there, controlled. He was approaching a state of shock, leaning over the very edge; but he couldn't allow that to happen, not if he was going to live, to survive. Don't quit. Don't stop. Don't give up. His mind raced, grasping for any thoughts which might carry him away from the nightmare he'd just entered.

His orthodox training overshadowed all of his thoughts but a burst of fleeting logic, as he tried desperately to escape the atrocity of the moment, callously forewarned and reminded him he would not be allowed to sit shiva, the traditional Jewish seven day period of prayers and mourning for the deceased, for his mother and his family.

I will live, echoed with each fallen tear. I will survive, pounded with every aching heartbeat. Over and over. Like a phonograph record stuck in the same life-supporting groove.

The drab brick barrack was large, a hundred and thirty feet long by thirty feet wide. Outside the front door was a simple black-on-white sign identifying it as barrack number 14. Inside it was barren, stark, row after row of wooden bunks stacked three tiers high and capable of housing a thousand prisoners when jammed body to body, six to a bed. The floor, which was also the sleeping area for the lower tier of bunks, was cold, hard dirt.

The group, still mournfully aghast from their confusion, disorientation, and the tragedy they'd just experienced, assembled inside the building. They were immediately confronted by a man coming from a small room to the left of the door.

"I'm your block senior," he announced. "Every one of your worthless lives is now in my hands." His voice was gruff, gravelly, clearly defining who was in charge. "When you're inside this block, you're responsible to me. Violate the block rules, my rules, and you'll die. I've lost track of the number of people I've killed, so a few of you won't make much difference one way or the other." He let this sink in for a moment. The only sound in the entire room was tears as they splattered on the dirt floor.

The block senior, carrying a whip like the ones they'd seen earlier, turned the group over to his equally malicious assistants who marched the men up and down the narrow rows issuing bunk assignments.

Yakoff was ordered into a middle bunk with five others. The slats were made of thin strips of wood which gave off a damp foul smell of yesterday's urine. There was no mattress or any sign a blanket had ever existed in the small enclosure.

It was a struggle for the six men to force themselves into the limited space at the same time. Their bodies were pressed tightly together, making any movement virtually impossible. The aroma that remained from others before, mixed with the lingering stench from the disinfectant, created a new gagging effect in all their throats.

Just after the men settled into their newly assigned sleeping positions, an announcement was shouted from the center of the room. "The latrines are outside, straight ahead and down the road about a hundred yards. You can't miss it." This was followed by a sick, perverse laugh. "Anyone who wants to, can go now."

Three men crawled wearily out of Yakoff's bunk but he was too tired to move. Tomorrow would be another day. Tomorrow he'd go to the bathroom.

There were muffled prayers being offered in the background. Low, painfilled sobbing could still be heard. Yakoff listened to the agony around him, trying unsuccessfully to escape it. In less than four hours he'd seen brutality and violence unlike any he'd ever witnessed.

He'd been stripped of every meager possession he owned, beaten, shaved, and tattooed with a painful mark that would never go away. He'd been ripped apart from his mother and family and seen their scorched ashes rise from the chimneys to the heavens. He'd been separated from his father and seen him marched away to an unknown, unthinkable eventuality. He was a prisoner in a concentration camp, alone, completely and totally dehumanized, and his world and life would never be the same.

All Yakoff wanted to do at this most horrible moment in his life was sleep, to get away if only for a moment from the agony which burned in his young heart. He closed his eyes and faces flashed before him.

I will live, I will survive. Over and over as he clenched his pain-riddled teeth tightly together. I must sleep. I will survive. I must sleep...

Chapter III

Wind ripped through his hair causing the long woolen scarf wrapped tightly around his neck to stand nearly straight out behind him. The icy chill on his face brought tears to his eyes. They crawled out of the corners and were swept across rosy cheeks. The sun, a blazing golden ball, hung low in the sky, creating a magical wonderland as far as the eye could see. And right now all Yakoff could see was the bottom of the hill and the end of that fabulous ride. His toes and fingers were chilled, nearly frozen, but even that didn't matter. The ride was the only thing.

Yakoff was flying, steering the fastest sled in town, or at least his side of the river. And he loved it. He could hear friends from the neighborhood and classmates screaming encouragement, "Faster! Faster!," as he flew past. The smile of satisfaction was as wide as could ever be expected or imagined.

Yakoff didn't need one of those fancy sleds, the kind you buy in a store with metal rails underneath. He and his friends managed just fine with the ones they constructed themselves. Slats from an old barrel tied together, or a long plank with warped ends, made a perfect toboggan.

He slammed into a large snowdrift at the bottom of the hill and everyone standing around cheered. Then they all laughed. They were each bundled in more layers of clothing than most of them could count, the younger ones looking like round little puffs about to roll away at any given minute. When they played outdoors, especially sledding on the hill, they never noticed the subzero temperature. How could they, bundled up that way? Except of course for their feet; Yakoff's feet never seemed to get warm during the long and harsh winter months.

The only momentary exception to that somewhat freezing absolute was when his father took him and his younger brother Moishe, to the mikvah on Friday afternoons. It was a treat of varied and mixed proportion.

It wasn't so much that Yakoff disliked the public bathing room. After all, it was the warmest place in town. Next, obviously, to his mother's fireplace in their kitchen. The steam and heat from the water did much to relieve the stinging numbness in his feet, a painful reminder of six and a half days of cold.

The mikvah was down the street from Yakoff's house and around the corner, occupying most of the first floor of a fair-sized building. The actual bathing area was in the center of the room and close to fifteen feet square. Steps leading into the water were made of tile, smooth to the touch.

The kind elderly gentleman who ran the bathhouse, which was actually owned by the Jewish community, kept the coals in the fire white-hot and a pot of boiling water was always ready whenever one of the neighborhood men would shout, "More steam." Yakoff liked that.

What he didn't particularly like was bathing in everyone else's dirt. The hot steaming water had a permanent layer of scum floating on the top, impossible to avoid. Even more impossible since this was the only bathhouse on the Jewish side of the river. No one in the neighborhood had any electricity or running water so this was where they all came to bathe. The women were restricted; Friday mornings only. It was open to the men the rest of the time.

The part Yakoff most enjoyed was just after the bath was finished. His father would take a wooden bucket filled with hot water and pour it over the youngster's head, rinsing away soapsuds and scum from the other bathers. It was a clean feeling through and through.

However, the final rinse was the part Moishe liked least. He was far too young, being only six, to appreciate it. He'd cry and shiver and his frail little body would tremble. So Yakoff would hold his little brother still, keeping him from squirming away while his father doused him with the fresh clean water. When the ordeal was finally over, the three would laugh, dry off with thick towels they'd brought with them, and walk back up the hill.

It was like that every Friday during the fall, winter, and spring. The entire family would bathe and then put on their other set of clothing, the good one, and go to the synagogue when the sun went down.

In the rear of the same building as the mikvah, was a small store. Here the chaced, the ritual slaughterer, would cut the throats of all the live poultry. Yakoff found it interesting and amusing to sit outside the shop, particularly on a Friday, and watch the neighborhood women as they lined up holding their chickens, ducks and geese by the neck.

The combined sounds as they clucked their last clucks and honked their last honks in choir-like unison intrigued him. The level and volume of their boisterous output increased as they grew closer to the chaced's knife, like they knew what fate was in store.

But the chaced wasn't a butcher. His only task was to correctly kill the fowl. For the women in the neighborhood to maintain kosher kitchens, the poultry's necks had to be cut in an exacting and very proper way which conformed with the laws of the Jewish religion. Friday was usually the day this ceremony most often occurred so the wives and mothers could prepare special meals for Saturday, the Sabbath.

Just across the street from the mikvah was the community well...

"The well!" Yakoff screamed, remembering. He pulled his sled out of the snowdrift, bid a hasty good-bye to his friends and started to run back up the icy hill. Footing was treacherous. The boys had all been carefully attending to that since the first, much anticipated snowfall.

He slipped, falling several times before reaching the top. Each fall created a chorus of laughter and each time Yakoff joined in the merriment. Through it all he never ceased his persistent scaling of the mighty hill.

It was a good time to grow up; and Sierpc was a good place to grow up in. The neighborhood was friendly and clean, everything you could possibly want or need was close at hand, walking distance obviously, since no one on their side of the river owned a car, a luxury which was punctuated by the fact that there were only two gasoline stations in the entire town.

A little over twelve-thousand people lived there, half Jewish. Even though they constituted fifty percent of the population they were still a much maligned minority. No one was quite sure why and little was ever spoken about it. That's just the way it was. Yakoff often wondered why this was so, but never received any valid or truly understandable answers. In time, he ceased his questioning and viewed the situation with a dull acceptance. One thing he knew for sure was a Jewish person dared never venture across the river and into a gentile neighborhood at night. Never.

For the most part, the town was peaceful. There was little violence or crime to speak of, a quiet village just getting along by itself without any outside intervention. It was fifty-fifty, half Jewish and half Catholic.

After awhile, Yakoff didn't even mind that only the Jews, and not the Catholics, were required to tip their hats, bid a cheerful good-day and step aside whenever they approached a policeman on a public sidewalk. That's just the way it was. They dutifully followed suit to prevent altercations, avoid scorns, eliminate unpleasantries.

The reasons or justifications for the disdain were never clear, never certain. Strange, because the Jewish population provided valuable and critical services to the community. They were the shoemakers, carpenters, tailors, shopkeepers, merchants, businessmen, and landlords. They rented space to gentiles for their own businesses as well as providing places for them to live. Attempts were never made to convert anyone to their own faith.

The Jews were peaceful, maintaining their assigned positions and stations in life, not bothering anyone. They went about their own business and took care of themselves. Their lives were steeped in rich tradition that was adhered to carefully. Tradition along with thousands of years of persecution had been ground into their souls like sand into glass. And none of them really understood why. That's just the way it was.

With his makeshift sled tucked neatly under his arm he dashed past the front of his own synagogue, the one he and his family attended regularly. From here, because of the regularity, it was easy for Yakoff to compute the number of necessary steps as well as the elapsed time, to the exact second, before he was standing at his own front door. He ran past the entrance to the four-story grey apartment building that Mr. Fejkiel owned. Other than the City Hall in the main square, this was the tallest building in town, an architectural wonder. Who on earth would want to live that far off the ground, Yakoff regularly asked himself.

The apartments were mostly occupied by gentiles, the only ones on this side of the river. Their existence and life-style was not much different than the Jewish community which surrounded them. They eeked out a meager living and seldom bothered anyone. The exception to this rule came with the celebration of birthdays and holidays.

Christmas was always the big one. Yakoff would stand in his grand-parents' apartment with his nose pressed flat against the frost covered windowpane, and watch in confused amusement as the Catholics beat the hell out of each other. Their celebrations always included great volumes of vodka, and after much consumption, the men became boisterous. Arguments would ensue over who among them was the strongest and most manly. Following the yelling and screaming, which served as a general call for the neighbors to prepare themselves for the festivities, the challengers would step outside and engage one another in the most knock down, drag out, bloody exchanges imaginable.

It didn't make any sense. None at all. But the fighting was as regular as clockwork, providing dubious entertainment for Yakoff and his friends.

The only other notable service the gentiles provided for the community was manual labor on the Sabbath.

According to the laws of the Jewish faith, no work of any kind can be done on the Holy Day, a time frame which begins on Friday at sundown and continues through Saturday when the sun once again recedes. This twenty-four hour period is set aside purely for prayer and inner contemplation. Nothing else.

As a result, the few local gentiles were hired to fulfill certain and necessary functions such as starting fires and serving meals which were previously prepared. The arrangement was mutually tolerated out of necessity more than anything else. The Jews needed the services and the gentiles needed the money. Other than this wordless encounter one day each week, the two religious factions practiced separatism, leaving each other alone and coexisting in relative harmony.

When he rounded the corner and looked up the small incline to the top of the hill, he could see his building. Even though Yakoff had scarcely ventured outside the city limits, there was always a warm unexplainable glow felt each time he saw his home. A feeling no doubt attributable to the closeness of the family and the affinity he felt towards the place itself. He was born there, as was his brother and all of his sisters.

On the day of each of their births, the older children were scurried out of the room, usually to stay with their grandparents for the duration. A midwife from the neighborhood would visit and boil great quantities of water. Soon, through the thin walls separating the apartments, a baby's first cry could be heard.

When Moishe was born, Yakoff concluded it had something to do with the water. But by the time Miriam arrived, he basked in the smugness of his older and wiser understanding concerning the event.

His grandfather, Yzchak, owned the two-story building. There were eight compact, one-room apartments, four up and four down. The wooden frame had turned a drab grey from years of fighting the harsh elements and losing but it was home, the only home he'd ever known. His entire family lived there. His grandparents as well as an uncle who had ten children of his own. Time spent in solitude was a rarity.

Yakoff climbed the well-used steps and turned down the hallway. When he opened the front door his mother was waiting, holding a wooden pail, her other hand on her hip. A look of scorn and impatience covered her face, but Yakoff's sparkling eyes and beaming smile quickly erased any hint of dissatisfaction. Besides, the boy knew she was only kidding.

After a tender but quick hug she pulled away. "Your cheeks are so cold," she said, laughing. She was a good person, gentle, kind, warm. Her eyes were filled with compassion, understanding, forgiveness.' She gave her love openly and equally to all members of the family and was one of the first community volunteers whenever anything needed to be done.

Yakoff took the pail and teasingly hugged his mother again, making sure to rub his rosy-red cheeks against her own. This time she didn't pull away. Their affection was solid, genuine, cherished by them both.

He'd been on time and knew without a question she was only kidding, a game they often played. The children each had their own chores and responsibilities and the thought of trying to avoid them or cut corners in any way was unthinkable. They were a family and they each did their own part to help.

Yakoff's chores included chopping wood for the fire and providing water for the cooking and washing. Today would take only one trip to the well while on wash days, which were once a week, the trips were countless. The trips, with the combination of chopping more wood to keep the fire blazing, eliminated playing or other childlike activities with his friends.

But that was fine. There was no such thing as forgetting your assigned chores. Nor was there ever any complaint. The chores were done first, then the homework, then playing with friends. It was a lifestyle he'd grown up with and never challenged.

Bounding back outside and into the snow, he petted the family dog waiting by the front door. He was a mangy sort of mutt and would never be mistaken for a house pet. The hair was matted, thick, and he slept under the shelter of the stable roof. Leftovers were nonexistent but somehow the dog, who was never given a name, scavenged for his own food and remained remarkably loyal to the family.

At least the well isn't crowded, Yakoff thought. There were only two people in line. Pleasantries were exchanged along with neighborhood gossip as they lowered their buckets deep into the well then slowly turned the handle, drawing it back to the top, laden with fresh ice-cold water.

The steps that he took climbing back up the hill were carefully chosen. Too many times he'd slipped on the ice and watched his precious cargo wash down the street, only to be retrieved after waiting in line again. Today Yakoff determined that wouldn't happen as the chill in the air was becoming more severe and he longed for the warmth of his fireplace. He looked down at his feet, cautiously avoiding potholes and patches of ice, a smile came to his face.

Soon the ice would be thick enough for his father to replace the wheels of the buggy with rails, converting it to a sleigh. Several times last winter the family had bundled up and gone for wonderfully exciting sleigh rides through the countryside. The moon would shimmer off the deep snow creating a picture-postcard effect. Branches on the trees would bend gracefully toward the earth from the weight of their newly acquired dressing. And the family was together.

A familiar sound diverted Yakoff's attention from the street below. It was a warm, friendly sound, one he always enjoyed hearing; the steady, rhythmic clip-clopping of his father's horse trotting up the hill. As usual, the horse was unattended.

Yakoff's father, among other things, was in the carriage trade. Every day, other than the Sabbath of course, he'd be waiting at the station when the trains arrived at four in the morning and then again at five each afternoon. Seated stately in the driver's seat he'd transport arriving passengers to their downtown destinations or to one of Sierpc's three small hotels.

During the winter months Pesach was also a member of the board which regulated and oversaw the one Hebrew school in town. As such, one of his duties and responsibilities was to make sure enough coal had been rationed and delivered to the janitor to keep the school warm while the classes were in session.

After the five o'clock passengers had been satisfied and their needs attended to, he'd drive across the river to a rented shed, a small enclosure just large enough to protect the buggy from the elements. He'd unharness the horse and push the buggy inside by hand. Every night, the instant the harness was removed, the horse amazingly knew the day's work was finished. He'd turn slowly away from the shed and begin his rhythmic clip-clopping across town, up the hill, and into his stable for the night.

Seeing the horse trotting past him meant Pesach would soon be home. That meant Yakoff's favorite part of the day was drawing near, the part when the entire family was together in their one small room.

His father would ask each of the six children what they'd done today and they, in turn, had to report at least one new thing they'd learned. The children vied for their father's attention. Love and mutual respect was abundant. They were crowded, to be sure, but they were happy.

As the conversation continued, Yakoff's mother and older sisters would set the table and serve the evening meal. During the week their diet consisted of staples: soup, bread and potatoes. On the Sabbath they tried, whenever possible, to have a treat in the form of a small portion of meat or poultry. There was never a feeling of having too much to eat but on the other hand no one left the table hungry.

Then the father would speak, he'd lean back, fold his arms across his broad chest and tell of conversations with his daily passengers. Places they'd been, sights they'd seen, people they'd talked with and knew. It was the most exciting time of the day for Yakoff as well as his only real contact with the outside world. He heard of faraway places filled with wealth and glamour but strangely enough, fostered no desires or ambitions to ever leave the safety and comfort of either his home or his hometown.

This night was different. Pesach entered the room and greeted each of the children with a kiss on the cheek; then a warm embrace for Shaina. The joy that always filled his face when he viewed his family together was strangely contorted. He was clearly troubled, pained by something yet to be explained, noticeable to the point that the children suppressed their recounting of the day's activities, waiting anxiously for their father to speak.

He slowly removed his long warm overcoat and hung it on a hook in the corner. Then he motioned for the family to join him in the living area of the room.

"I've just come from the main square," he said, referring to the one directly across from the City Hall. His voice was low, almost a whisper, filled with concern and uncertainty.

Shaina could feel the apprehension. She spoke quietly, "What is it, Pesach?"

"A report just came over the public radio..."

"Yes..."

The children remained silent.

"One of the European military powers just announced a new leader." Shaina's eyes opened wide. She didn't want to hear the next sentence. She knew what was coming so the news didn't surprise her. It frightened her.

It was January 31st, 1933. Adolf Hitler had just been appointed Chancellor of Germany.

Chapter IV

The shrieking, piercing bell sent shock waves through every available brain cell. It rocked nerves and twisted imaginations back to stark, cold reality. The sound was eerie, harsh, frightening; followed immediately by vile and abrasive screaming.

"On the floor or I'll bash your goddamn face in!" The man yelling smashed the ends of the three-tier bunks with his long sturdy stick. He gave little concern or attention to whether or not he cracked open any unsuspecting human heads in the process. He was a room senior, one of several ruthless assistants to the block senior, responsible for cleanliness and tidiness in his area of the block.

The room senior's first duty of the day was to roust the sleeping, half dead men and get them outside for the morning roll call. Once accomplished, his day was virtually his own. It was a position earned from the Nazis by exhibiting brutality as well as cruel and inhumane treatment to fellow prisoners.

Yakoff's eyes sprang open, uncertain momentarily as to where he was. The room senior's stick smashed dangerously close to his face and he reeled back, now fully awake.

"What do you think this is, a goddamn hotel?" As the man screamed he hit the wooden slats of the bunk. Over and over, harder each time, now trying to make contact with any of the scurrying bodies. The six targets in the bunk frantically avoided the raining blows and miraculously made it to the floor unscathed.

The screaming continued. The veins in the senior's neck protruded in grotesque fashion. He herded the new arrivals in Yakoff's section towards the door they'd entered just hours before; the only door in the building.

There was a mass of striped humanity there, bunched up, all trying to make it through the small opening at the same time. Positions of safety were vied for with much pushing and shoving. This was no time for consideration or cooperation as the other room seniors forced their own men forward, striking viciously at laggards unfortunate enough to bring up the rear of the group.

Outside, the cold early morning air caught Yakoff like a slap in the face. It was pitch-dark and the first deep inhale brought back a vivid reminder of the immoral and unbelievable tragedy of the preceding night. The vision of his mother and the rest of his family being forced into that truck was etched indelibly on the inside of his eyelids and it wouldn't go away. He wanted desperately to believe they were still alive but at the moment felt reservation about any thoughts of a positive nature.

He was still confused, disoriented, frightened beyond his own imagination, more so than the night before. His tongue felt the dried blood in his mouth. His teeth and their exposed nerves began to hurt again. A quick steady blast of agony shot through his cheekbones straight to the brain.

An important occurrence transpired. Obviously the pain had been there since he first woke up, but somehow it had been transferred out of and away from him. Concentration or intense mental involvement lessened the pain to the point of being tolerable. Yakoff didn't understand how it worked, he only knew that it did.

The sharp stinging pain came from the middle of his back, starting at one side and shooting all the way across. It was a burning sensation, like fire. The resounding thud accompanying the agony indicated otherwise. He quickly turned his head to see the room senior drawing back to hit him again.

Yakoff silently pleaded "What?" with his face and his hands. "What have I done? What do you want?"

The room senior pointed to the other men filing out of the block, indicating with his stick for Yakoff to follow. Timidly and painfully the youngster backed away from the scowling man waving the club.

Pain, inflicted from several sources and for little reason, weighed heavily on the intimidation he felt. It was another stage in a carefully orchestrated paranoia. It created mistrust, separatism, withdrawal into the deepest abysmic fathoms of the mind.

The new arrivals, unfamiliar with the early morning ritual, were pushed, shoved, kicked and beaten until necessity joined them with the others in forming neat rows of ten. The rows were designed to simplify the count taken by the block senior and recounted and confirmed by an SS man.

There was a great shuffling of feet as the prisoners jockeyed for position, trying to execute the straight lines. The newer men, unaware of the proceedings, were quickly ushered to the front of the line and occupied most of the positions on the outside perimeter of the group. And why not? No one mentioned anything to the contrary.

It was much too dark to see anything but Yakoff could hear positioning and shuffling like their own occurring from various surrounding blocks. He could hear dull, ominous thuds from sticks brutally applied to human flesh. The sound of inflicted pain rang in his ears like a cracked and dissonant bell, out of tune, not right. Not right at all.

Thoughts turned to his father, leaving unanswered questions about where he might be and the more disturbing and unnerving question about his very life. Was he still in the camp? Was he still alive? Was there a remote possibility of ever seeing him again? And of course there was no one able or willing to provide answers or information about anything. Only the silence reflected by dull, tired, frightened eyes.

A small contingent in the rear of the column was hand-selected and sent back inside the block. Probably special privileges, Yakoff thought. Probably going back to sleep. He longed to be one of the chosen few without any real knowledge of their mission. After a moment or two there was an unfamiliar sound coming from behind him.

He dared not turn around, keeping his eyes glued straight ahead, ever watchful for the men with the sticks. His ears told him the special, privileged squad just chosen, was dragging something out of the block and stacking whatever it was to the right of the door. There was a lifeless thump as each whatever was removed.

Yakoff had been forced to the end of his row by other prisoners who went through this ordeal on a daily basis. He stood at attention trying not to bother or disturb anyone. It was impossible to arrive at an accurate count but he could loosely calculate from the rows of ten that his block held nearly a thousand prisoners.

His imagination raced, wondering how many similar blocks were in this place. How many fellow human beings were being violated and incredibly abused? His temples pounded, and for a quick and fleeting second, a rage, a hatred, replaced his fear and uncertainty. The rage was begging to cry out at his tormentors, to confront them with their own insidious brand of inhumanity ... but remembrances of others whose rage had been uncontrollable convinced him otherwise. Yakoff had seen people beaten with rifles until they were bloody, lifeless pulps. He'd seen innocent victims shot down in the street for absolutely no reason, other than the fact they were Jewish. His tongue would be held. Again and again and again.

He gulped a quick breath of air to calm himself and the mid-December chill grabbed the exposed nerves of his four front teeth like a vice, refusing to relinquish, refusing to let go. His scream was muffled and barely audible among the shuffling in the nearly frozen mud. Then it was quiet. Deathly quiet. Even the shuffling, shifting weight from one foot to the other, trying to circulate some blood and achieve a small degree of warmth, ceased. And it stayed like that. The silence was only broken by suppressed and guarded coughs from several men standing in the straight rows of ten.

The coughs were low, guttural, more like a retching an hacking from deep inside the chest. It was the sound of terminal illness, the slow kind. And after several of the suppressed coughs were heard there was another sound, the now familiar sound of wood on flesh.

There were footsteps up ahead at the front of the columns but it was still too dark to see anything. Something was vaguely familiar about the metric cadence in the distance. Yakoff was still trying passionately to clear his mind, to eliminate or at least momentarily escape the agony he felt both inside and outside his body. He listened closely, pressing his lips tightly together to prevent the cold morning air from its relentless attack on his exposed nerves.

A mental picture slowly formed, accompanying the footsteps in the mud. It was a vile image of soldiers marching through the ghetto. Patrols, heavily armed, wearing helmets, helmets marked with the feared SS insignia on both sides. Patrols laughingly terrorizing innocent and unsuspecting people, especially the elderly and children. Often the patrols would stop and publicly humiliate a devoutly religious person by producing a large pair of scissors, wave them tauntingly in his face and then brutally defile him by shearing off his beard. Relatives and friends would weep soft tears over the callous indignity. The soldiers? The Nazis? The heavily armed storm troopers? To them it was sport. And when their amusement was over they'd reform the patrol and continue their marching down the street.

That was the sound, Yakoff thought. The goose-stepping cadence of an SS patrol. It was a sound he'd never forget. But this time it wasn't a patrol. It was only one man. Just one of him and a thousand of us. How is this possible? Why is this happening?

The marching steps finally halted in the darkness ahead. Yakoff was still lost and swimming aimlessly in his own mental pool. Reality returned in the form of a glancing blow to his chest and right arm.

"Hats off when you see an SS you stupid swine," the room senior hissed. Yakoff wasn't the only one brutalized in this senseless tirade. Others, especially those standing at the front of the rows and the sides were beaten ruthlessly with equal abandon. No one within striking distance escaped the punishment.

He jerked his cap from his head and the winter chill painfully reminded him that he no longer had hair as a protective cover. Grimacing silently, through the physical pain which now permeated his entire body, he realized that this was the reason for the jockeying of position during the roll call. Those standing on the inside of the group, and the further in the better, would probably elude the early morning sticks. But that's all it was; a probability, not an absolute.

The unprovoked beatings were a perverse performance for the newly arrived SS man, brutality in its sickest form to gain favor, acceptance, perhaps even privileges from the captors. Things not making any sense seemed to be the only thing making any sense. Protect yourself, trust no one, don't talk, don't move, don't ask questions, caps off in the presence of SS men. And most importantly, during roll call, fight for positioning in the middle of the group. Yakoff was learning.

The SS man spoke with the block senior and even though their conversation was loud and accentuated with short clipped words, it was barely audible to those on the sides and the rear. Being fluent in German, Yakoff could decipher several of the phrases floating through the silence.

The senior explained the new count, including the arrivals last night. He spoke in terms of bodies rather than human beings. Bodies, Yakoff thought. How interesting, how bizarre, how inhumane. The SS man, a noncommissioned officer in charge of the body count in the block, goose-stepped his way down the rows of the prisoners, carefully recounting and confirming the report he'd just received. No one trusted anyone.

Yakoff stared straight ahead, avoiding the remote possibility of eye contact with the uniformed adversary. When the count was completed and the SS man satisfied with its accuracy, he spoke a few hushed words to the senior and marched away into the blackness of the morning.

The group was dismissed from their tightly formed ranks without explanation as to what had just transpired. Yakoff and the rest of the new men cautiously followed the precedent set by the old-timers.

It was still dark. Faces were covered and shrouded in dull grey tones; hard to explain, hard to understand, hard to decipher. The reality was to instantly adopt a sense of conformity, a carefully contrived guise toward self-preservation, a ploy that might lend itself the greatest resultive end ... survival.

Yakoff remembered the earlier thumps from the whatevers he'd heard behind him. Succumbing to curiosity he turned and looked to the right of the front door. Momentary disbelief was his first reaction. He squinted and leaned forward a little, as if his eyes were deceiving him, playing some sort of sick, bizarre joke.

But it wasn't a joke. The grinding, churning stomach muscles started up again. This time it was beyond the hunger he still felt. These were the rumblings of being close to death. Close enough to touch it, smell it, feel it. The sight was hard, no, impossible to believe. But there it was in front of him. The thumps and the thuds that he'd heard were lying in a pile, stacked alternately in rows of five, seven layers high. They were bodies, human beings, all dead, men who'd died a silent death in the night and were now stacked like a cord of wood. They were mostly naked. Their eyes, sunken deeply into the bone-thin faces were racked with anguish, open as if pleading for some release, or perhaps thankful that they'd found it. The bodies were stacked in the neat rows for purposes of efficiency. It made it faster and easier for the SS man to confirm the total count in the block. And every single body had to be accounted for. Every single one. There was no escape from Birkenau ... only death.

A long, weary line of prisoners slowly began to move down the road directly in front of the block. They were headed south, walking in silence.

"Where are you going?" Yakoff whispered.

"Latrine," the man said, without looking up.

The youngster joined the line, carefully checking each direction for the men with the sticks. Within several yards they came upon another large group of prisoners standing in front of their own block and many fell in step with them. There was little talk, only the sound of the wooden clogs slushing through the mud. A man beside Yakoff mumbled something but he couldn't make it out.

"What did you say?" Yakoff asked.

"Are you new?" It was an odd tone. There was no emotion in the man's voice. Not curiosity, not even interest, just flat, bland words.

"Yes."

"... On the transport that came in last night?"

Yakoff shook his head and they walked a few more steps. Then the man spoke again. "The water," it was as if he were sharing a mystical secret, "don't drink it."

"The water..." Yakoff repeated, uncertain of the man's message. "Rotten ... gives you diarrhea, the runs. You drink it, you get sick. Too sick to work. No work..." the rest of the words faded away. Yakoff didn't ask but had reasonable cause to believe that in this place those who didn't work didn't live.

He could see the outline of the latrine about a hundred yards ahead. It appeared to be nearly the same size as the block building and there was a long line of men waiting to enter.

A foul aroma gradually attacked his nostrils. It was vile, putrid, the smell of human excrement. It was coming from all around and each step carried him deeper into the stench.

I can understand the smell from the latrine, Yakoff logically deduced, but why is it also behind us, and on both sides? How can that be? It was still too dark for the youngster to clearly see where they were walking and what they were walking in. Too dark to see that the road was covered with human defecation, bowel movements from men with diarrhea, hundreds who'd tried unsuccessfully to make it to the latrine that morning.

After a few more steps the gagging returned to his throat. To compensate he tried to breathe through his mouth but the cold morning air quickly reminded him of the exposed nerves in his front teeth. The smell reached deeply into his lungs and even though he hadn't eaten in nearly three days there was an uncontrollable urge to throw up.

Three more steps and that was it. He grabbed his mouth and turned back toward the block. There had to be some alternative. By now the road was filled with men, mostly the newer arrivals, bent over and vomiting. The majority of stomachs had not experienced the luxury of food in several days so the throwing up process was actually more of a dry heaving effect, the variety that rips stomach and chest walls.

Yakoff's upper body ached from the retching. Each time he coughed or tried to gulp air, he experienced new waves of agony. He quickened his step, trying to escape this particular nightmare and return to another. But by now the ground was treacherous. The mud and excrement from countless prisoners crawled over his wooden clogs, taking hold of his exposed toes and ankles.

He plodded through the vomit and the shit, trying desperately not to fall down, trying to maintain balance, equilibrium. So many thoughts, on so many things. His bladder betrayed him and he urinated in his pants. It was an odd sensation. At first he was embarrassed but quickly realized that no one in this hellhole cared. The next and greatest

40

sensation was the accompanying warmth. The steamy liquid covered his groin and slowly ran down his left pants leg, the warmest his body had felt in days. He wanted to do it again. He wished there was more. But the warmth was short-lived. The air quickly caught the thin, wet uniform pants, turning them instantly into a sheet of ice, gripping the sensitive skin, refusing to let go. Yakoff pulled the damp cloth away but with each step the painful cling returned. He tried to rub the area with the tail of his shirt but each touch brought more irritation, more pain.

The sun was breaking the horizon through the low-hanging clouds and ever present pungent fog that filled the air. Leon and several of the others from Sierpc were standing in front of block 14 when Yakoff returned. Most of them had been fortunate enough to go to the latrine last night, before the road was soiled.

Conversation was limited and guarded. What was there to say? They were singularly experiencing their own incredible personal loss. There were no words or gestures of consolation, only eyes glazed with sadness. Remorse, empty, alone. The Nazi ploy was brilliantly staged and effectively working.

Mind games, mental tricks, ways and me   Anything to get away from this place. God in heave   e I done to deserve this? What have any of us done   aimlessly, waiting for the next demeaning act, the n

The sun, now a third in the sky, cast a dre   the eye could see. Yakoff continued his mind games and re   state of confusion. Something was missing. Something integ   lways accompanies the arrival of morning. It was the birds, c   lack of them. Even in winter, the birds would brightly chirp   ning of each new day. But this place had no birds. Is it po   ed himself, that a place could be so evil it would keep away   ll the animals? His answer thundered in the form of siler

He looked to his right, down the road toward the latr to the ten foot high fence holding them in, controlling and their movements, keeping them prisoners. Just outside the fence stood a tall wooden guard-tower with a uniformed soldier behind a machine gun.

It was more than two hundred yards away and clear vision was distorted by the prevailing mist. Yakoff pointed towards the fence and nudged an old-timer standing beside him.

"What're those?"

"Those what?" the man said, never taking his eyes from the ground.

41

"Over there ... on the fence."

The man slowly looked in the direction Yakoff was pointing. There was a frozen look on his face, a non-expression which didn't change.

"Bodies," he said, without emotion. "The fence is electric. You touch it and you die."

"But didn't they know that?"

The man exhaled a heavy sigh. His face remained the same. "They knew," he said. Then much softer, "They knew." And then he walked away.

Yakoff looked at the bodies hanging in the distance. He remembered the dull humming he'd heard when they walked through the gate last night, the electrification singing its slow and constant song of death. He turned and followed the man, touching his arm, catching his attention. "But if they knew," he asked, "why did they still try to escape."

"Have they not done just that?" the man countered.

Yakoff's face clearly explained that he didn't understand what the man was saying. "But I..."

His words were cut short as the man lifted his face for the first time. He looked deeply into Yakoff's young and confused eyes. He spoke slowly, letting the words sink into the soul. "They have found," he said with resignation, "the only freedom that any of us will ever know."

There was controlled milling as the men moved toward the front door of the block, forming a line. Yakoff and the others quietly followed the mass without question. In silence and with growing anticipation they watched as other prisoners carried large kettles through the entrance.

Steam escaped from under the lids and it created a rush of excitement. Food. The word was reverently whispered and passed down the line. Hunger brings a weakness to the body and the spirit unlike any other. It's a personal, singular state of desperation which can only really be felt and understood by the affected individual.

But food, food for our empty bellies, the men thought in unison. Sustenance. Strength. Something to fill the hollow, aching pit, something to erase the grinding pain. The line began to shuffle forward, all but the newer arrivals carrying a metal dish, six inches across by two inches deep.

To the right of the front door was a small office area where the rations were issued. This was also where records and a sparce amount of supplies were kept.

Filing past the door, each new man was given their own dish with instructions to guard it with their lives. Then they received a ladle full of coffee from one of the steaming kettles.

There was no argument. No complaint. Yakoff followed the others moving about the block, trying to find a place to sit.

"This is it?" he asked a man beside him.

The man nodded without expression and pulled a small piece of black bread from his pocket. It was actually more a crust of bread, no larger than a man's thumb. But at this moment the size was unimportant. It was food. Solid food.

"Where do we get the bread?" the hungry youngster asked.

"You don't," the man replied. "You get the bread with your soup at night and if you're smart you save some for morning."

Yakoff's mouth salivated as he watched the man eat. He could tell by the sound it was hard, much harder than a thin piece of toast burnt through and through. But at this moment, it was the greatest delicacy he'd ever seen. The man took small, thoughtful bites, breaking the bread into carefully designed pieces no larger than crumbs, chewing slowly, savoring every morsel with his tongue before he swallowed.

I'm going to do that, Yakoff told himself. I'm going to save my bread so I can have it in the morning. He watched with envy, jealousy, then anger at the unfairness of some eating while others didn't. A heavy sigh of remembrance brought the unfairness into a quick and absolute perspective.

Fairness was a concept that had been violated and unused for a very long time. He actually and honestly couldn't remember the last time he'd been treated with fairness or even the slightest degree of parity. They always got less. And the reality was that their less was gradually and systematically diminishing. But at least he had his coffee.

He felt the warmth of the dish in his hands. There was an oblique sense of comfort in holding the metal bowl and he relished it. He hadn't noticed it before, but the coffee had an odd aroma; it didn't smell quite right. Closer inspection indicated it didn't look right either. The liquid was brown, murky, like a shade of mud. It had a foul, rancid odor which offended the senses, both eyes and nose. But at least it was warm. At least it was something.

It's the water, Yakoff remembered. It's made with the rotten water. He rested the bowl on his lap, trying to warm himself as well as dry his still damp groin, trying to contemplate the consequences of drinking. But logic has no bearing and carries no weight in the presence of real and sustained hunger. He knew without hesitation the ersatz coffee would find its way into his growling stomach.

Yakoff watched several of the others and followed their unusual example by raising the dish to his mouth with one hand and holding his nose closed with the other. The taste was bitter, vile, but he forced himself to swallow. He had to put warmth inside his body. He had to sustain.

A man seated two bunks down the row started to cough violently. He choked and then began to gag, spitting on the floor in uncontrollable spasms. When he threw up there was no solid food in his stomach so the only thing that came out was a slimy liquid, splashing those seated across the aisle.

One of the room seniors appeared from nowhere and began to beat the man with his stick. He beat him on the back of the head and the neck. The man fell to the floor, face down in his own vomit, but the room senior continued his relentless attack. Viciously, growling with each blow, enjoying the power and control that he wielded. Blood flowed freely from both of the man's ears, dripping to the floor creating a sick shade of pink as it mixed with the man's slime. The senior continued to beat, long after the man was dead, cracking open his skull with each well-placed stroke.

Then he stood straight up and flexed his chest, a sign of authority. "This is for you new men," he began. "This is what'll happen to any of you who shit or throw up in the block." He offered a cursory glare, to those seated closest to the execution. Then a sneer, and a sick smile of satisfaction. He raised his stick to hit one of the other men. The prisoner cowered, dropping his half-full dish on the floor, covering his face with his arms.

The room senior lowered his stick, shook his head and smiled at the man whose eyes reflected terror. "Get a mop and clean it up, " he said. "This block will remain clean at all times." Then as an afterthought, "And drag that worthless piece of shit outside."

The man turned and walked away in march-like fashion, as if imitating or even worse, emulating the Nazis, their captors, the very people responsible for this. Odd, Yakoff thought, this man trying so hard to be like them. Particularly odd since the room senior was Polish, a fellow countryman.

Yakoff looked at the man with the bashed skull on the floor, lying in a swirling pool of his own blood. He put his fingers to his nose and drank the foul, brown liquid.

Chapter V

'Raus!! Raus!!"

It started again. Sticks. Flying in all directions as the men were quickly herded back outside. The newer men, neophytes with regard to rules, regulations and policies, watched others clutching the damp dishes preciously to their sides and sheepishly followed their lead.

The sun was nearly full but the sky and the air surrounding this place was grey, drab, lifeless. Yakoff could see forests in the distance, well past the wires. The area had been cleared and was barren for fifty, perhaps a hundred yards between the fence and the trees. And still there were no bird sounds.

The sounds Yakoff heard were the sickly hacking, coughing, the muffled, woeful moaning, the subtle shuffling prisoners, trying to obtain some degree of warmth; the orders, always screamed and always in German, and the wooden clogs, sloshing through the nearly frozen mud. They were all sounds reflecting pain. They were all sounds flirting with death.

There was a feeling in the air which deftly severed any sense of optimism. The older men from block 14 moved cautiously around the front of their building, trying to avoid an unknown inevitability the new arrivals would certainly experience. No advice was offered, no caution was issued. Only blank, silent stares.

The inevitable arrived in the form of kapos; prisoners elevated to the positions of captains of various assorted work patrols both inside and outside the perimeter of the camp. They wore armbands signifying their dubious stature and shared a common trait. For the most part they were Germans, priding themselves on their loyalty to the fatherland, and also convicts who'd been transferred to Birkenau from prisons throughout the country.

In an incredibly bizarre sense, the kapos were the most elite of all the prisoners. Their rank was earned and maintained through their unchallenged ability to control others. Their control was extended to the

45

limit of life itself. A successful kapo didn't work; he directed a group of others, responsible for their daily output. His word was law and seldom questioned. His discipline was delivered in the same form as the block senior; the stick, usually without the slightest provocation, sometimes for mindless amusement and never without incredible pain.

Several kapos marching in unison approached the front of Yakoff's block and began to handpick workers for their own individual patrols. They pointed their sticks and jabbed strong forefingers into chests of men who were too physically exhausted or suffering from malnutrition to accomplish any degree of work, let alone hard labor.

But this was a concentration camp. Those too weak or sick to work ... died. And as young Yakoff had seen, death came quickly. Life in Birkenau was cheap.

The selection process was carried out swiftly and at random. The prisoners followed obediently, without question, argument, or discussion. Total submission at its most dehumanizing level. It was sickening, cowardly, but more important, more than anything else ... it was survival.

First three then five then more of the kapos came with work assignments for the day. Thirty men, fifty men, a hundred men. Always in even numbers and always marching away in precise and exacting rows of five.

Everything was symmetrical, everything was organized. The rows of ten for the count, the rows of five while marching, the rows of bunks inside the block, the levels of command and authority. Yakoff had no clear-cut explanation as to where he was or why; but one thing was certain, the Nazis were remarkably adept at whatever it was they were doing.

He watched in silence as the men walked away from the block, grouped together in tight columns. Close attention was paid toward any unusual movement, especially from men carrying sticks. Yakoff waited anxiously to be picked, but each time the kapos passed the front of the block making their selections, he was overlooked. This continued for a half hour until only a handful of the thousand men remained behind.

Yakoff had entered a deep state of shock. His world and life had literally been ripped away. The only reality was pain. His pants, still wet, caused chafing to his inner thighs. Each step, mixed with the chilling wind, brought a stinging, burning sensation to his groin. Feet and toes were nearly frozen. His left arm continued to ache from the tattoo and the needles and jabbing. The four front teeth, hanging tentatively from his gums, reacted violently with each exposure to the harsh, foul air. Welts on his back had formed, creating intense discomfort with each simple movement.

All these were minor when compared to the aching and emptiness he felt within. There was an overwhelming urge to succumb, to give up. But from somewhere, a place deeper inside himself than Yakoff had ever known, burned one tiny flicker of hope. Yes, he was in pain. Yes, he was instantly alone in a new and unknown world bathed and shrouded with grey smoke, the odor of human flesh and cruelty. But this flicker, tiny as it was, somehow superseded the desire to give up. Implanted in the vast gaping void was the beginning of a mechanism known as survival.

For some unknown and unexplained reason Yakoff wasn't selected for a work patrol his first day in Birkenau. Nor was he allowed reentry into the block. He stayed outside near the wall, trying to avoid the wind as it whipped between the buildings. A few others also eluded the selection process. It was from these men, in whispered guarded sentences, that Yakoff learned about his new surroundings.

Birkenau, often referred to as the camp of death, was specifically located in a swamp with a murderous climate. The Nazis had carefully chosen the area for its remoteness. Towns within thirty square miles were completely evacuated to maintain secrecy about the true purpose and function of the camp. Few people were aware of what actually occurred behind the electrified wires. Security was vast, immense. No one had ever heard of a successful escape and no one ever brought up the prospect.

The camp was huge, stretching further than the eye could see. It was nearly a thousand yards wide and two thousand yards long. The block buildings, some brick, some wood, faded endlessly into the distance. There were hundreds of them, with each block designed to hold between six hundred and a thousand prisoners. Birkenau was capable of detaining and brutalizing two hundred and fifty thousand people at a time.

The numbers were staggering, too large to comprehend, let alone believe. It was a city within the wires. A city filled with prisoners guilty of no crimes against anyone; kept there for the express purpose of forced, hard labor. The fruits of their labor came in the form of a death which was certain and inevitable. Sometimes it was quick and unexpected. Other times it was slow and agonizing. But always it was a certainty. Some died from starvation; the slow, one day at a time kind. Others from disease, several of which were prominent in the camp. Some were beaten to death by the SS or kapos or block personnel for little reason other than sport. Many died from sheer exhaustion while trying to complete worthless but assigned work tasks. There were countless suicides, not only from rushing to the wires but also from just walking away from a work patrol, asking for the inevitable bullet in the back of the head. Some who had given up completely ate the dirt on the ground, which was covered with lime, slowly and painfully poisoning themselves. Those who survived the cold, work, starvation and constant beatings, were all scheduled for eventual execution. There was no escape from Birkenau.

The day was a blur. The information Yakoff received was for all practical purposes irrelevant. There was no food, no shelter, no warmth. Only the sounds and smells and overriding feeling of death.

Marching. Far away. In the distance. Coming closer. Familiar sounds. The wooden clogs sloshing through the mud, thousands of pairs, droning in tired unison. The men filed wearily through the large steel gates and returned in columns of five to their assigned blocks. Their faces were sullen, drawn, empty. There were eyes without hope, faith or belief, resigned completely to their horrible circumstances. Most were bone thin, some actually walking skeletons, barely able to extend one tired foot in front of the other.

Yakoff was cognizant of something noticeably different. There were far fewer men slowly milling about than earlier that morning before they left.

As the rear of the column drew nearer, Yakoff could see what the difference was. Men who still had some degree of strength were carrying others on their backs. Makeshift stretchers had been prepared and more bodies, heaped and piled on top of each other, were being dragged, into the camp.

Out of the thousand men who left that morning, every single one returned. The difference was, nearly two hundred and fifty were dead. They were placed in neat rows of five and stacked on top of each other in preparation for the evening count.

A long line of prisoners started to move toward the latrines. Yakoff, pants still damp, joined the others as they trudged through the slime. The skin on both inner thighs was rubbed raw and he knew additional moisture would produce open sores. He marched, gulping short painful gasps of air through his mouth, each breath comparable to a nail being driven into his gums. The alternative was throwing up from the rancid, foul stench he was walking through.

Returning to the block the men were again forced into lines of ten for the evening count. Sometimes they called it a roll call but no roll was ever taken. It was a count, plain and simple, to make sure all the bodies were there and no one had attempted an escape.

The SS man in charge of the block returned and marched up and down the rows, checking and rechecking. Then he carefully counted the stacked bodies, most of them naked by now. The bodies were nameless, insignificant hulks of flesh, blood and bone. The only identification they had were the tattoos burned into their left forearms.

The block senior, clipboard in hand and with absolutely no emotion, pulled each limp and lifeless left arm from the pile and found the corresponding number on his list. With a dark pencil he drew a line through the number and that was it; the number ceased to exist. Thoughts, feelings, or concern for the human being were never felt and certainly never shown. With a simple, brief stroke of a pencil it was as if the person was never born. And in this place there was no one who cared.

The SS man and the block senior completed their assigned tasks and after satisfaction with the final tally, dismissed the men.

Dismissed, Yakoff thought. Dismissed to what? To where? If it hadn't been for the abundant pain permeating his entire being, the thought and concept might have proven humorous. How bad can it be, he asked himself. It couldn't get any worse. Could it?

The men shuffled at the same, slow, exhausted pace back inside the block. The two small wood burning furnaces in the center of the room barely provided enough heat to warm their hands. But the body warmth emitting from seven hundred and fifty men, crowded tightly in a small confined area, helped the temperature to rise considerably. Never to the level of comfort but at least away from the point of freezing.

Prisoners huddled in small groups, clutching their dishes to their sides. It was apparent food of some sort was coming, but faces of the older prisoners indicated little anticipation.

Food ... the thought hit Yakoff like a fresh summer breeze, pouring over his mind in visions of great consumable feasts. He envisioned meats and cheeses and cool tall glasses of milk straight from the cow. And his mother's apple strudel. Delicious. The best in the whole wide world. A delicacy, a delight. It was a gastronomical daydream, filled with pastries and sweets and good things. Then it occurred to him he couldn't remember how long it'd been since he'd eaten. Was it four days? Five? Six?

His last meal had been in the Stregova ghetto, just before the Nazis came in the early morning with their rifles, screaming and herding them into the train. The real food from six days ago had been scraps that were scavenged and begged for. A crust of bread, a small slice of stale, moldy cheese, barely a bitefull. But there they had water to drink. Not like here.

The front door creaked open and several prisoners came in from the cold. They were carrying vats, like the ones from earlier this morning, and boxes stacked on top of each other. It was the food. Dinner had arrived.

When the lids were removed from the caldrons a steamy mist rose to the roof. An aroma like that of the foul tasting imitation coffee filled the room. The food, whatever it was, had also been prepared with the rotten, dangerous water. But it was food and the steam created a magnetic effect on young Yakoff.

Lines moved past the unusual smelling pots and each man received a ladle of soup. Several of the older prisoners, obviously exhausted from the work patrol, appeared to be hanging back, almost to the point of wanting to be at the rear of the line.

When Yakoff reached the food station he received a small rusty spoon, his soup, and two tiny crusts of hard bread, the consistency of dried clay, tasting like a combination of lime and sawdust.

"You'll get used to it," a man said, noticing how he still held his nose as he tried to swallow. "After awhile you won't even notice the smell."

Yakoff nodded and gagged down a mouthful. Several prisoners sitting around the block were noticeably thinner than most. Their eyes were like black hollow pits, every bone in their bodies protruded distinctly through their loosely clinging skin. They never seemed to acknowledge or react to anything, as if they were in a deep state of catatonic shock. The body moved but the brain didn't.

Most of the men in that condition sat hunched over, holding their dishes in their laps, staring straight ahead with fixed, unmoving eyes. None were eating. Another prisoner approached one of the transfixed men and took his soup. There was no resistance, no conversation. He took it and walked away.

Yakoff nodded and the man beside him continued, "He's a Muzzleman." It was stated as a fact, certainly no great revelation or wondrous piece of information.

Yakoff shook his head, indicating ignorance to the reference.

"The thin ones, with the hollow faces, the walking dead." The man paused for a second. "Soon he'll be gone ... maybe two days."

"Why?" Yakoff whispered, not fully understanding.

"Because they've given up and they're ready to die. They don't care anymore. Look," he said, pointing. "They don't eat, they don't talk, they don't feel pain."

"How can that be?"

"Their souls are already dead, gone. The guards beat them till they're unconscious pulps. Still they get up and move among us until they die of starvation. They never cry out. They never make a sound. They just die a slow, quiet death."

Most of the men finished eating and placed their dishes upside down at the head of their bunk. Yakoff did the same. He learned they had one free hour until a strictly enforced curfew was effected. During that period they were allowed to move about anywhere within their own enclosure. Another prisoner told him it would be wise to stay near his own block if he chose to venture out into the night air. There were two reasons for this. One, there were many prisoners who would think nothing of robbing him of his overshirt jacket, thin and threadbare as it was, for additional warmth for themselves. And two, was the possibility since he was new in the camp, of becoming lost. Prisoners who missed the curfew paid dearly for their tardiness. Sometimes the form was gross, violent punishment. Sometimes those who returned late were never seen again.

The biggest percentage of men climbed wearily into their bunks in futile search of an extra hour's sleep. This was the only hour of confinement when they could truly escape the constant harassment and brutality.

The thought of sleep carried a slight degree of solace. Yakoff watched as the men placed their caps on the dishes, creating a rock hard but better than nothing pillow. He remembered what he'd promised himself earlier and saved one of the tiny crusts of bread. He had it safely tucked down deep inside his pants pockets, which by now were nearly dry. His skin, however, was still raw and tender.

If you can get used to the rancid odor in the coffee and the soup, he justified, I suppose in time I can also get used to the latrine. In time, he thought, repeating it over and over. In time. In time. What does that mean? How much time is there? For me or for anybody else?

Solitude was upon him like a blanket providing neither warmth nor shelter. He felt to some extent it was the solitude and loneliness which drove the Muzzlemen, the walking dead, to their level of self-degradation and destruction. He couldn't let that sense of total isolation consume and destroy him. He had to be strong. He had to survive. He had to talk with someone.

Leon was standing in front of his own bunk, down the aisle about twenty feet away. Yakoff looked at his cousin, virtually his same age, and wondered, should I talk to him? Was there anything they could talk about? Could either of them offer the other any consolation at all?

In time, Yakoff thought, the phrase returning. In time perhaps there'll be something to talk about. But not now. Everything is too close, too fresh. His mind ached for comfort and closeness of a friend or relative. He casually knew most of the new men in the block, but only out of circumstance. Only because they'd been forced to live together within the close, constrictive walls of the Stregova ghetto. For the most part they were strangers sharing the common bond of repression.

Yakoff took a hesitant step towards Leon, then stopped. The bread crust in his pocket rubbed the raw skin, irritating it with a sharp stinging sensation. Without thinking, he removed the precious morsel, placed it underneath his overturned dish, and gingerly walked the twenty feet separating Leon and him.

Neither spoke. When their eyes met, it was a sharing of mutual despair. The exchange lasted only a brief second. Yakoff finally opened his mouth to speak but no words would come. Only a raspy, gurgling silence. The young men didn't touch. They didn't have to. Their eyes expressed what was deep within their hearts. There was a slight nod of understanding and Yakoff returned the few short steps to his own bunk.

A terrible thought flashed through his mind. A question which could be answered by a simple wave of the hand or even less; confirmation by the flick of a finger. Yakoff stared at his overturned dish, hating himself for his own stupidity. How could he be so ignorant to leave his one singular piece of food unprotected? How could he be so dumb?

Wait a minute, he told himself. We're all prisoners here. We're all in this together. Surely no one would actually stoop so low as to steal food, the most precious of our commodities, from another prisoner. Most of us are Jews. We've already tasted in clear and certain terms the oppression the Nazis administer. Support, he rationalized, that's what we have to do. We have to support one another. Mentally, physically, spiritually.

It was a mind game and Yakoff knew it. Or at least was afraid of it. Tentatively he moved his right hand forward, placing it on the dish. The metal was cool to the touch but it conveyed a sinking feeling of emptiness. He didn't want to lift it from the bunk. He didn't want to know. He didn't want to hurt anymore. But he had to find out.

Fingers gripped the edge of the dish and he exhaled a heavy sigh of anticipation. It was not a pleasant moment. Tiny beads of sweat began to form on his forehead and under his arms. He lifted the side ever so slowly until the dim, filtered light drifted under. Then his worst fear was realized.

The empty area under the dish was the size of a canyon. It was bone, stark, empty. The precious, life-sustaining piece of food had disappeared. Yakoff raised the dish off the bunk and looked inside, as if miraculously the bread might be clinging to it. He stared at the barren planks of wood, not believing his own stupidity. Men seated around him focused their eyes straight at the floor. This crime, one of the worst of all, would not be followed by confession.

Hunger gripped him again, this time magnified tenfold. The evening meal was little more than warm smelly water; vile, foul, distasteful. A stomach still empty was growling for substance in any form. A lesson was learned, painful to be sure, but a lesson nonetheless.

The other first evening lesson was proper positioning in the soup line. The further back, the better your chances for a scrap of potato peel, or skin from an onion floating close to the bottom. Though sparse and rotten, these items proved to be delicacies when added to the thin brown water.

They were lessons in survival. Basic, simple and also necessary if one was to exist in this barren field of futility.

Slowly Yakoff climbed into his bunk, shifting for position among the other five men in the limited space. The pungent odor was a combination of hard-earned perspiration along with an indication that he had not been the only one among them who relieved himself in his clothing. Reflection of "You'll get used to it" sifted through his aching brain like a fine mist. He maneuvered carefully, trying unsuccessfully to locate a position of comfort. He envied those more clever for keeping the precious bread crusts on their person. He ostracized himself for his act of innocence and ignorance. He reflected the day's as well as the night's events.

The block was settling in for the short evening's rest. Gagging, choking and coughing echoed from the walls and ceilings. At least the sticks were silent. One of the men in Yakoff's area coughed in violent uncontrollable spasms. Phlegm flew from his mouth spraying those nearby, moving the other five with each attack. Sleep was the only relief even remotely available. Finally the man drifted off and the coughing subsided.

Yakoff was close to sleep, the only escape from the Nazi hell. At first it was a minor irritation on his left leg. He smacked the area with his hand and it seemed to stop. Then it came back, this time worse. He smacked the leg again but the irritation continued. It was buglike, a crawling sensation, moving up his leg. He scratched it, hard, but it kept on moving. Then he could feel it on his chest and underneath his right arm.

It was a stinging, like tiny, driving needles. Each time he smacked, the stinging appeared somewhere else. Yakoff opened his shirt but the light was too dim to see anything. He touched his chest, feeling with his thumb and forefinger for one of the irritated areas.

He could feel it. There was something in his grasp. Something tiny and moving, crawling for freedom. Holding it closer he could finally see what the vile little creature was. They were invaders, crawling on his body, his neck, back, groin, a hundred tiny stings. Brownish-green little monsters, smaller than ants, impervious to destruction.

Others in the bunk felt the same sensation, the same painful irritation. They were all, except for the man who was sick, smacking themselves, scratching for a relief that was not to be. The bed, the bunk, the entire block was infested with lice.

Chapter VI

The material was heavy wool, the itchy kind. The first time he tried it on it felt like a quarter of an inch thick. The fact the pants didn't quite match the coat didn't matter in the least. It was new to Yakoff, brand new. And it felt wonderful. Even in mid-May with the summer sun beating down and sweat pouring profusely from his armpits it was wonderful.

Yakoff's father had taken two old suits to the local tailor and had them altered to the youngster's size. He was thrilled with each fitting and the absolutely grown-up idea of having his first suit. Actually, the prospect of owning and wearing his very first pair of long pants was considerably more exciting.

He was thirteen, trying desperately to look like an adult in the three-way mirror as the tailor made the final adjustments. A smile of satisfaction, attainment, accomplishment, beamed across his clear-skinned face. His eyes, glowing with anticipation, watched every subtle move the short, bald-headed tailor made.

Pesach nodded acknowledgment at the length of the trousers and the two older men spoke in glowing superlatives of Yakoff's upcoming manhood. He was the undisputed pride of the neighborhood.

At the mikvah earlier that afternoon there were pats on the back and congratulations from all in attendance. Yakoff's posture appeared to be improving. He was standing considerably taller, both in his own eyes as well as those of the others. He felt good, his young chest filled with pride. Tomorrow would be the most important day of his life, the official day of reaching manhood in the Jewish faith, the day of his barmitzvah.

Preparations had long been completed for the highly honored recipient. Learning the ritual itself was a relatively easy task since Yakoff could both read and write in Hebrew, the language of the Torah, the Holy Book. There were two minor rehearsals at the synagogue and his father was always available to explain exactly what, where and when the young man was to read.

Being the first born son made the occurrence even more solemn. It was a time of joy and celebration. Yakoff's mother had spent days preparing food for the kaddish, the party following the ceremony. Sweet aromas from her famous apple strudel filled the entire apartment building. Yakoff was inwardly tempted on more than one occasion to secretly sample the delicacy while the rest of the family slept. Instead, he lay awake, savoring the aroma and imagining every delicious bite that was soon to be.

Chuling was also prepared, a meat and potato dish cooked slowly overnight in a sweet dough. It would be exactly ready for devouring when the family returned from synagogue. This particular dish was a rarity, served only at the most special occasions.

The entire family was excited, Yakoff's parents were proud. They had a fine young son about to become a man and their pride showed clearly in both faces. Sleep was long in coming that Friday night.

Dressing the following morning was a flurry of activity, everyone putting on their finest clothing for the upcoming event. Words were unnecessary and unspoken. The feelings each member of the family had were recognizable and universal.

It was the first time the rest of the family had seen Yakoff in his new suit with the long pants. Shaina clasped her hands together as a tear of joy appeared in one eye. Even in the excitement of the moment, Yakoff noticed and gave his mother a quick affectionate hug showing appreciation and love.

Proudly the family walked the block and a half to the synagogue, Yakoff and his father leading the way. Without looking, they knew the eyes of the neighborhood were watching.

The synagogue was good-sized. It was one of three in town and capable of holding more than four hundred people. On this gloriously clear Sabbath morning it was full to capacity. Most of the congregation attended on a regular basis, some daily, but many were there to see young Yakoff enter manhood.

The woman's section was separated from the men's by a wall with several tiny, sliding wooden windows. When the windows were open they could hear the ceremony, but vision was limited to the first few rows. On this day of honor the entire family was assigned front row seating.

Following tradition, two readers conducted the service. One led the worshipers in prayer and the other was a learned man who read passages from the Torah. One of them had a rich, baritone voice. "Yakoff Ben

Pesach," he announced. A giant wave of pride flowed through the collected multitude as Yakoff rose and walked onto the elevated area in the middle of the synagogue.

The boy stood straight, proud, erect. Today he was given the Haftorah, the highest honor, to publicly read from a portion of the book. The Haftorah was basically an interpretation of the Torah but unlike the most holy of books, contained punctuation marks, adding to the ease of the reading. Yakoff's voice sang out in clear, strong tones and brought honor to his family.

The party, filled with celebration, was held in their one-room home and attended by family members only, a result of limited space as well as the cost involved. The price of Yakoff's new suit and food for the event nearly depleted the family's savings. But it was worth every cent. The food was delicious and the mood was festive.

Others recently barmitzvahed in Yakoff's class at the Hebrew school received wonderful gifts along with the congratulations. Some were treated with new suits, some with shoes, others with books. Some actually received money to spend as they wished.

Yakoff was keenly aware of his family's financial situation and only slightly envious of those more fortunate than he. They had a good life, secure in all aspects, a clean home and enough food to eat. They were blessed with exactly what they needed to survive in relative comfort. And it was his father who actually instilled the lesson of sharing with others less fortunate than they.

Leon, a first cousin and his family, also attended the party. It was reciprocal in that Leon was barmitzvahed only two weeks earlier. A mutual friend of theirs, who belonged to another synagogue, had also gone through the ceremony that same morning and invited all of his classmates to his own kaddish. Their friend was from a well-to-do family and food would be plentiful.

Yakoff bade goodbye to the adults and followed two of his cousins toward the larger and more elaborate celebration. It was a festive day to be certain, but somehow Yakoff felt removed from it all. He was strangely alone and in search of solitude.

"You guys go on," Yakoff said.

"What's the matter?" Leon was confused. This certainly wasn't a day to be troubled.

"Nothing. I'll catch up later."

Leon and his cousin each shrugged and walked down the street. Yakoff watched until they rounded the corner and disappeared from sight.

Slowly, deliberately he walked across the street into a small, tree-filled park and sat on one of the empty benches. Since it was the Sabbath most people were in synagogue and no one would bother him for awhile. The thirteen year old ran his hand across the thick wool covering his right leg, his first long pants, pensively staring into the distance.

It wasn't the size of the party that bothered him. Nor was it the fact there hadn't been any presents, like some of the others received. Yakoff knew his parents did the best they possibly could and he loved and respected them both. To complain about anything or be less than totally appreciative was unthinkable.

Perhaps it was the excitement of the day and the importance of the event. He didn't know and couldn't quite put his finger on it. He only knew he wanted to be alone for awhile. Just he and his brand-new suit, savoring the warmth of the mid-May morning.

Yakoff liked the warmth. Summer was his favorite time. Winter was all right but occasionally the cold was unbearable, intense, something he couldn't quite accustom himself to.

But the summers ... what wonderful times. Pesach leased a large orchard late in the spring and the entire family moved to the site as soon as school was over. They lived in tents and on warm clear nights, slept under the stars. Yakoff's mother and older sisters cooked over blazing open pits and the food always tasted better prepared outdoors.

The arrangement was a cash-lease. His father would negotiate with the landowner until they mutually agreed to an equitable price. Then he would pay one-half the amount at the time of the settlement and the other half at the end of the summer. Any profits that accrued from the sale of the harvest, went to the family.

It sounded better than it actually was. The fruit trees always carried the possibility of not producing up to capacity due to inclement weather, insect damage, or ripening too soon. Also, a certain percentage had to be figured for loss by theft.

Sometimes people from the city would steal into the orchard at night and carry away bushel baskets filled with apples, plums or whatever they could get their hands on. The family, as a result, took turns standing guard to run off any predators venturing into their territory. A sharp yell or announcement of someone's presence in the shadows was enough to send trespassers scurrying to another nearby field.

There was a sense of authority and accomplishment each time

Yakoff discovered a would-be thief. He'd lower his voice as much as possible, shouting hollow threats of jail terms and other unpleasant repercussions for their deeds. Then he'd smile proudly to himself as the burglars turned their backs and disappeared into the darkness.

The days were long and the work was hard, sometimes back-breaking. Countless row after row of trees had to be picked clean and carefully, to avoid bruises and destruction. Yakoff became quite proficient and enjoyed the work. To him it was still fun.

The soft dirt in the fields brought a sense of comfort to his bare feet. Shoes? They were for sissies. Shoes were never worn in the summer-time, except for synagogue when the family returned to town together. Then he always wore his one pair of thick-soled shoes and his brand-new, long pants suit.

Sometimes, on market days, Yakoff would ride into the city with his father, helping him sell fruit to the local townspeople. It was a bargaining process for nearly every piece. Occasionally the open-air negotiations became hot and heavy with people screaming at each other, trying to save a precious penny or two. Yakoff learned well and became a good trader, a valued asset to the business.

His face was well-known in the market and his self-confidence as well as ability to deal with the public was respected. He drove a hard bargain but customers knew the youngster was always fair.

Yakoff enjoyed being with his father. He cherished his spoken words like precious gems. He valued the closeness of his wisdom. He appreciated the sharing and the teaching of the ways of life. He respected him more than anyone he knew.

Even though the orchard was situated well out of town and even though the long trip was made to the weekly market, Yakoff's father still arrived in the city early each morning to tend to his carriage trade. The daily drive was arduous and time consuming but the income was neces-sary. And, it perpetuated the family tradition of evening discussions concerning the day's events.

Yakoff liked school and missed it in the summer. He was a good student. Not great, but good. Once, when his grades fell behind, his father hired a tutor for assistance with world history. The youngster was honored that his father was concerned over his education, but embar-rassed that family money was spent in his behalf. He experienced deep feelings of guilt over taking something away from his brother and sisters and vowed his grades would never drop again. The vow was kept.

The one thing Yakoff didn't miss about school was the trip to and from. The walk, though it only took ten minutes, forced him to cross the bridge and traverse through a sizable portion of the gentile neighborhood. Often, in discussions with classmates at the Hebrew school, Yakoff mentioned that anti-Semitism in Poland was a national pastime. There was little discussion about the problem, and questions, even tentatively posed, were never satisfactorily answered.

"Suffering and oppression is a way of life with us," the teachers would say. "The entire history of the Jewish people has been laced with unjustified persecution. Turn the other cheek. Don't rock the boat. Don't cause any more trouble than we already have."

This was a difficult pill to swallow and palatably absorb while rocks thrown by older gentile children were hurtling toward you. Direct confrontations were few and far between. Those only occurred when the gentile antagonists far outnumbered younger Jewish children who were defenseless.

The Polish gentiles, usually older and larger, would hide near the top of a hill and pepper young Jews with rocks as they tried to make their way to school. It was a mindless act, bred from ignorance and cowardice. As a result, older Jewish children would function as unofficial escorts, guards for the smaller ones. It wasn't organized and no one was openly asked to protect another. It was an assumed responsibility, deeply felt and adhered to religiously.

A fair-sized lake, filled with sparkling blue water, was on the far side of the public school. During the wintertime the lake would freeze solid, providing entertainment for the townspeople. Few of Yakoff's friends could afford their own ice skates but it was still great fun to go down to the lake, take a long running start, hit the ice, and slide for an eternity. The feeling of exhilaration was cut short by large groups of gentiles throwing snowballs made the day before, now solid ice and hard as rocks. The lake, like everywhere else on the other side of the river, was an unsafe place. So, the Jewish children converted most of their energy toward riding down the hill on their makeshift, homemade sleds.

The gentiles' animosity toward the Jews in Poland seemed to be inborn. Other than necessary business transactions, there was little contact between the two. The mistrust, dislike, and protected acts of violence against the children were a way of life. Gentile children were told to be guarded and especially careful around all Jews during Passover, the highest of the Jewish holidays. Parents explained the Jews would capture them, slit their throats, and use their blood in the preparation of a liquid broth indigenous to the Jewish faith. Generations of unjustified hate had been built on this and similar stories.

The summer, a result of hard work and dedication, was successful. But the following spring proved even better. Yakoff's father, a member of the board from the Hebrew school, was involved in events and happenings from their very conception. He cast an important vote as to what the school should and shouldn't do.

Dinner that particular evening was normal by all standards. Each of the children had taken their turns talking about what they'd done during the day and the one thing they'd learned. After the children, as was the custom, Pesach leaned back, folded his arms across his broad chest and spoke.

But this night there was no explanation about what had come over the community radio in the city square. No discussion about the passengers he'd carried to and from the railway station. This night he talked about the Hebrew school and its most recent board meeting.

"We had a vote today," he said in an authoritative voice. "We've decided the upper grades should take a trip to Warsaw to study museums, see a different culture than our own and visit the Hebrew seminarium."

"What's a seminarium?" Moishe asked.

"It's a college where our people learn to become teachers, musicians and scholars."

Yakoff missed his younger brother's question altogether. His heart was pounding and his mind was racing. Warsaw, he fantasized, what a trip. What excitement. What fun. And the opportunity to visit the seminarium ... he stopped himself in mid-thought. He knew a trip of this magnitude would cost far more than the family could afford. He silently envied those fortunate enough to go, but knew better than to ask. His participation was certainly out of the question.

Pesach's pride was veiled in smugness. "Yakoff will make the trip," he said, repressing great smiles of satisfaction.

Yakoff looked across the table. Was he hearing things?

"Father," he asked tentatively. "What did you say?"

"Your ears have not deceived you my son. You'll be making the trip with your classmates."

There was a stunned moment of silence, disbelief. Then great shouts of joy filled the room. Could it be? Was he really going to go? But his father had spoken and his word within the family was law. Pesach was a cautious man. He weighed each word carefully before speaking. It was a trait Yakoff was learning well. The ability to think before you spoke was a valuable asset in their life and time. But even so...

"Really, Father? Really?"

Pesach smiled and nodded. The entire family was thrilled. Other than Yakoff's father, no one within the confines of that room had ever been more than ten miles away from Sierpc.

Yakoff couldn't sleep that night. Anticipation overwhelmed him, but it was strangely tempered with a subtle fear of the unknown. Warsaw was a big city. The largest in Poland. More than two and a half million people lived there. One of the thoughts flashing through his mind was the increased amount of anti-Semitism which must certainly exist. If it was as pronounced there as it was in Sierpc, and with the increase in population ... he stopped himself. What a silly thought. It was going to be a marvelous trip.

The four weeks between the announcement and the departure seemed an eternity. Twenty-five students from the fifth, sixth, and seventh grades plus four teachers, were eventually scheduled. The fortunate children were kind and exercised wisdom beyond their years by not talking or discussing the upcoming event in front of others who couldn't afford the excursion.

The train station was painted a pale light blue with white trim everywhere possible, reminding visitors of the famous gingerbread house from the familiar story. It rested atop a small incline with brick steps leading up. Once inside and past the ticket windows, it was necessary to walk down more steps to reach the lower level in the back, where the two daily trains stopped for passengers.

The children and teachers met in the mid-afternoon in front of the Hebrew school. They were taking the late train and excitement covered every happy face in the crowd. They each carried knapsacks usually filled with their schoolbooks. Today they carried a change of clothing and other essentials the children would need over the next five days.

Once assembled they walked together to the station. There were no parents or well-wishers to send the children on their way. As they rounded the final comer, Yakoff could see his father's horse and buggy standing in the street.

He knew his father was doing exactly the same thing as the rest of the fathers in town; his job. Still, the sight brought a warm glow to his heart. As the children filed past the buggy and started up the steps Pesach stepped down to the sidewalk and smiled broadly at his young son.

Without embarrassment, Yakoff ran to his father and hugged him. Then he kissed him on the cheek. "Thank you father," he whispered.

Pesach, still smiling, nodded and patted his son on the back. Their closeness and affection was noticed and apparent to the entire group. The father stood straight, tall. "Have a good time," he said. Yakoff said he would and joined the others as they climbed the steps. "And learn something new... every day."

The words echoed in his mind as they entered the passenger car. He would, he promised himself, fulfill his father's last request. Then, on his triumphant return to Sierpc, he'd share his new-found knowledge of the world and its ways with the entire family.

His first train ride. How exciting. How honored. The feeling was mutually shared by the rest of his classmates. They were organized and polite, never causing any trouble to their teachers or fellow passengers.

The teachers wisely gave the group about ten minutes to settle down. The motion and speed of the train was exhilarating, a sensation of flight; much better than the sled ride down the long icy hill. Trees and telephone poles buzzed by and the children passed time trying to count them. Chaperons kept a watchful eye on the children, making sure they were all in their places, keeping track, being responsible.

After awhile, one of the teachers led the group in a sing-along. Yakoff was purely and completely happy. He had the serene beauty of the   peaceful, lush green, rolling countryside right outside his window. He had the companionship and closeness of his friends and classmates surrounding him. He had the love, trust, and respect of his parents and family. And right now, this very moment, he was off on the adventure of a lifetime.

The train ride to Plock lasted just under forty-five minutes, each one filled with pleasure and excitement. Anticipation and unlimited curiosity brought hundreds of questions which the teachers assured would all be answered in due time.

Plock was a fair-sized city, much larger than Sierpc. The buildings were taller, some of them five or six stories high. And people were everywhere, viewing the group of children as if they were a sideshow odyssey. Here the teachers were even more emphatic about the group staying close together. They marched in twos out of the station and turned to their right, heading downhill.

After a few moments walking they saw it, a magnificent sight heretofore only seen in picture books. The ship was huge, a giant vessel with a twenty-foot tall paddle-wheel covering the entire width of the rear deck. It was unlike anything Yakoff or the others had ever seen. There were three spacious decks and the ship had a bright, festive appearance. It was white with red and blue trim. Wide walkways surrounded each of the decks providing unobstructed vision in all directions. The crew members, standing at the ready, were dressed in pure white uniforms with shiny brass buttons.

There was an aura of pure ecstasy as the classmates walked across the gangplank. So many things to see, so many things to do, so many things to learn. The children were awestruck to the point of silence. But only for a moment. Then questions poured out like raindrops from a mighty thunderstorm. How is this? Why is that? When will we ... ? The teachers laughed, reassuring everyone the answers to their questions would come.

Several cabins were booked well in advance and the children already had their assignments. They were eight to a room and the excitement of the moment far outweighed any sense of overcrowding. After all, Yakoff's one-room home, which housed and slept eight people was only slightly larger than this.

A long, mighty blast from the ship's whistle and they slowly pulled away from the dock. The children ran to the rail watching, as several hundred people waved good-bye to the boat and its temporary occupants. With the first rocking movement, several knees were a little shaky. But the river was wide, flat and smooth. Soon even the most queasy, gained strong sea legs.

The children watched off the rear deck until the city disappeared in the distance. The land on either side was dark green with a sweet, fresh smell, all clean and brand-new. Each deep inhale was refreshing, pure.

The travelers from Sierpc, knowing there wasn't a restaurant on board, brought along their own food. There was an abundance of fresh fruit and the mothers had prepared enough sandwiches for a small army. Like the daily occurrence at school, they all exchanged things among themselves. A cheese and onion for an egg sandwich with salami slices. Trading and bargaining until everyone was happy as well as delightfully full.

Within an hour, darkness began to fall. It'd been a long, full, busy day and time was taking its toll. Yakoff was the last to return to his cabin, choosing to spend a few extra moments watching the huge, powerful paddle-wheel turn over and over, its hypnotic churning leaving a long trail of white foam behind.

There was much scurrying as the children rushed to dress. After a peaceful night's sleep they were fresh, revitalized and ready to go. Warsaw stretched out for miles before the ship came to dock at the main port. Decks were lined with people pointing fingers at things they'd never seen before. Visions their eyes reported were far greater than stories they'd read or heard.

Warsaw was huge, sprawling, modern. With skyscrapers and things never imagined in Sierpc. Millions of people. Seeing this for the first time made their hometown seem a million miles away. The children were in awe.

They saw traffic signals at intersections. Electric traffic lights controlling the flow of tens of thousands of automobiles. The cars and constant traffic were unbelievable. Three cars at the same time in Sierpc was a rarity, generally talked about for days.

There were trolley cars connected to overhead electric cables. The children had seen busses before, one came through Sierpc every day. But nothing like this. And the buildings ... by noon nearly everyone in the group was suffering from a sore neck, a direct result of staring upwards at the heights of the stone and brick giants.

The first day they visited two art museums and a huge outdoor sports arena where great soccer matches were held. Legs were exhausted since most of the touring was done by foot but they pressed on, trying to see and do as much as possible during their limited stay. Plus, they were still carrying their knapsacks, deciding to forgo the time necessary to check into their hotel until later.

The children were tired, some completely worn-out as they limped into the hotel lobby. But spirits were lifted and second winds grabbed up like wildflowers along a deserted highway. The hotel, deep in the heart of the Jewish neighborhood, was gorgeous, palatial compared to anything they'd ever seen. And they were actually going to spend two nights in this garden of beauty.

Wood paneling on the walls was dark and rich. Furniture was brown and green leather, overstuffed and more comfortable than any of them could remember. Paintings of elusive beautiful women and castles of the wealthy were everywhere. Large chandeliers hung from the ceiling, twinkling, bringing light to everything below. The hotel even had its own elevator, a box behind a sliding door in the wall which carried people up in the air and then back down again. All quite remarkable.

The rooms were magnificent. The children slept two to a bed and four to a room. The beds were soft with thick ornate wooden head-boards, and they each had a heavy comforter with sheets. It was the first time in Yakoff's life he'd slept in a bed with full linens. For a moment he just stood there, running his hand over the softness awaiting him.

Dinner was beyond belief. They ate family style at tables for six in the hotel's restaurant. There was one entire plate heaped tall with meat. The children were speechless. It was seldom, if ever, they'd seen so much meat in one place. And it was all for the six of them. Shyness subsided as ravished empty stomachs guided their actions.

There were overflowing bowls of cooked vegetables, trays of steaming dinner rolls with fresh butter, even a cake with creamy smooth icing for dessert. If not heaven, it was deliciously close. It was the most complete and delightful meal Yakoff had ever eaten. For the youngsters from Sierpc, it was a feast fit for a king.

They thought it was too good to be true, even discussing it among themselves after dinner and before retiring to the soft linen covered mattresses for the night. But the early morning breakfast discounted their questioning completely as each were served hot sweet rolls, warm milk, and fresh cool slices of cheese. It's difficult to believe but no one argued or sent anything back.

There were more visits to museums with viewings of priceless pieces of art. Parks, with great statues carved from marble, depicting Poland's history as well as heroes. The tomb of the unknown soldier, a large glaring reminder of bloody wars fought. The magnificent, tall columned building where the senate for the country held session. Even the castle where the president lived. All the excursions were directed by professional tour guides offering valuable information with each stop.

Yakoff was filled with wonder, his eyes bright and shining. Warsaw was alive, vibrant, exciting. They saw great mansions inhabited by the very wealthy. Houses much larger than anything Sierpc had to offer. He rode a trolley car for the first time and saw people on the street wearing fine expensive clothes. Nearly all the streets were paved. It was like a fairyland.

They changed hotels after two nights but stayed within the area of the well-defined Jewish neighborhood. The second hotel was comparable in appointments and luxury to the first, with one noticeable and remarkable difference. Each floor, at the end of the hall, had a special room. The walls and ceilings were covered with white tile. Silver coated faucets and nozzles were protruding.

"Yakoff! Yakoff! You've got to see this!"

The voice was familiar, coming from down the hall. It had a sense of urgency and Yakoff sprang from his bed.

As he entered the room several classmates were there, all staring in amazement. "What?" he asked. "What?"

One of the boys reached forward and turned a silver faucet to the right. Yakoff jumped back as a fine stream of water poured out of the nozzle, drenching his shoes. His mouth fell open and he stared in disbelief. Like so many other things, this was the first time he'd seen a shower. The hotel even had hot and cold running water. The mikvah would never be the same.

They visited synagogues, huge compared to Sierpc's standards, and covered with ornate gold trimmings. They were exquisite with memberships numbering in the thousands. It was breathtaking and incredibly memorable. But their last day in Warsaw proved to be the most important of all.

The Hebrew seminarium was a four year college, self-contained in one large building. Two of the teachers took the children through the school, explaining with great pride each of the various departments as well as their functions. The one which intrigued Yakoff the most was the college of education. Teachers were looked up to and highly respected. The youngster from Sierpc listened intently as the guide explained various classes available as well as the pressing need for Hebrew teachers.

The thought captured Yakoff like a vice. He consumed every piece of literature available and talked privately for hours with several teachers at the school. Yes, they told him, if his grades were sufficient there was certainly a chance for admittance. His hopes soared, fleeting for a moment at the very prospect.

Next year he'd be out of school and need a career or business to pursue. Following in his father's footsteps was out of the question as well as personally unappealing. After a long day's thought and continued discussions with teachers from his school, he decided what he really wanted to do with his life was attend the seminarium, graduate and become a teacher of the Hebrew language.

At the moment his vision was little more than a lofty desire. The college was expensive. Loans were difficult to obtain and he doubted his family could afford the additional burden. Still, the seed was planted. The dream had begun. Somehow, someway, Yakoff was going to become a Hebrew teacher.

Graduation from the Hebrew school was unceremonious. There

were no parents in attendance as diplomas were distributed. But there was a great sense of joy and emotion with hugging and well-wishing between all the classmates. They'd spent seven years of their lives together and it was coming to an end.

Most of the others were going into their father's trades or businesses. It was tradition. Yakoff had spoken with his father on several occasions about his dream born in Warsaw. Pesach was pleased that his son was desirous of becoming a teacher but the seminarium was too expensive. It would be necessary, he told him, to work for awhile and save some money before attendance would be possible.

Yakoff never argued or pressed the issue. If his father said that's the way it was, then that's the way it was. He'd kept his vow and improved his grades during his final year in school. He'd become a good student and academically was qualified for higher education. Still, the dream of college would have to wait, at least for a year.

Pesach concluded the arrangements for Yakoff to work as a tailor's apprentice. In exchange for learning the trade, he would work for an entire year without pay. After one year, if promise was shown, he would receive a minimum wage and could begin to save some money. As was tradition, the decision was made by his father and Yakoff had no voice in the matter.

The work was boring and tedious. There were four tailors in the shop, including the owner, and they enjoyed playing tricks on their new employee. They'd send Yakoff out to find buttons with one hole, the order issued with straight faces and great seriousness. Yakoff would shrug his shoulders and set out to find them. After much embarrassment and looking like a fool, the red-faced apprentice would return to the shop to find the tailors doubled over in hysterics.

The same trick, in various forms, was played many times to the amusement of the others. Yakoff never complained or talked back to their insensitivity. He went about his work and tried his best to learn the trade. Anything less, or to show arrogance in any form, would bring disrespect to his father and the family name. That was unthinkable, something he would never do.

Ofttimes Yakoff longed for the comfort and security of the two-story red brick schoolhouse. Things seemed easier then, somehow better. He was with friends in a comfortable environment. Now the opposite was true. He missed the camaraderie and closeness of his fellow class-mates. Even though they lived within a few blocks of each other, they were seldom seen except occasionally on the street, sometimes at the mikvah, and usually in synagogue. But there was no social life in Sierpc.

It was an unhappy time for Yakoff, difficult to keep his dream alive. He was in a lowly position, without pay, doing something he didn't really want to do. That alone was bad enough, without the abuse being heaped upon him. And then there were the daily reports on the public radio in the town square, announcing the escalation of the war and Hitler's bloody march across Europe.

Chapter VII

"Yakoff," Pesach announced, placing a large calloused hand on his son's shoulder.

"Yes father..."

"You've worked hard this past year and your mother and I are very proud."

Yakoff nodded his thanks and smiled. He remained quiet, choosing to let his father continue.

"The orchard was better than usual this year and we've managed to put aside some money..."

"Yes...," his voice was tentative, hoping. Was his father actually about to speak the words he longed so desperately to hear?

"We've enrolled you at the seminarium in Warsaw." Yakoff was delirious with joy. "You start to school next month." It was too good to be true. His dream was going to become a reality. A teacher of Hebrew, looked up to, respected, a scholar.

It was all he could think of or talk about. The only thing which wasn't perfect was the separation from his family. But Warsaw was only two hours away by train or truck. He'd find a part-time job in the city and still be able to visit home. The neighborhood was abuzz over Yakoff's good fortune. There weren't many young men fortunate enough to attend college. He indeed was a lucky one. His respect for his parents and the sacrifices they were making soared to new heights.

School was barely two weeks away. Plans were completed and everything was in order. Yakoff still couldn't believe it, even as he excitedly related the story for the hundredth time to his coworkers in the tailor shop.

A low buzzing in the sky diverted their attention. It was coming from the southwest, growing increasingly louder, a constant drone like a huge bumblebee. The tailors and Yakoff walked outside and looked across the clear September sky. Airplanes were unusual in this part of the country. The sighting of a plane above Sierpc was a unique experience.

"There!" one of the tailors shouted, pointing. The others trained their eyes on the tiny speck in the sky. It was coming towards the city. Several other shopkeepers joined them on the sidewalk for this uncommon occurrence.

The plane dipped lower, its single engine growing louder, still headed straight for the city. The group on the sidewalk looked at each other and shrugged, no one having any idea what was going on. Within seconds the street was filled with curious watchers, their eyes squinting, their faces covered with a strained sort of wonder.

By now the plane was over the far edge of the city and appeared to be diving. Then the pilot pulled the stick straight back as the plane nosed up and began to climb. When the assent began, something looked like it fell from the wing.

But before anyone could offer a comment there was a thunderous explosion which rocked the ground. A huge fireball danced a hundred feet in the air and debris was seen flying in every direction.

There was a moment of shock, disbelief, stunned silence. Then the screaming started. People panicked, running in all directions. Soon Yakoff was the only one still standing on the sidewalk. Everyone else was scurrying about, trying to locate family members or loved ones and return to what they erroneously believed was the safety of their homes.

Another plane appeared in the smoke-covered sky and another explosion followed, this one louder, considerably more powerful. The panic and screaming intensified. Still Yakoff didn't move. His legs were frozen to the cement. Immediate, pressing thoughts vied for his conscious attention. The town, via the public radio, was aware not only of the blood pouring, a result of Hitler's bullets, but also his intense hatred of the Jewish race. Yakoff's own ears heard Hitler's voice on the radio proclaim in screaming anger his answer to what he referred to as the Jewish problem; The Final Solution.

But who could believe such a madman who would actually announce to the listening world he fully intended to annihilate an entire race of people. It was beyond ludicrous, impossible to believe, insanity .. yet it was happening.

The bombs dropped well on the other side of the river so Yakoff's concern for his family and home was temporarily pushed aside. They lived on the outskirts of town, literally beside a farmer's field, so their safety for awhile seemed secure.

Without forethought he began to run towards the area of destruction. He could hear bells and sirens from the fire truck in the distance. Streets were filled with citizens, running, screaming, crying. Flames, ten to twenty feet high, were blazing, coming from the direction of the train station. Adrenaline pumping, heart pounding. It was late afternoon and his father would be there with his buggy waiting for arriving passengers.

The train station had been spared. Perhaps intentionally, perhaps by accident. No one knew. The tracks behind had proven to be the target. Thick, long pieces of steel were twisted from the ground like dainty weightless ribbons. Railroad ties were shattered to toothpick size. Cavernous holes were black from gunpowder. The entire area was ablaze. Thank God, Yakoff thought to himself, the buggy and his father were nowhere to be seen.

There were casualties. Cries of agony from those fortunate enough to still be alive echoed above the wailing and hung painfully in the smoke-covered sky. Great crowds of people were swarming, trying to free others trapped by the twisted steel or help the wounded and bleeding from flying shrapnel.

Yakoff turned and ran full-speed the entire way home. Turning the final corner he stopped dead in his tracks and exhaled a deep sigh of relief when he saw his father's horse in its stall. His own relief was mirrored by the rest of the family. Yakoff was the last to return to their apartment.

Hugs of comfort and looks of concern were interrupted by a neighbor pounding loudly on the front door. They listened as their friend told them Shaina's brother, Yakoff's uncle, was wounded by one of the bombs and had been carried to the hospital. Without concern for their own safety, both Pesach and Shaina instantly decided to return to the heart of the city to do whatever they could to help.

Streets were filled with confused citizens, the panic and screaming continued. There was a steady stream of people, a large column of army ants, going back and forth between the train station and hospital. Wives were holding husbands' hands. Sometimes that's all they were holding.

Damage was greater than anyone expected. Victims fell to their knees, praying out-loud through tears and grief.

"Listen!!" It was a voice faraway, loud, above the others. The street grew quiet. Then they all heard it, the low, droning buzz in the sky. The planes were returning. Bodies scattered, taking shelter under the nearest available roof. Was this it, several asked themselves. Was this what Hitler was referring to as his Final Solution to the Jewish problem?

Was the answer to bomb, maim, and kill every Jewish resident of Sierpc as well as the rest of the world? The German bombs were powerful and indiscriminate. They killed gentiles as well and as frequently as Jews. There had to be more to it, some thought, huddling together, holding on tightly. The thought was grotesque and abhorrent.

The planes flew lower this time, targeting themselves on the road the multitude was following. The flight path was well-defined, leading Nazi bombers directly to the hospital. Was the first run a diversion to later establish the real target? Could anyone actually be that cruel and inhumane? No one knew.

Tightly packed dirt from the street erupted on contact with each metal sphere. Fragments, lethal projectiles flew everywhere, cutting some down at the legs, others in the chest. Blood flowed freely across the sidewalk and into the street. Several with head wounds died in their hiding places. No shelter was safe from the attack.

When the salvo of bombs hit the hospital, an entire wing of the three-story structure was leveled. Patients, recently wounded, doctors, nurses and other hospital personnel collapsed in the rubble. Tiny particles of brick mixed with stagnant clinging smoke created a cloud-like mist hanging for more than a hundred yards. Visibility was cut to zero. All was quiet except for the low, agony-wrenched moaning.

The buzzing returned. Oh, my God, they're coming back. No one could clearly see but it was apparent from the sound more airplanes were filling the sky. Residents listened to the noise, transfixed, unable to see through the reddish-grey mist.

They heard bursts of machine gun fire. Then again. The engines revved up, slowed, then revved up once more. The shots rang louder, as if the dogfight were directly above. It was the sound of insanity, futility, the sound of hell. They heard a clinking ringing noise, bullets ricocheting off metal. Then several clunks were clearly discernible; direct hits on something. An engine sputtered, tried for life, then sputtered some more. It died and the unseen sky above the mist was only half as loud.

Whining followed. With their ears, they traced the path of the disabled airplane winding its way towards the earth. Whose is it? Ours? Theirs? All was quiet, waiting for the inevitable crash and explosion.

None came. Somehow, miraculously, the pilot managed to land the aircraft without power. The intensity of the question of whose plane - increased considerably. If it's ours, a hero's welcome is in order. If it's theirs, the pilot must quickly be captured and put to death for the carnage and destruction created.

The German pilot was semiconscious as they carried him by stretcher into the remaining portion of the hospital. He drifted in and out of various states of awareness and mumbling incoherent gibberish. "Mein Fuhrer, fatherland forever, death to all Jews." Things like that.

A great portion of the town's population cautiously gathered to watch the impending spectacle. It was actually Shaina, Yakoff's mother, who saved the German pilot's life. Her brother had just been viciously murdered in the hospital bombing, so it certainly wasn't compassion compelling her to speak to the assembled mass outside the smoldering building. Rather, she appealed with concern and logic for all of their safety.

"This," she said, "is probably the first of a great wave of Germans to invade us." The crowd quieted, listening intently. "When they come, if we've been civil to one of their own, perhaps..." Her voice trailed and the group became deathly silent..." Perhaps they won't do to us what we hear on the radio they've done to so many others."

The tears filling her eyes and passion consuming her voice was not for the Nazi killer lying three stories above. It was private and personal. It was for her and her family. It was for all the Jews destined to be a statistical factor in Hitler's Final Solution. To an extent it was even for the Polish gentiles who were residents of Sierpc, the anti- Semites who taught their children to hide at the top of the hill and throw rocks at her own people.

After much discussion the Nazi pilot's life was spared and he was nursed back to health. The town was on edge, waiting. The public radio in the main square repeatedly broadcast messages from the Polish government admonishing the attack and announcing "We are strong. We will never surrender. We will never fall." But the Polish army was taking a severe beating at the front and no men were available to protect the city. Even the tiny police force, if it chose to put up any resistance to the impending attack, would be the cause of immeasurable damage and destruction to the town. Only a handful of the citizenry owned weapons. To resist would have been futile as well as suicidal. So they waited.

It was early morning, before sunrise, when it started. People jumped from their beds and ran to the street. The noise from the engines was deafening, the ground shook under the mighty weight of the heavy equipment. An unspoken exclamation of "Oh, my God" filled the hearts of every watcher. An endless stream of rolling stock moved through the town in a slow, confident fashion.

There were trucks, tanks, heavy artillery and more soldiers than Yakoff thought possible. The parade-like column went on for hours as citizens lined the street watching in silence. No one had ever seen such an awesome display of power.

The invasion of Sierpc was peaceful, uneventful. Other than the noise from the trucks, it was quiet. No resistance or aggression was shown by either side. Most of the column and support equipment was lumbering to another unknown location, but a large contingent of soldiers remained to secure the town.

Yakoff's curiosity won him over and he walked across the river and into the main square to observe these foreigners he'd heard so much about. At first he was surprised at their apparent normalcy. He saw no display of overt violence, women weren't raped and children's throats weren't slit. The Germans seemed to be regular people who were hot and tired from a long arduous march.

Many were resting on the grassy square, some removed field jackets and shirts and washed at the pump. Some began to walk nearby streets like tourists, looking for souvenirs. The townspeople stayed well out of their way and no words were exchanged.

Yakoff, from a safe distance, and with an insatiable curiosity, followed a small group of soldiers down a side street and into the local drugstore. The owner unlocked his doors rather than risk the chance of having the windows smashed. He stood behind the counter wearing a starched white apron. His hands were flat and in front of him but his fingers were trembling when the soldiers approached.

Their tone seemed polite as they asked the owner for something using their native tongue. He replied in Polish he didn't speak German and using his arms, gestured and indicated for them to take anything they wanted. The soldier's demeanor remained unchanged and he calmly asked another question, again in German. The two men stared at one another in confusion.

Yiddish, as a language, is slanted toward German with many words the same or at least close. Yakoff, watching from the rear of the store, understood what the soldiers wanted and hesitantly approached the counter. In Polish he explained to the druggist the Germans were after shaving materials and soap.

The store owner shrugged, retrieved the requested items and laid them on the counter. The German nodded and reached into his pocket producing a large roll of Polish currency. Then he asked, "How much?" The druggist looked dependently to Yakoff for interpretation. He told Yakoff to tell the soldiers to take whatever they wanted with his compliments. After this translation the German politely insisted on paying. It was all very unexpected.

Prices were totaled, the cash register rung and money was paid in full. Then the most amazing thing happened. Not only did the German thank Yakoff for his assistance but he also insisted the young lad accept a tip for his services. When the soldiers left the store, Yakoff and the owner stared at one another in total disbelief.

Yakoff was a rarity. The majority of Jews, knowing the Nazis' feelings toward them, stayed within the confines of their homes. Yakoff's curiosity had proven to be financially sound. The coin felt warm tucked deep inside his pocket.

More soldiers entered the store and the process was repeated. They ordered, Yakoff interpreted, the druggist rang the register and the Germans thanked the youngster by giving him a tip. It was one of the best days ever for the gentile store owner. Any other time, had Yakoff entered the man's store, he would have been watched like a hawk and followed like a common thief.

Today however, he was a hero, the man of the hour, perhaps even a lifesaver. Not only did the druggist thank him repeatedly but also insisted he return the following day.

Yakoff's pockets were filled with coins, more money than he'd ever had in his life. The reaction of his family was contrary to what he'd expected.

"Didn't they know you were Jewish?" his mother asked, her voice trembling with fear and concern.

"They didn't ask...and I didn't say."

"Perhaps you were lucky and should stay at home tomorrow." Pesach's voice was stern. He was not pleased with Yakoff's mysterious, unknown absence.

Yakoff never argued with his father about anything and this time was no exception. He calmly and logically explained the financial rewards which could accrue from helping the gentile druggist. It was safe, he told him. The Germans were polite, filled with gratitude for the services he provided.

"And besides," Yakoff rationalized, "the money I'm making will be used toward my tuition at the seminarium."

Finally, but reluctantly Pesach agreed with his son's logic and decided to allow him to return to the drugstore. That night as the kerosene lamp was extinguished, no one could see Yakoff's face as tears came silently from his eyes and crept down his smooth cheeks. No one could feel the disappointment in his heart, for he knew without question that his dream of attending the seminarium and becoming a Hebrew teacher had slipped evasively through his fingers. Emotionally he resolved himself to the fact that for awhile, and no one had any idea how long, his dream would have to remain just that, a dream.

The next few days passed with guarded optimism. Soldiers appeared to be staying out of people's way. There was no violence reported or open hostility from either side. The Poles blandly accepted their conquerors presence and life was returning to some degree of normalcy. Jews for the most part, remained in their homes, refusing to open their businesses or allow themselves to be seen and potentially ignite unpleasant or dangerous situations. The condition was tense but apparently stable.

Yakoff continued to work as an interpreter. Vast numbers of troops and transports kept moving through the city. It went on night and day. The sounds of the large trucks were constant. Each convoy carried death and destruction for all who dared oppose it.

Then one day without warning or explanation the soldiers who'd occupied Sierpc fell in line behind one of the convoys and marched out of town. The citizens were in awe. Was that it? Was it over? It was quiet, as if the temporary occupation hadn't occurred. No celebrations were planned, no dancing in the street. Instead, an unspoken feeling of gloom and despair hung over the city like a low black cloud, ready to erupt and rain down on the innocent Polish citizens.

The Jews continued to stay in their homes as the tension mounted. For three more days and nights the German convoys thundered through the streets heading northwest, deeper into Yakoff's homeland. Trucks by the hundreds, motorcycles with sidecars, heavy artillery, open touring cars carrying officers of the Third Reich, even mobile kitchens to feed the growing army. The smell of diesel fuel was everywhere. The columns kept moving, stopping only for water, or to purchase toilet articles from the drugstore. No one stayed behind.

But one foul, grey afternoon, they did. Several open cars carrying officers pulled out of the convoy and waited. They were joined by three trucks filled with heavily armed SS troops. These officers were different. Their uniforms were black and the insignia on their high peaked caps was a silver skull and crossbones. Their attitude and demeanor announced that the town was now under their control.

Yakoff quickly learned these men were the most ruthless in all of Hitler's army. They were the highly trained and intensely dedicated Gestapo; an abbreviation for Geheime Staatspolizei, the secret state police.

The officers met briefly with the town's governing body and explained how things were going to be from now on. Then they returned to their cars, heavily guarded, and conducted a short, motorized tour of the city and selected temporary quarters for themselves.

Those unfortunate enough to reside in the largest and nicest houses in town were forcefully evicted without notice. Families, peacefully eating dinners, had their front doors broken down and were escorted at gunpoint into the street and instructed not to return. In one frightening second they were stripped of everything they'd taken a lifetime to acquire. Ornate houses with white picket fences, flowers of the season and fine trimmed lawns were surrounded by SS troops guarding the newly obtained command posts.

Secret, separate meetings were held in whispered darkness, gentiles and Jews, each trying to predetermine what their fates would be. Frustration mounted to new heights for no one had any idea. Discussion of revolt or resistance was quickly quashed.

There was much valid argument that the Germans, as their oppressors, meant no real bodily harm. History recorded, time after time, when one country successfully invaded another, the rarity of indiscriminate mass murder. The oppressed usually became slaves or working-labor for their captors. Certainly their lives would be changed. Certainly their freedom would be curtailed and possessions confiscated. But certainly also, they rationalized, the Germans would follow the paths set by predecessors and feed and keep alive the greatest captured working force in the history of the world.

Pointless discussions and conversations continued far into the sleepless night. The following day was quiet, uneventful. Citizens were lulled into a dulled sense of believing that a normal, regular life might somehow be maintained. The presence of the Gestapo was seen and felt but nothing occurred that was out of the ordinary.

Yakoff snapped quickly out of his light sleep when he heard the commotion outside. People screaming, doors opened then slammed shut.

Heavy footsteps pounding on the wooden floor then down steps. He dressed as quickly as possible, following the rest of the crowd.

Once outside there was a reddish-orange glow in the sky. More people filled the street, all running toward the corner. Around that, they painfully saw what was causing the panic. The oldest and largest synagogue in town was ablaze. Jews were screaming, crying out in hopeless, frustrated agony.

In the distance they could hear the siren of the fire truck making its way up the narrow street. Individuals waving frantically, confused, disoriented. The synagogue Yakoff attended had been left untouched, at this moment a fact which brought little comfort. As he neared the scene of the sacrilege the roaring flames illuminated thousands of people watching helplessly. Many were on their knees, praying for a miracle, tears streaming down their faces. But not all.

The flames also outlined the smiling faces of the Gestapo members and their SS guards. Instantly Yakoff realized they were the ones responsible. The fire was purposely set and the misery it caused provided them great amusement.

The crowd parted as the fire truck rounded the corner, only to be stopped by a column of SS men pointing loaded rifles at the driver. It was apparent the Gestapo wasn't going to allow the truck near the fire. The holy place was doomed, the wailing increased. One of the Gestapo, still smiling, calmly suggested a bucket brigade be formed and the fire extinguished by hand.

Jewish men in attendance ran full-speed to their homes and businesses to obtain wooden receptacles. The screaming siren and glow in the sky brought a large contingent of gentiles from the other side of the river. When they arrived, they stood passively behind the line established by the Gestapo, refusing by their gestures to assist.

One by one the men returning to the scene formed a line from the pump across the street to the flaming building. Heavy buckets were passed from man to man then thrown on the blazing house of worship. It was an exercise in futility. On occasion, an SS man would approach the line and trip one of the brave fire fighters. When he fell, spilling the precious cargo and disturbing the timing of the operation, the Germans would roar with delight.

One man, after being tripped, rose and faced the uniformed soldier who'd done it. There was anger burning in this eyes, a rage, a hate. He took one step toward the man in the steel helmet when another, carrying a sub-machine gun, fired a burst into the sky.

All became very quiet, only the sound of the crackling wooden structure. In an instant the water began to move again. The Jews worked, the gentiles watched, and the Germans continued their laughter.

The front of the synagogue collapsed into the street and it was obvious all was hopeless, the building was lost. The flames began to slowly subside but the bright glow from the smoldering white-hot coals clearly indicated there would be nothing left to salvage. Depressed, confused, and shocked, the crowd didn't notice as the SS men formed a perimeter surrounding them. When some of the mourners turned to go back to their homes, they were callously met with rifles pointed directly in their faces.

Another volley of machine gun fire quieted the crowd and one of the Gestapo stepped forward. He had a sinister, evil smile, and warned the group that failure to follow his instructions to the letter would result in instant death.

"Resistance in any form," he screamed, "will achieve the same result." He approached some of the elderly Jewish men who had been valiantly working on the bucket brigade. After more than an hour of transporting the heavy water, they were completely exhausted.

"Form a line" he yelled, "and dance your way around the synagogue. We'll have a celebration."

The order was met with silence and shock. The Gestapo produced a long handled pair of scissors and viciously trimmed the beard of one of the religious, pious men. No resistance was offered. Jewish rituals had taught them for several thousand years to turn your cheek to others who offend or ridiculed your beliefs or ways of thinking. Several rifles also made this a poor time to take exception to the teachings. The Nazis roared at the man's humiliation and embarrassment.

Again the order to dance was repeated and again the men stood in stunned silence. An SS fired a full clip of bullets into the ground directly in front of the tired and beleaguered men. The bizarre form of motivation was effective. Their complete attention had been captured.

After a momentary recovery period the men slowly moved forward, leaving their wives and terrified families behind. They were forced into a circle and driven like animals around the smoldering building. Shouts of "Faster, faster!" filled the crisp night air. How could they possibly know this was only the beginning?

The pace wasn't satisfactory so all were ordered to stop. A different Gestapo walked directly to one of the eldest and most frail men forming the circle.

"Take your pants off," he shouted.

Increased disbelief permeated the crowd. The man shook his head, indicating he didn't understand the German command. A sharp slap to the face, knocking him to the ground, corrected any misunderstanding. He unbuckled his belt and slowly lowered his zipper.

"Faster!" came the command again, this time, punctuated with a clenched fist to the old man's stomach. The Gestapo stood the man straight up, deciding to help along the process. Violently he ripped the trousers and underwear to the man's ankles, leaving him half-naked in front of the entire Jewish population in town.

Women in attendance lowered their eyes to the ground, humiliated, embarrassed. But not for themselves, for the naked old man. Gasps rippled through the audience, quenching the Nazi thirst for cruelty.

But it wasn't enough, their perversion called for more than one helpless naked old man mumbling prayers. The Gestapo, above their laughter, shouted the same obscene order to several others standing nearby. Threats as well as violence, slapping, hitting, and rifle butts created more than a dozen men with trousers bunched at their ankles.

More rifle fire into the air quieted the wailing women. The men were forced at gunpoint to crawl on hands and knees around the burning synagogue. Wounds opened and soon they were following an endless trail created from their own blood.

Nearby houses were broken into and anyone found hiding was ordered to put on prayer shawls and forced into the street. Once there, the Nazis made them join the circle of men, dancing in bizarre, macabre fashion around the burning building until the last standing exterior wall tumbled to the ground.

Then it stopped as quickly as it started. The synagogue was lost, reduced to little more than smoldering ashes. The accumulated tears and agony amused the Gestapo and SS men. They viewed the sorrow as a continuing sign of Jewish weakness.

A black uniformed man appearing to be the highest ranking officer, stepped forward and the crowd grew instantly quiet. He spoke in German, words ringing clear, filled with authority. He informed the crowd that by three o'clock that afternoon, a committee of Jewish leaders should be formed.

"The group will consist of the most wealthy and influential individuals in your community. Failure to comply with the order..." he let his words trail off and smiled. He knew the Jews were aware of the Nazi presence and seriousness. The biggest question in everyone's mind was the Germans' intention.

At the meeting, the twelve Jewish men chosen to represent their neighbors were told they would be known hereafter as the official Jewish Advisory Bureau. They would be responsible and accountable for carrying out Nazi orders and compliance with all requests.

"Your cooperation," the Gestapo said, "will guarantee the safety of you and your families. Do you have any questions?"

Of course there were questions. Hundreds. But none were asked. Silence and submission made a great deal more sense.

The Gestapo was firm, but some in attendance swore they could detect a sense of compassion and understanding in his voice, as if he really didn't want to hurt or harass anyone. It was this tone he used when he told the Bureau another meeting was scheduled for the same time tomorrow. At that meeting, he said the Nazis expected the Bureau to deliver the equivalent of ten thousand dollars in gold and silver.

There were mumbles of disapproval concerning the impossibility of the request but none were vocal. The Nazi assured the Board in a sincere and convincing fashion if this request was met their homes and families would be secure and safe from worry.

Heated discussion followed as the Nazis and their guards left the room.

"Who can believe anything a Nazi says?"

"But the man seemed so sincere."

"What other choice do we have?"

"What will they do if we don't pay their ransom?"

"How will we collect it?"

"And where?"

As the board canvassed the neighborhood soliciting money supposedly in exchange for their safety, it was impossible for them to know of similar collections concurrently, taking place throughout hundreds of cities in occupied Poland. Discussions were little more than futile exchanges of air. The Jewish citizens had no idea if the Nazis would live up to their promise but based on the atrocity of the previous night they were clear on the repercussions if they didn't.

Amidst much valid complaint, the money was raised as the hour for the meeting approached. This time the Nazi in charge was smug in his indifference. The full spectrum of his arrogance had returned. He was aloof, removed, clearly in his own mind, above the Jews in attendance.

When the gold and silver was exchanged there was neither a thank you nor a document defining the earlier promise of safety. The currency was counted by an underling and swept off the table into a black valise with a lock on its handle.

Without question or discussion, the Gestapo announced the Jews had forty-eight hours to raise the equivalent of twenty thousand dollars or the entire population of the town would be transported to concentration camps. He took the money and marched to his waiting car.

Their worst suspicion was realized. They'd been robbed. Clearly, openly, blatantly. The ransom money they'd delivered under unspoken protest would be sent, all or at least part, to Berlin to help finance Hitler's awesome war machine. They were actually helping to pay for their own annihilation.

The Bureau, individually and collectively, was aghast, incensed. They were also helpless to do anything about it.

"What if we do raise it?" several asked.

"Will the Nazis laugh in our faces again?"

"And steal that money too?"

"Without delivering anything in return?"

Probably, was the answer but the results of noncompliance were deathly frightening. Sketchy rumors of Nazi concentration camps filtered across the countryside and found their way to Sierpc. They were unpleasant stories about slave labor, starvation and brutality.

This time the Jewish community provided resistance to the Bureau. They'd been deceived and they knew it. Try as they might, the twelve men couldn't raise what the Nazis demanded. They worked diligently until the eleventh hour, going home to home, trying to convince neighbors to participate in what they all knew was a robbery.

The Gestapo received the news without emotion. The Bureau asked for an extension, assuring adamantly the money could be raised if they had a little more time. The terse, scornful answer resounded as shiny black boots marched out the front door. The Bureau remained, trembling, their fate now in the hands of madmen.

Three days passed without incident, proving only to be the calm before the storm. Few Jews ventured out of their neighborhoods or crossed the river to the gentile side. They continued to watch the movement of the convoys and waited. There was nothing more they could do.

Escape from the city was possible but escape to where? Where could anyone go? The roads were filled to capacity with tanks and other equipment; Germans everywhere. They certainly must have invaded the rest of the towns and villages as well. There was no communication, so idle assumption was the best anyone could offer. For all practical and intrinsic purposes, they were trapped.

Tension, already peaking, continued to intensify each time a Gestapo car was seen driving through the neighborhood. Women and children were kept indoors. Services at the two remaining synagogues were conducted in extreme secrecy. All rights had been stripped from the Jewish population.

It was predawn during the third sleepless night when trucks were first heard coming up the hill. The rumbling shook the ground like a mighty beast bent on destruction. Yakoff managed to sleep through the commotion as hundreds of troops piled out of the backs of the vehicles.

The first sound Yakoff heard was screaming from the streets.

"Raus! Raus! Out! Everybody out! Everybody on the street in ten minutes and packed! Anyone not on the street will be shot!"

That was it. That was the sum total of the instructions given.

Surprisingly, the pandemonium was controlled. Packing of essentials was carried out quickly with little or no panic. The thought of a dreaded concentration camp was secondary to being shot. Discussions concerning this potential eventuality were previously taken care of. The children moved rapidly, putting a limited number of things in their packs.

"Shaina," Pesach said, concern filling his face. "Shaina ... you've got to hurry. You've got to pack."

Yakoff's mother was calm, resolved. She let out a heavy sigh before speaking. Her voice was clear, unwavering, "You know my parents are staying..."

"I tried to talk them out of that." There was urgency in his voice. "They'll be killed..." then he stopped, staring momentarily at his wife, the mother of his children. An awareness came quickly. "You're not going are you?"

Shaina shook her head. "I'm not sure why," she began softly, "but if I stay to help and look after my parents, I don't think we'll be harmed..."

"But..."

"There's no reason and they'd have nothing to gain by it."

The children stopped what they were doing and ran to their mother's side.

"It'll be all right," she assured them. She was strong, comforting each of her babies. "I want you to go with your father. You'll be safe and in a short time we'll all be together again. You have to believe that."

Time was running out. A great clatter of footsteps ran down the wooden stairs and assembled outside. Slowly Pesach turned away from the tearful goodbye and resumed packing. His heart was broken, knowing he was going to leave her, but he knew she was right.

Shaina hurried the children back to the more immediate chores at hand. They were all growing up quickly and none of them liked it.

"Two more minutes!" came a calloused shout from below.

Shaina walked into the small kitchen area and returned carrying some chicken parts and two loaves of bread. "You'll need them for the trip," she said, fighting back her own tears.

"But where did you..."

"They're for the children ... and you." As they embraced, each wished with all their hearts time could somehow stand still and that very moment could last forever. Trembling in each others arms, they knew the reality of what was, and reluctantly let go.

"One more minute!!"

They filed down the narrow hallway, stopping so each of the children could hug and kiss their grandparents goodbye. Yakoff, the eldest son, now a man, tried desperately to control his emotions but tears gave him away. His grandmother, old and frail, held him close and told him to take care of the younger ones. He turned to leave, promising he would.

One final clinging hug from his mother. "We'll be together again, Yakoff. You must believe that ..."

"I do mother. I do..." was all he could manage through the tears.

Once forced inside the large trucks and bellowing noisily down the hill, the questions began. Would he? Would he ever see Sierpc again? He fought the question, trying to direct his mind to a thousand other thoughts but there was only one. The same haunting question over and over. The one hurting the most in this moment of complete and absolute insanity. The one about his dear mother and his promise to believe what she'd said ... would he ever see her again?

Chapter VIII

The goddamned bell started to shriek again, jerking the prisoners from their sleep and back to this unbelievable reality. It was a restless night. Sometime during the darkness, another group of unsuspecting terrified newcomers were shuffled into block 14, issued stern orders about the rules and regulations and stuffed into the makeshift bunks. But not before three of them were beaten until they were bloody and unconscious, a lesson for the others.

The man sleeping next to Yakoff continued to cough violently throughout the night, spitting with each retching hack. And then the lice. Stinging and digging their way under the skin. There was no escape, not even through sleep, which lately was as precious a commodity as freedom or even food.

Then the screaming started. The incessant top of the voice screaming by the block seniors, accentuated with their deadly swinging sticks pounding the ends of the bunks. As always, it was highly motivational. The men scurried as quickly as possible, trying to avoid the sharp sting of the wooden weapons.

The routine was the same as before. Through the front door of the block, hopefully without receiving a vicious blow. Into the cold, black morning air and the near freezing mud. Lining up in neat, easy to count, rows of ten, jockeying for an internal position among the group.

Yakoff blinked twice, quickly recalling yesterday morning. The strongest remembrance was the recurring pain, a result of standing on the outside perimeter of the column. He slithered and maneuvered his way to the interior of the group. There was bumping and pushing as the men vied for positions of relative safety. Newcomers innocently and unknowingly assumed stances on the outer edges.

They'll learn, Yakoff thought to himself. They'll learn. A heavy sigh punctuating the thought created a fire-like pain shooting through his gums and exposed nerves. He closed his mouth quickly, breathing through his nose, only to be sickened by the pungent aroma hanging heavily in the surrounding air. There wasn't a place or spot, no matter how small, in his body, mind or heart that didn't hurt.

He heard goose steps in the distance, coming from the gate. When the SS man reached the front of the column, Yakoff quickly yanked his cap from his head, listening peripherally as those on the sides learned the lessons taught by the sticks. Compassion and concern for fellow prisoners was diminishing rapidly, those brain cells and energy sources being filled and totally consumed with necessary individual survival.

There were bits and pieces of conversation between the SS man and block senior, a report of the new arrivals. He heard the sound of the nightly dead being dragged from the block and stacked behind him in neat rows of five. Thuds and muffled screams were heard through the darkness from blocks on either side. The actual count, thank God, was right the first time. The prisoners were dismissed for their morning pilgrimage to the latrine.

The walk through the remains of the previous night began. Slop, slush. Slop, slush. Through mud, excrement and stench. Yakoff felt choiceless. The latrine was a must and the excursion had to be endured. The irony preceding each nauseating step was that the sickening, vomit provoking aroma blocked out the painful fragrance of burning flesh.

People threw up on the sides of the road. Others, the weaker ones, slipped, falling into the grotesque slime. Which caused more pain? Which was the easiest to bear? Breathing through his nose or his mouth? You'll get used to it, he remembered. How, when, and more importantly, why?

The latrine was the size of each of the blocks, consisting solely of several hundred open holes in an elevated slab of cement. The stench within the confines of the walls was unbelievable. Men passed out on the floor from the incredibly foul smell. Vomit covered the walls. There were no toilet seats or toilet paper. The Nazis wouldn't be that extravagant for prisoners destined for death.

Yakoff gagged and his chest and stomach began to heave. He was close to throwing up, but deathly afraid of the ordeal which would follow. He swallowed hard, pain shooting through his mouth. The pain, he thought. The pain will stop the gagging reflex. He reached for his mouth and grabbed the four dangling front teeth between his thumb and index finger.

The instant he ripped the teeth from the exposed nerves, tears shot straight out of his eyes, nearly two feet forward. His mouth, face and brain were on fire. The hammering, nail-driving effect returned, this time much more powerful and pronounced than before. His knees buckled and he nearly collapsed to the slime surrounding his clogs. Somehow he maintained his balance. Somehow he contained the cry of agony stuck deep in his throat, begging for release. Somehow he managed to sit with the hundreds of other men, relieve himself and then quickly and carefully escape this sick and perverted Nazi joke.

The exposed nerves were sensitive to the touch but he knew they had to come out. It had to be swift, quick, one solid jerking motion for each. Survival, he thought to himself. It has to be. He opened his mouth and measured the tiny hanging remains. Then, remembering and acting only on his last conscious thought, he gripped the nerve firmly between two fingernails and yanked. More pain. Much intensified. More agony. He couldn't stop now. Delay was impossible if he was going to complete the horrid task. He ripped out the remaining three with equal but cautious abandon. Breathing was heavy. Knees weak. But it was over and he knew in time the gums would grow, covering the gaping sockets. Eventually the pain would subside.

While waiting in line for the muddy brown water, Yakoff renewed his promise to never leave bread anywhere but inside his own pockets. Constant hunger is a good reminder. Envy for those wiser than he, relieved to a small extent, the stinging in his mouth.

The smell from the water was the same as before: rotten, foul. He had to be overly careful, pouring the bitter tasting liquid over his lower lip, to avoid contact with his bleeding upper gums. To complete this maneuver, he was forced to hold the dish with both hands. You'll get used to it, he heard again, drinking the vile, make-believe coffee without the benefit of holding his nose closed.

"Out!! Out!! Faster!! Move!!"

More screaming, followed by wildly swinging sticks and ruthless accompanying punishment. Back into the cold relentless air and waiting for selection to various work patrols.

The sun was beginning to illuminate the surrounding marshy haze. Still no bird songs. Chimneys in the distance glowed brightly, sending wave after countless wave of ash-filled black smoke into the vast, waiting sky. No doubt, Yakoff painfully deduced, the wives, children and parents of the new arrivals.

Kapos came and began their selections, each handpicking the number of bodies required for the day's work. Ten here, fifty there, one took a hundred – always in a number divisible by five so they could easily be marched in countable lines through the humming gates.

The kapos came, the prisoners marched away and Yakoff waited. Would this be a repeat of yesterday? An oversight? Left alone to fend against the wind and cold? It wasn't to be.

"Over here..." the kapo's finger was pointing at him. Hardly anyone else was left. Yakoff started moving toward the menacing figure. "Faster!" he shouted, drawing back his whip. Evidently his movement was satisfactory, for the whip was lowered. He was joined by three other selectees.

Odd, Yakoff thought. Every other patrol has been selected in groups of five and we only have four. The answer came when he discovered this patrol wasn't going to leave the fenced-in compound. Instead they marched to the rear of a nearby block where a rickety shed covered a large wooden wagon. In German, the kapo instructed the four to pull the wagon, over fifteen-feet long with sides close to four-feet high, behind him.

Obediently they lifted the heavy tongue, following the man with the whip to the front of the block. He stopped when they reached the stack of lifeless bodies piled neatly in rows of five.

The kapo indicated with his thumb, mumbling in a low, gravelly voice, "On the wagon." Yakoff didn't understand. His eyes darted back and forth between the grotesque pile of naked bodies and the kapo. Two of the others on the patrol had been there before and knew exactly what to do.

The two, both in their mid-thirties, approached the corpses as a team. One grabbed a body by the wrists and the other, the shorter of the two, took hold of the shoeless ankles. With a one, two, three, swinging motion they hurled the man, impervious to pain, into the bed of the wagon. There was a dull thud as the body hit the wooden boards and rolled over twice.

His left arm was bent, twisted behind him, snapped at the shoulder so his hand was touching the back of his shaved, lice-infected head. There was a compound fracture at the elbow, and the bone, covered with dirt, protruded through the loose fitting skin, leaving a narrow trail of blood across the wagon.

Yakoff was transfixed, appalled, in a state of shock. His knees were weak, momentarily refusing to follow a direct order from the brain. This condition was instantly remedied as the kapo walked toward him, smacking the deadly stick into his own left palm. The third man grabbed Yakoff's shirt and gave it a yank. The burly Kapo eyed them both suspiciously and for some unknown reason chose to postpone the beating.

Souls finally and hopefully released to a place filled with peace and understanding. Yakoff had never touched a dead person before and the thought churned the empty walls of his stomach. The other man grabbed a pair of wrists, his face showing no sign of emotion. Yakoff hesitated. "Now!!" the kapo screamed, taking a step closer. Yakoff gripped the slimy ankles lying before him. The skin was cold, clammy, loose fitting. The body was so thin and emaciated his fingers wrapped completely around the bones. The touch brought a sickness to his throat, and his chest hurt from deep inside. The body, starved down to eighty-five pounds, seemed to weigh a ton. Then the swinging to and fro, the rhythmic one, two, three before letting the body loose to slide and bounce across the splinter laden floor.

Yakoff gagged and his breathing became heavy and irregular. Why this? he asked himself. Can't we at least provide the decency to lift these poor innocent bodies into the wagon and treat them with some sense of respect? Is this place so devoid of morals? His mind screamed the words his mouth was afraid to speak. The stick came crashing down on his right shoulder, buckling his knees.

"You want some more, asshole?" the kapo hissed.

Yakoff stared into the hateful, callous eyes. They were deep-set, cold, without concern or compassion for any member of the human race. Without changing expression, the youngster turned and grabbed the ankles of the next man in the pile. Then one, two, three...

The rest of the morning was a blur. Body after body. One, two, three. Over and over and over. There was a neat pile stacked in front of each block. After awhile Yakoff lost count. They filled the wagon until tattooed arms and broken legs hung limply over the sides. The feeling of sickness never went away.

Most of the corpses were Muzzlemen, incredibly thin, the walking dead, people who'd slipped away under the cover of night, only to be replaced by another innocent victim from the next transport. The bunks would remain full, the work would be done. The bodies were insignificant, totally irrelevant.

A prisoner carrying a medium-sized pot approached the crew and the kapo ordered the four to stop. It was lunch time. They would receive just enough food to give them barely the strength to continue their bizarre, obscene duty.

Yakoff was exhausted. News of the break, no matter how short, was well-received. The men carried their porcelain dishes with them whenever they went on a work patrol and kept them nearby. Yakoff turned and saw his dish face down in the mud, underneath the smiling Kapo's foot.

"Is this yours?" the man asked in a menacing tone. Yakoff nodded it was. "You better keep an eye on it." The inflection was sarcastic. "You lose it and you won't get anything to eat."

Yakoff stared at the man and nodded.

"What do you say, boy?" the Kapo said, spitting out the words.

"Yes sir," he replied quietly.

He retrieved the dish and wiped out the mud with his fingers. Even a makeshift polish with his shirt tail couldn't restore its cleanliness. The prisoner with the pot was dishing out contents and if Yakoff was to eat, it had to be now. Quickly he thrust the dish forward, receiving a ladle of the foul smelling soup. The thin, murky brown liquid tasted worse than it smelled, but at least it was lukewarm. At least it was something.

He held the dish with both hands, carefully sliding its contents over his lower lip, tenderly avoiding the bleeding gums. The kapo walked away leaving the four men alone. Yakoff's face asked the question and one of the old- timers answered. "They don't eat our food..."

"How's that?"

"He'll go back to his own block and eat some real food. Maybe a potato, or a turnip, or even a piece of cheese."

Yakoff envied the man's position. They all did. He discovered through guarded whispers, the kapo they worked for, comparatively speaking, was actually one of the nicer ones. He'd only hit each of them one or two times during the entire morning.

Yakoff turned, looking toward the wagon full of bodies, barely twenty feet from where they sat. There was a heavy, mournful sigh bred from hopelessness and confusion. He gazed pensively at the ground.

"You can't let it get to you," one of the men said, noticing Yakoff's condition.

"How can you not?" the youngster replied.

The man slowly shook his head from side to side. "I don't know," he whispered. "I just know you can't. Not if you're going to survive. You do what they tell you and try to stay out of their way. That, and don't give up."

Yakoff continued to stare without speaking.

"See those bodies?" the man said, pointing at the wagon. "They gave up ... and nobody cares..."

The meal break lasted less than thirty minutes. There was little conversation. Quiet-time was spent in reflection, searching for hows and whys, trying to grasp any small wisp of understanding, dotted with fleeting attempts to mentally escape the horror of it all.

The Kapo returned patting his well-fed belly, emitting a loud belch lasting nearly four seconds. The ridiculous sound had a privileged ring, serving the purpose of adding to the men's envy and misery.

"Back to work!" he grumbled, still patting. "No more rest today." The men slowly pushed themselves up from the mud. One was a little too slow so the Kapo took his afternoon exercise in the form of four roundhouse crashing blows with his stick. Each one was directed at the man's head. No retaliation was offered or words spoken. There was no need. The thud, thud, thud, thud, said everything, a complete summation. The man tried to shield himself with his arms but three of the blows found their mark. He was on his knees in the mud, blood trickling from an open wound over his left eye. Yakoff and the others watched helplessly. They knew without doubt or question that any attempt to help or protect their comrade would result in their own punishment and more than likely, death.

"Now," the Kapo said, looking down. "Are you gonna work or do you want to ride in the wagon?" Mustering every ounce of energy the man possessed, he stood straight up, acknowledging his readiness. It was understood that the alternative the kapo presented was a one-way ride to the furnace.

Is it possible, Yakoff asked himself, the Nazis would put into their ovens a man still alive? The thought of fire and flames triggered a crystal-clear image etched deeply in his mind and on his brain cells; the night the Gestapo burned down the synagogue in Sierpc, forcing at gunpoint the religious men to dance around the smoldering carnage with their trousers pulled down to their ankles. Yakoff gulped, deeply but quietly. He'd found his answer.

It was a struggle to pull the heavy wagon through the deeply rutted road. The mud was slippery, footing was impossible, knowing the consequence of falling down changed the perspective. During their rounds, Yakoff saw two other wagons, each pulled by four stripe-suited prisoners. Two other wagons carrying the same load as their own.

The perversion of the situation was too extreme to comprehend.

They were pulling a wagon full of dead bodies, skeletons, covered with disease and crawling insects, and the kapo might as well have been taking a leisurely Sunday stroll. He walked beside the pile of death, impervious to it all, swinging his stick to and fro like a police baton and whistling a bright German tune.

They halted at the main gate of the compound but their rest was short-lived. A huge black transport truck drove through the gate, turned around, and backed up to the wagon. The driver, an SS man, got out of the truck, flashed a non-caring, non-inquisitive look toward the prisoners and wagon full of corpses, nonchalantly lit a cigarette and walked away.

The two prisoners who'd worked this patrol before, moved without instruction. They lifted the tarp covering the back of the enclosed truck and lowered the tailgate. Then, jumping down to the ground, began to mechanically and methodically throw the bodies from the wagon into the rear of the truck. A cursory glance from the kapo prompted Yakoff and his still bleeding partner to follow suit.

In the time it took to transfer the naked bodies, the SS man enjoyed a brisk walk and three German cigarettes. The old-timers closed the tailgate, lowered the tarp, sealing the cargo from sight, and the Nazi returned to the scene. After a brief, hushed exchange with the kapo he smiled, patted him fatherly on the shoulder and climbed back into the driver's seat.

The engine roared to life and the macabre excuse for a hearse lumbered back through the heavily guarded gate. Yakoff watched as it drove a hundred yards down the side road and then turned left, toward the chimneys, still belching smoke and ash into the sky. The moment was particularly difficult for the youngster. The black beast of a truck was exactly the same as the one which carried his mother and the rest of his family to their death. That was what, he asked himself, trying to gain a perspective of time. A long time ago. Yes, certainly, it had to be. He counted with his fingers, trying to remember. So much had happened in so short a time. Reality didn't work anymore. So much of this was unreal. All of it was. Wasn't it? Or was it? But his fingers didn't lie and the pain and agony were a constant and lingering reminder. Yakoff arrived in Birkenau and watched his entire family trucked to their death only two nights ago.

The patrol picked up the tongue of the wagon and traveled a line parallel to the humming barbed-wire fence. Up ahead Yakoff saw a clump of something lying in the grass. As they made their way closer he could tell it was a body. This one, unlike the bodies they'd dealt with all morning, was still clad in the striped uniform. The man was lying on his back with arms and legs spread-eagle, rigid, eyes wide open and a face filled with terror. It had not been a peaceful death.

The rest of the afternoon they collected bodies of the men who "went to the wires." Men who couldn't take the pain, hunger or degradation anymore. Men who garnered enough strength to pull themselves from the lice-infected beds of plank, or freezing dirt, and walked purposely into a hail of Nazi bullets or the deadly fence itself.

The two old-timers attacked the corpse like vultures. The kapo watched dispassionately, no regard one way or the other. Yakoff couldn't understand what was happening and shook his head to clear the cobwebs. Like experienced scavengers, the two men ripped through every pocket in the limp uniform. Empty. Empty. Empty. Then one flashed a broad, brown-toothed smile at the other. "Success," he proudly whispered.

When he removed his probing hand from the dead man's pocket he unclenched a fist, showing the others his treasured find: two small crusts of black bread. The other man nodded, returning the smile. The man on his knees broke each of the small crusts in half and offered one to Yakoff. "We share," he said. "We share what we find."

Yakoff felt a rush of outrage but held his tongue. His mind screamed at every fibre in his body. Ingrate. Low, slime, vile creature to desecrate this human being. How could anyone...

But the man's actions interrupted Yakoff in mid-thought. "Watch," he said, quickly popping two pieces of the bread into his own mouth. See how I chew and swallow and eat." He paused, to see if Yakoff was learning the lesson. "This man chooses to die. That is his escape. I choose to live," Yakoff was speechless. The man on his knees was reading his face and mind like a book. He continued, "You think this bread will do any good for a dead man? Well it won't. And I feel nothing about taking it and eating it except less hungry."

The lesson was clear but repulsive nonetheless. Yakoff watched with painfilled eyes as the two carefully fingered the thickness of the dead man's overshirt. When they lifted the body from the ground, the discoverer of the bread crusts removed the shirt and put it on himself. A cold face turned to Yakoff. "This won't do him any good either."

It was then Yakoff noticed the dead man's hands. They were black, scorched from the electricity; and the smell, apparent for the first time, was atrocious. But the atrocity, when related to all Yakoff had seen in the last two days, seemed small by comparison. His mind distortedly repeated the phrase, "You'll get used to it," over and over as they walked to the next body.

The search and seizure process was repeated. This corpse carried no food but was wondrously wearing a pair of socks. They were thin with holes in both heels, but worlds better than none at all. They were no doubt a result of a trade in which the lifeless form exchanged his food, perhaps his last uneaten meal. The other old-timer received the socks and within seconds was wiggling his toes, exhibiting the prize for those less fortunate to see.

Most of the men who went to the wires, died from merely touching or grabbing the fence. This one, the one with the socks, managed to draw up the strength to hurl his entire body into the deathtrap. His hands were singed brownish-black. His shirt was crisscrossed with x's, burned by the steaming wires. But it was the man's face that turned Yakoff's stomach.

His face was charred beyond recognition. Any flesh touching the wire ceased to exist. The blood and veins were cauterized at the exact moment of impact. The skull had become an instant skeleton. The only remaining sign of life was the crawling, festering lice.

The next corpse experienced the same vulturous ordeal. Some bread was found and divided among the four men. Yakoff, still unable to force himself to eat, accepted the tiny morsel, placing it in his pocket. Maybe later, he told himself. The old-timers, watching Yakoff's actions, smiled at one another.

"You'll learn," one said.

And the other one finished the sentence..."If you're going to stay alive."

They found this body, face down in a ditch, the one dug by the prisoners themselves. It was four-feet deep at the bottom and circled the entire inner perimeter of the compound, thirty feet from the fence. Its purpose was to be a deterrent, a slowing device for those crazed, starved souls running to the wires. It also functioned as a boundary. Anyone venturing beyond the ditch would be shot without warning by guards in the watchtowers.

This body, making a suicidal run the night before, was illuminated in the floodlights and cut down by a machine gun. The chest was riddled with gaping, oozing holes, fresh and pungent. The uniform was ruined, there wasn't much left. As they lifted the lifeless form, Yakoff stole a glance toward the guard tower outside the fence, less than fifty feet away.

A guard, with features recognizable from this distance, watched the patrol go about their work. His face remained blank, unmoved by the scene unfolding in front of him. Is that the man? Yakoff asked himself, lifting the bleeding cadaver. Is that the murderer who shot down this starved, defenseless creature in cold-blood? Without a warning?

They were recovering bodies on the interior side of the enclosure, directly adjacent to the main road leading to the chimneys. Thirty feet to the fence, twenty feet to the guard tower, and over a hundred more to the road.

Something was moving in the distance, far off to Yakoff's right. It was people. A large column, marching with armed guards on either side. As they moved closer Yakoff could discern what was happening. They were women and children, some of them babies carried by mothers. Old people, elderly, frail, all wearing a pronounced yellow, six-pointed Star of David, the symbol of Judaism, sewn on their clothing in a prominent, visible place.

Yakoff turned his head to the left, toward the glowing chimneys, then quickly back toward the unsuspecting column. The chimneys, the people. Chimneys. People. Mother. Sisters. Grandparents. Little brother. How can God allow this? What in the name of anything holy is happening here?

His face turned a bright shade of crimson. Scarlet. A rage surged inside him, begging to be set free. Temples pounding, nostrils flaring, eyes blazing with confusion and hate. The pain was gone. Only the hate burning deep inside remained. The people, the old people, women and children, they must be warned. They must be told what lies ahead at the end of this road. I can't let them innocently and unsuspectingly walk to their own demise. He opened his bleeding mouth to scream...

"I wouldn't do that..." It was one of the old-timers watching the pain build to a boiling point. Yakoff stared at the man, then the chimneys, then the people, then back at the man.

"I wouldn't do that," he repeated.

Yakoff glared, his entire body trembling. The man spoke softer this time, with compassion, trying to make the youngster understand.

"If you yell at those people," he said, "you'll accomplish two things. One, you'll sign your own death warrant. Right here. On the spot. Instantly..."

"What's the other?" Yakoff asked, following a long silent pause.

"If you try to warn them, to tell them where they're going, they'll panic. They'll break rank and run, trying to get away..." Yakoff remained silent.

"Look around you," the man said. "Get away to where? They can't get out of here. None of us can. This way, if they don't know what's coming, at least they can die a peaceful death."

"Yes, but..."

The man interrupted, "But you want to warn them ..."

Yakoff waited for the man to finish. He was still trembling.

"You want to see those old people running down the road, chased and bitten by the dogs. You want to see babies dropped and trampled to death in a stampede to nowhere. You want to watch those little children drop like flies from machine gun bullets in their heads..."

Tears welled up in Yakoff's eyes and slowly trickled out, one by one. The man gently placed his hand on the youngster's shoulder and looked down into his innocent face.

"Let it go son ... there's nothing you can do."

By the time another wagon load of bodies was transferred to the black truck, the outside work patrols started returning. The columns of five spread endlessly into the distance. Faces, minds and bodies were covered with fatigue, exhaustion, despair. Eyes soulfully studied the mud in front of them. They carried and dragged bodies of men who hadn't made it through the day, men who'd be searched, stripped, and stacked outside the front of the blocks.

The routine was the same. Standing at attention, freezing, while the SS man in his long, warm overcoat, slowly went through the stupidity of the evening count. The numbers tallied, both the dead and the alive. It only took an hour and a half.

The prisoners were dismissed and began their evening trek to the latrine. By now Yakoff was starting to feel like an old-timer. The gagging, retching and coughing continued, but at least during this trip the unbelievable stench didn't weaken his knees. It was a minor victory but nevertheless acknowledged and appreciated. The man in Yakoff's bunk who was hacking and spitting-up throughout the night, managed to make it through the day. When Yakoff returned from the latrine the man was lying down, refusing to get up when the evening rations arrived.

"I can't move," he said. "What's the use?"

Yakoff tried to talk him into joining the line. He even offered assistance but the man refused. Another prisoner, eyeing the exchange, grabbed the man's bowl from under his head. "I'll bring something back," he lied, disappearing into the five hundred starving men.

The food was the same. Foul, bitter, muddy water and crusty black bread. Yakoff accumulated three or four stolen crumbs from the afternoon patrol and had them tucked safely in his pocket. These would not be left in his bunk he vowed. But they did give him the confidence to eat the two small pieces the room senior distributed.

Eating was difficult with open holes in his gums. The brick-hard pieces had to be slowly and carefully chewed with his remaining back teeth, then washed down with the vile liquid. The good Samaritan who took the sick man's bowl never returned.

Then came the hour of free time before curfew. Some of the others, with relatives or friends in adjoining blocks, ventured into the cold night air. Yakoff was not among them.

He left the coughing, hungry soul in his bunk and walked down the narrow crowded aisle looking for Leon and his other two cousins. He found them together, quietly discussing their various work patrols that day. They'd all worked outside the fence on different construction activities. Yakoff learned this amounted to little more than carrying large rocks from one location to another.

When questioned about his own work patrol he deftly avoided it. He wanted to forget the bone-thin bodies and open staring eyes. Leon and his brother Nathan appeared to be all right. They were noticeably suffering from shock and disbelief over everything going on around them but physically looked like they were holding up.

Shaya, Yakoff's other cousin, looked much weaker. He'd lost at least ten pounds over the last two days. His face was drawn and he was short of breath. He had a pained, uncomfortable look. Yakoff asked the obvious question with his eyes and Leon took him aside.

"It's the runs," Leon said. "He has the diarrhea. It won't stop."

"From the water?" Yakoff asked, knowing the answer.

Leon nodded. "His system can't take it."

The two cousins offered one another hopeless sighs of exasperation. They knew there was nothing they could do. Absolutely nothing. Shaya would miraculously heal or perish. They'd already heard about the hospital, the lone building isolated at the end of the compound. It was quietly but clearly rumored if someone went to the hospital he would never return. Suddenly Yakoff heard the phrase in his mind; if you don't work, you don't live. This time, ringing closer to home, the remembrance came with a chilling effect.

Feeling worthless, Yakoff slowly made his way through the prisoners in the aisle and returned to his bunk. There was a low babble of voices which never seemed to be raised, only the block senior and room seniors were allowed that privilege. He heard muffled prayers in the distance, always singularly. Group prayer or any organized religion was dealt with severely. That was one of the maximum punishable offenses. The man in the bunk continued coughing and retching. Yakoff couldn't tell if he was asleep or awake. Painfully he dragged himself up into the bunk and laid down, again trying for the temporary mental escape.

He finally fell asleep, his eyelids reflecting the faces of the day, the agonized eyes staring into nothingness, infinity, yet strangely seeing everything. The voices, if they could still speak, seemed to be cautioning; be careful with my body and how you throw it on your wagon of mercy, your wagon of absolute escape. The huge rumbling black trucks stereoed their way across Yakoff's brain. The same goddamned trucks ... the pleading, crying eyes and outstretched, begging, tattooed dead arms dissolved and segued into orange glowing chimneys. Ashes, white-hot, making their escape before the freezing night air of Birkenau turned them a solid, permanent black.

At first Yakoff didn't notice. Not with the piercing bell, the room seniors screaming, and sticks flying every which way. The man beside him was still. Very still. There was no more coughing or involuntary body jerks. In his rush to exit the bunk, Yakoff didn't notice the quiet body had also turned cold and rigid.

The men charged for the front door and the bone chilling morning air, ever watchful of the swinging sticks. With little more than a fleeting glance Yakoff's eyes made contact with another bunkmate, also preparing for the mad dash. Their communication was telepathic as well as swift. The other man nodded slightly and his new partner instantly understood.

The second man acted as a lookout, standing guard while Yakoff jumped back into the bunk. Their combined premonition was accurate. The noncoughing man was dead. Without hesitation Yakoff's hands found their way into the corpse's pockets, rapidly and desperately searching. There was no smile of satisfaction when he felt the uneaten crust of bread. He stuffed it into his own pocket and quickly rolled the body over. The dead man's shirt was in good shape and wasn't going to be wasted or stolen by someone else.

Hurriedly, in the cramped and limited confines of the bunk, Yakoff removed the overshirt and quickly returned to the floor just as a menacing room senior turned the corner. The timing was fortunate. Two more seconds and he'd have been discovered. Their luck continued. They made it through the door and into the morning blackness without the painful reminder of someone else's absolute authority.

Yakoff ripped the crust in two, shared it with his partner, and tunneled his way into the sea of shivering men. The additional layer of clothing helped considerably to cut the chill of the brisk, foul air. He had bread in his pocket and an extra shirt on his back. He was already way ahead of most of the men standing around him in learning the ways of survival in Birkenau. Scavenging through the pockets was accomplished without feeling. There was no sorrow or remorse. The absoluteness of life versus death is a quick deterrent against sensitivity.

The man on the work patrol was right. Food won't do a dead man any good. Nor will his clothing. As the columns shuffled from foot to foot, side to side, trying to achieve the wonderful sensation of warmth, Yakoff reached into his pocket and cradled the waiting treasure.

When he removed the crust and held it in the light he was momentarily sickened. The bread was covered with lice. Hundreds. Crawling every which direction. Making their way across his thumb and forefinger, then down his wrist.

The first reaction was to throw the stale morsel to the ground and bury it in the mud beneath his clog. But "morsel" was the most important word in the unspoken sentence. It was food. With his left hand he brushed the swarming insects away. He flicked them with his finger and wiped the crust on his pants leg.

On reexamination, he sadly discovered the creatures were coming from inside the delicacy. But it was food and couldn't be discarded. It was too valuable to throw away.

Yakoff heard footsteps from the SS man goose-stepping toward the column. He felt the crawling insects in his pocket, left over from the bread. He slapped his leg, trying to kill the stinging beasts, then turned the pocket inside out. Just as quickly, he stuffed the crust into his painfilled mouth and swallowed it whole.

After the count, latrine, and rations, he was selected for the same patrol, picking up bodies throughout the compound, throwing them on the wagon, transferring them to the black beast and watching helplessly as they roared toward the glowing chimneys.

During the afternoon collection, the four-man patrol shared several crusts of bread. For Yakoff, each bite was less distasteful. The youngster realized it was something that had to be done. There was no right or wrong attached. It just was.

He had seen in three days the agony and pain inflicted by their tormentors. It was understandable to Yakoff as well as the other prisoners how someone would purposely reach out for an instant death rather than grovel in it for hour after agonizing hour.

But the determination some of these suicidal souls possessed was virtually beyond Yakoff's comprehension. They collected a body penetrated by more than two dozen Nazi machine gun bullets. His entire chest was an empty hollow cavern. Even so, his persistence and desire to guarantee his own demise carried him all the way to the fence. The body traveled the last thirty feet to the electricity long after the soul was dead. A guard in the nearby watchtower looked dispassionately as the violated carcass was lifted onto the wagon. And the lines of women, children, and elderly, continued to march unsuspectingly down the main road.

The next morning as the men hustled through the door of the block, Yakoff confronted Leon. Even in the dim light he could see his face was pale and empty.

"What is it?" he asked, as they shuffled for position.

"It's Shaya," Leon said. There was a remorseful ring in his voice and sadly Yakoff knew further explanation was unnecessary. Leon choked a little then spoke again, "He didn't make it through the night."

Yakoff's voice failed him but he expressed concern, compassion, and feeling with his eyes. Leon nodded appreciation for the gesture and disappeared into the crowd. The count that morning seemed longer and colder.

Later, after collecting a hundred more dead bodies and before the evening rations, Yakoff silently offered prayers for his cousin. It was a reflective time, quiet. A stranger, a man Yakoff hadn't seen before, appeared at the end of the long row of bunks and slowly made his way down the aisle, stopping at each group and mumbling something in a low whisper. Yakoff was curious and watched with interest. Finally, while talking to a group no more than twenty feet away, one of the listeners turned and pointed in Yakoff's direction. Then he nodded to the stranger.

Yakoff's mind raced. Now what? Who's this and what could he possibly want? All the rapid-fire possibilities were negative. Heavy sigh. The stranger approached.

First he looked around, checking for room seniors. Then he whispered, "Are you Yakoff Skurnik?"

Yakoff stared at the stranger, not changing his expression. Without thought he placed his right hand over his left forearm, as if the stranger could see the tattoo through his shirt.

"Why?" Yakoff replied coldly.

"If you are.." the stranger said, looking around again, "I have news..."

There was a brief hesitation as Yakoff studied him. Who was he? Could he be trusted with so minor a confession? Finally..."What news?"

"Are you Yakoff?" the man persisted.

Yakoff nodded. What did he have to lose..."I am."

The stranger spoke slowly, carefully, making sure the youngster understood each word. "Your father is alive...he wants to see you... later tonight... I'll take you to the place."

Chapter IX

For the first time since he arrived, the cold night air had no effect. Yakoff's heart, beating rapidly, pumped gallons of warm blood through every vein and artery. The stranger hadn't spoken another word after the incredible announcement, except to tell Yakoff he'd return for him after the evening ration.

Eat? Who could eat? He was too excited, too overjoyed. The stranger also managed to locate Leon and share the same incredible news with him; his father was also alive. It was too good to be true. That was his only reservation; it was too good to be true.

Yakoff remembered the man's face during the tattooing process when he asked about the Sonderkommando, the special squad. He remembered the blank distant avoidance and the refusal to answer his innocent question. The time spent since that moment was too painful to ask the simplest questions of anyone. The time, Yakoff thought. The time. It seemed like a year, or was it two, or a lifetime? But now, watching the others slurp the evening rations, he had to know.

The first nine or ten people he questioned didn't look up from their soup or acknowledge his presence. The response didn't alter his determination in the least. Finally a man raised his hand. From the expression on his face and the sunken hollow eyes, Yakoff could tell the man had been there for awhile. His teeth were yellow and rotting and his breath was foul. He motioned for the youngster to join him, sitting, on his bunk.

Yakoff guessed, without asking, that his tattoo read in the sixty thousand range. That would make him a rarity. There weren't many people left with a number lower than sixty thousand on their arm. If his supposition was correct, the man was a master of survival, from whom much could be learned.

The voice was shaky, raspy, perhaps a result of too many sticks to the side of the head. But it also had a ring of authority, knowledge, a heavy Polish accent, Jewish. They spoke in Hebrew.

"Sonderkommando," he repeated, stretching out the word. "The special squad. Yes, I'll tell you about the Sonderkommando. They're personally chosen by Commandant Schwarzhuber for their size and strength."

The man looked up, waiting for a question but Yakoff remained silent, allowing him to continue.

"They're isolated within our walls and kept away from the other prisoners..."

Still no question.

"... so none of us will be aware of the horrible deeds they perform." The man nodded toward the west, the direction of the chimneys. Then he grew quiet.

Yakoff was hesitant, afraid to ask but he had to know. "What deeds?" he finally said. "What deeds do they do?"

The man took a deep breath and let it out slowly. "You know about the gas chambers ... and the crematoriums?"

Yakoff nodded but his knowledge was vague, far from accurate or complete.

"When the women, children and old ones are marched to the gas chambers they are told they're going to take showers and get cleaned up after their trip ..." The man swallowed hard with an audible gulp.

Yakoff nodded, encouraging him to continue.

"It's the Sonderkommando, in the dressing area, who assures the victims everything's going to be all right, that it's just procedure and they're going to be with their families as soon as their shower's over."

Yakoff was shocked. The information carried an electrifying effect and showed noticeably. The man's voice level remained the same.

"They'll be shot on the spot if they don't cooperate. Think for a moment, if you can, of our people. We're all going to die," then added softly, "All of us. Not having to live with that knowledge makes it far more peaceful. It's easier, much easier, if you don't know." He paused another second, breaking one of his crusts of bread in half and swallowing slowly. "Their last moments alive are probably the most calm they've known for years."

Yakoff pictured his father consoling people, convincing them everything was going to be all right, just as he'd done so many times with passengers in his carriage. This time the ride would be much shorter, and then again, much longer.

Yakoff emitted his own exasperated sigh, stood and thanked the man. "There's more," the man said. "If you really want to know."

For the first time, Yakoff didn't. But he knew he had to hear it all, the whole horrible story, so he sat back down.

He learned once the people from the transports were locked naked inside the gas chambers the Sonderkommando carefully inspected their hanging clothes. Items of value were collected and turned over to the kapo in charge.

The Jews, having no idea of their destination, let alone their destiny, carried money, food, jewelry, silver and gold. Under armed SS guard it was collected, sorted, and turned over to the kapo. He retained the choicest pickings for his own personal use and then passed the booty up the chain of command. After everyone rummaged through the remains of the dead, it was boxed, including all clothing, and shipped to Germany to help fuel the fire raging in Hitler's furnace.

But that, the man said, was the easy part of what the Sonderkommando was forced to do. The thievery was accomplished while the people in the carefully sealed room took their "showers." After the gas was turned off and the room aired out, the Sonderkommando had to enter the enclosure and remove the dead bodies.

Corpses were taken from the underground gas chambers to the crematoriums on the first floor. Here they were further desecrated. Hair was sheared which was saved and used to stuff Nazi mattresses. Under careful watch, with a Nazi dentist in attendance, every gold filling was callously ripped from every mouth. Much of this gold remained in Nazi pockets. Some was melted down and used by the Third Reich to purchase guns, tanks and airplanes, all to further the vicious cycle of mass murder.

Then, the man continued, came the worst part. The bodies were placed, three at a time, onto steel slabs, resting on wheels and pushed by hand into the ovens. The stench was unbearable, the burning took twenty minutes, the act itself caused many incidents of insanity. The men forced to perform this unbelievable atrocity went stark raving mad on a regular basis.

When insanity occurred it posed little problem or concern for the SS in charge. The men driven crazy, in several cases a result of having to burn their own family members, were shot on the spot and thrown into the ovens.

The only remains exiting the furnace were the charred, steaming skeletons, the bones. Even these were saved and used as part of a chemical formula in the manufacture of soap. Common soap. Yakoff's stomach churned again. The thought was appalling. Germany was washing its face and hands with the remains of the Jewish race.

The three walked in silence to the end of block 14 then turned right, heading north. Yakoff wanted to say something to Leon, to offer a condolence about Shaya, but chose instead to not do anything which might put a damper on the excitement of the moment.

As they passed the fronts of blocks 20 and 21 the stranger stopped several times, speaking in hushed whispers to other prisoners. He appeared to be well-known. Yakoff wondered more than once what was going on but didn't question, he maintained his silence. The stranger's business was his own and Yakoff's only real concern was seeing his father, embracing him, feeling the strength only he could offer.

More plodding through the mud and finally they reached block 22. Still the stranger didn't speak. They walked past the block and took a left, between 22 and 23. Directly in front of them was a brick wall nearly eight-feet high, spanning the distance between the two blocks. There was no gate or opening. Several men, 50, perhaps 75, were leaning against the wall and milling about. Many seemed to be talking to themselves. The stranger led Yakoff directly to the wall.

"Stand here," he said. Actually it was more like an order.

Yakoff couldn't contain himself any longer. "Why?" he asked, irritation creeping into his voice.

"Because your father's on the other side. This is where you're to meet."

Yakoff's heart raced. He nodded and the stranger walked away with Leon to another point at the wall. The waiting moments seemed like hours. What appeared to be numbers of people talking to themselves was now understandable. These men were talking to family members or friends on the other side of the wall.

He grew impatient, wondering if the whole thing was a sick, bizarre joke, another carefully contrived device to break down his will and desire to go on living.

"Yakoff..." It was a whisper, floating over the wall. It was a question and a statement, both at the same time. But most importantly, it was Pesach, his father.

"Father?" he whispered back. "Is that you?"

There was a hesitation, like someone was catching their breath or calming themselves. Then, "Yes son, it's me."

Yakoff had planned a thousand things to say and at least a thousand questions. They were all gone. Relief swept through him like a tidal wave and he was momentarily empty.

"Yakoff?... Are you there?"

Quickly, "Yes, yes. I'm here."

"How are you my son? Are you all right?"

"I'm fine father. How about you?"

"Yes, I'm fine too."

There was an unpleasant pause. What would they talk about now? Their situation? They both knew reiteration was unnecessary as well as uncomfortable. The rest of the family? Hardly. The knowledge of what happened to the rest of the family was far too painful a subject to broach.

Yakoff broke the silence, "How did you find me?"

"The man who came to your block?"

"Yes?"

"I paid him to find you and bring you here'

Paid, Yakoff questioned. Paid with what? Who inside these fences has anything to pay anyone with?

"How father? Paid with what?" Yakoff wasn't sure but he thought he heard a deep sigh from the other side.

"With food," Pesach said. "I ... I sometimes have access to food in my job."

"Oh the youngster softly replied, remembering the story from the old-timer with the foul breath. "I know of the Sonderkommando."

"I figured by now you would."

"Are the stories true?" He was hoping for a negative response.

"Probably..." Another long pause. Then, "But the important thing now is our survival. Our staying alive. Do you understand that."

Yakoff nodded, forgetting momentarily his father couldn't see him.

"Yakoff?"

"I'm sorry father. Yes, I understand."

"Are you getting enough to eat?"

His first inclination was to shade the truth. Not lie. He'd never do that. Just alter reality. "Not as much as I'd like," he finally said.

"Come back to this same spot tomorrow night. I'll have some food for you."

"Are you sure? I mean, sure that'll be alright?"

Yakoff wanted to say no, to refuse the offer, knowing the source of the food. But the superseding motivation was survival. Rejection would slowly lead him down the painful path of starvation, the path traveled unwantingly by the Muzzlemen.

"Tomorrow night," Pesach repeated, more forcefully this time.

"When will I get to see you?" The question was mixed with naivete and optimism.

"We're locked in here and not allowed to see or mingle with other prisoners. Only ourselves. For awhile this will have to do."

Yakoff understood.

"You better go now...take care of yourself...we'll talk tomorrow."

"Yes father...tomorrow..."

Curfew was nearing and the other men were also leaving the wall. As he walked back to his own block Yakoff was overcome with emotion. His father was alive! Alive... He reflected on their nightly dinners in Sierpc, when food was plentiful, tasty, abundant. Now it was taken from... He chose not to complete the thought. He fondly remembered how his father would ask each of the children what they'd learned today and now asked himself the same question.

Today I learned about the Sonderkommando, he told himself. And more about the Nazis. A foul taste entered his mouth and he tried to erase the images which followed. And food, The thought rolled slowly across his brain. The importance of food. Until this moment, food had been a necessary ingredient in the process of survival. Now he'd learned it was also the monetary exchange of the camp. With food you could obtain things, you could buy favors, you could get information. You could even find your son in a compound filled with more than twenty-five thousand prisoners.

A new transport arrived the preceding night and the bunk was again filled with several hungry souls. Yakoff reached into his pocket, removed as many lice as possible off a crust taken from a man at the wires, and savored its taste as if it were the finest meal he'd eaten in Warsaw during his class trip.

Knowing his father was alive and well made sleep come a little easier. He wished he could see him but from what he'd heard, was aware of the improbability. The worst part of the story was the eventuality facing every member of the Sonderkommando.

No man selected for the special squad was ever recirculated among the regular prisoner population. Their selection for the squad was also the guarantee of their death. Nazis, wishing to maintain the secrecy of their killing and burning, kept the squad completely isolated until their usefulness was fulfilled. Then, because of physical weakness or insanity, the special squad members were swiftly disposed of with a club to the head or assassin's bullet in the back of the neck.

One day at a time, Yakoff told himself. One day at a time. He's alive and that's all that matters. I'll deal with it tomorrow. He rearranged his cap on top of his dish, trying to make it a little softer. There was a high-pitched voice crying in the distance. Not muffled sobs, like usual, but open crying. Probably one of the new arrivals, a green-horn. Several thuds from the now familiar wood on flesh and the crying ceased.

Sleep brought the temporary escape he longed for so desperately. It'd been a long day and he'd learned much. His ability to cope was deepening, his will to survive was sharpening, his knowledge in the ways of this place of hell was growing. His last conscious thought was that somehow, someway, he was going to make it.

Survival is instantly reduced to a one-on-one situation. It's you against everybody and everything else. It's cruel, harsh, and repugnant to anyone who has never been forcefully pushed beyond the edge of that impossible to comprehend abyss.

It was just as well the old-timer with the rotten teeth and foul breath kept some information to himself. Just as well Yakoff hadn't heard the numbers and accurate statistical data surrounding the monster to the west of his block. Just as well he never knew the unlimited capabilities of the, enclosures resting in the bowels of the earth, directly under the glowing chimneys.

The Nazi's greatest wish was that the world should never know about the four crematoriums to the west of Birkenau. The secret of their hidden gas chambers, the showers, each ruthlessly murdering two-thousand people at a time, should never be told. And the ovens, burning to capacity, snuffing out the evidence of ten-thousand human beings an hour. This information must stay forever in the birdless swamp.

The old-timer was correct in his withholding. The numbers were far too vast for Yakoff to begin to understand. They were far too vast for anyone to understand. But they were what they were, and this despicable page of history could never be erased. Never.

When Yakoff returned to the wall, the number of men lingering about sharing guarded whispers with unseen voices was the same as the previous night. He went to the spot as instructed and waited an eternity. Finally the sound of Pesach's strong reassuring voice drifted over the brick divider.

Their time was limited so conversation was to the point. Yakoff told his father about Shaya and others from Sierpc who had perished. He also related stories about the ones still alive, apparently doing alright. Food and work were the main topics. While Yakoff spoke quietly about collecting dead bodies, no mention was made of the horrible job his father was forced to perform. It remained unspoken, something they both tried desperately to avoid and block from their memory cells.

When it was time to leave, Pesach quietly announced he was going to throw a package over the wall. Yakoff was attentively looking into the air and didn't notice as several other prisoners slowly shuffled closer to where he was standing. At the moment, the contents of the package outweighed wherever it came from. Food. What a deliriously delightful thought. He hadn't had a bite of real food in over ten days.

Hunger brings with it a constant nagging pain, starting at the pit of the stomach and hurting all the way to the collarbone. Ribs ache from internal pressure and the kidneys and liver beat out a regular tune of desperation. The back never stops throbbing and the entire torso is locked in the grips of an ever tightening vise.

Soon that'll be over, Yakoff thought. Soon this package over this dreadful wall will eliminate the pain and I'll have food which means strength and the ability to go on. Real food without lice in it. Solid food. What will it be? His mind danced with the possibilities. Meat. What if it's a chunk of real meat? Impossible. Too much even to consider. Perhaps a vegetable. A potato, maybe even a turnip. Heart pounding, excitement level rising, he still didn't notice the crowd of stripe-suited prisoners moving closer.

The small, tightly bound package appeared in the moonlit sky. It hung there for a second, magically suspended, out of reach, another dream shot to hell. A huge forearm appeared from nowhere, smashing Yakoff in the chest, knocking him backwards, then down. He was trampled and stepped on by eight, maybe ten other prisoners, jumping wildly in the air, each fighting desperately for the precious package.

One man grabbed it at the height of his jump. He was tackled by two others, thrown to the ground and punched in the face. The package was ripped from his grasp by another who made it ten feet before being tripped and pounced upon. Fists were swinging, blood was flowing, kicks were flying. Yakoff watched in disbelief as one of the nondescript men snatched up the prize and outran the others into the night.

The following evening a much more suspecting Yakoff appeared at the wall at the appointed hour. This visit however, he could feel the scrutinizing eyes following his every move. He chose not to relate to his father what had happened the preceding night. Rather, he thanked him graciously and let it go. Their discussion was the same. What's happening with so and so and obviously, food.

As the curfew approached and it was time to return to the block Pesach again reported he was going to throw the package.

"One second, father," Yakoff replied, his heart racing. Prisoners, probably the same ones from the night before, began moving closer, saliva dripping from their thieving mouths. Yakoff, much wiser, was aware of their presence and prepared.

Leon, and five or six other friends with fathers or relatives on the other side of the wall appeared from nowhere, forming a semicircle around Yakoff. Their backs faced the wall and expressions and demeanor told any of the would-be thieves they had a long, bloody road to hoe if they were going to steal any food this night.

It was a stand-off. Nobody moved.

"Now father," Yakoff said. The package came flying over the wall landing safely in his arms. There was shuffling and unpleasant mumbles but no one tried to break through the barrier of protective bodies. The plan had worked. For his cleverness he earned himself an onion and half a potato.

The tight-knit group met regularly at the wall, each protecting the other, as loved ones on the other side risked lives to deliver the precious commodity. The meager scraps provided sustained life in several cases. Each succeeding time the group formed their semicircle of protectiveness, they were never challenged. Indeed, Yakoff's plan worked.

He remained on the body-collecting patrol for three more grueling days. The work was abhorrent but provided the opportunity to obtain additional food. Once a pattern of regularity was established with his father, the need no longer existed.

After the morning count and latrine, which by now was nearly bearable, Yakoff drifted unnoticed to the front of the next block. He was selected with fifty others for construction work outside the fence. The kapo in charge had a mean look, a permanent menacing scowl.

The kapo told his unwilling recruits he had no aversion whatsoever to killing any of them on the spot if they failed to perform the work he assigned. It was not the most pleasant way to begin the morning. He continued, with great braggadocio, explaining he personally was responsible for beating to death at least four people every work day.

"Five on Sundays," he added with a sinister laugh.

Carrying their bowls the men formed columns of five and marched to the compound gate. There they turned left and walked to the main road. Then a turn to the right and toward the main entrance. It was the first time since his arrival Yakoff had been outside the interior fences of his enclosure and it gave him an odd but limited sense of freedom.

It also gave him a minor concept of the size and scope of the camp. Other work patrols were approaching the main road from all directions. There were thousands of prisoners. Tens of thousands, dressed alike, plodding in lines of five through the mud. The scene was awesome. A sight never to be forgotten. A massive sea of blue and black striped prisoners, more than anyone could possibly count, all destined eventually for the chimneys behind them.

They walked past the stiff, frozen bodies of the men who went to the wires the night before. The sight was so common no one bothered to look. Eyes down, in the mud, straight ahead. One day at a time. One step at a time. Death was everywhere, covering Birkenau like a freshly fallen snow, evenly blanketing everything in sight.

At the main entrance, the kapo reported the number of prisoners he had with him to an SS man who noted the figure on a clipboard. The column marched through and was joined on the other side by five armed guards who would spend the day with them.

The helmeted Nazis talked loudly among themselves about the numbers of prisoners they'd shot in the back while attempting to escape. They laughed about the notches they should each have on the stocks of their rifles. Their conversation, planned well in advance, was effective. The worst part was, it was also true.

A man tripped in the mud. The kapo was instantly on him with his stick, beating wildly, screaming like a crazed madman. The rest of the prisoners stood back, well out of the way. The guards nudged each other, smiling, slowly sucking German cigarettes.

The work made little sense to Yakoff. It consisted of carrying heavy rocks from one large pile to another over a hundred yards away. After the fifty men had transported the entire stone mountain, they were ordered to return the rocks to their original position. It was hard, trying work. Arduous, senseless. An exercise in exhaustion. Back and forth. Back and forth. Under the smiling eyes of the guards and vicious stick of the kapo.

Men dropped in their tracks, too tired to continue, until the kapo administered his merciless brand of motivation. A prisoner was beaten to death in front of Yakoff's eyes.

"That's one," the kapo gleefully shouted to the others. The tone was nauseating. "Faster!! Faster!!" the kapo screamed, blood dripping off the sides of his stick. Without reason or regard, he hit each man walking. One dropped his heavy load after a resounding whack and the kapo ordered all activity to cease. He had the man bend over at the waist and delivered twenty-five blows to his back, the last five while the man was face down in the mud, unconscious. It was impossible to tell at what point during the beating the man died. The kapo kicked the lifeless body in the face and blood oozed from his sunken eyes. The corpse was left where it was, another obstacle to walk around or over.

"That's two!"

This went on until the midday break for rations. Those who performed slowly, in addition to the beatings, were forced to stand at attention during the entire break period and even denied the foul tasting soup. The soldiers continued to be amused.

The afternoon was more of the same. Haul the rocks. Back and forth. Pile to pile. Mindless, senseless, stupid. Only designed to exhaust the prisoners and break their will. And it worked. More beatings without reasons.

"That's three!!"

Smiling guards. Men collapsing. Bodies everywhere. On and on. Over and over and over.

At the end of the day they were ordered to stop the ridiculous ordeal. The bodies were gathered up and carried or dragged back into camp. The survivors were near death. Few had the strength to speak. Worse than that, there was nothing to say if they could.

As they plodded back toward the main gate Yakoff heard a foreign sound in the distance. At first he thought he was hearing things, that his mind had finally, actually snapped. Each step convinced him otherwise. It was music. A band was playing out here in the middle of nowhere. It was a German marching tune. Bright, airy, happy, with a strong steady beat.

The road was filled with thousands upon thousands of prisoners. Tired, dragging, ready to drop. As each column neared the gate its kapo moved among the men, striking violently, forcing them to walk in step with the music.

Yakoff, strong enough to pull a body behind him, turned to the man on his right.

"What the hell's going on?"

"For the count," the man moaned. "It's to keep us in straight lines so the guards can count by fives when we match through."

Yakoff nodded and wishing to avoid the painful sting of the stick joined step with the rest of the group. Of the fifty men who left that morning, only thirty-six kept cadence with the music.

Chapter X

Cold December winds blew ruthlessly through the open swamp. Each day the temperature dipped lower and lower. Pesach delivered a pair of socks, thin but without holes, in one of his packages. They were welcome and never removed. The mud, which at first had a freezing effect, formed a cake-like shell, hard, conforming to the foot and providing insulation. Warmth, in any form or extent was much appreciated.

The next day Yakoff avoided the killer kapo and joined another patrol. Construction work was the same, hauling rocks from pile to pile, back and forth. No sense. None at all. It would have been ridiculous to say the work was easier because it wasn't. The appreciable difference was the lack of methodical killing. The dead men returning to camp were a result of literally being worked to death. They numbered ten.

This went on six days a week. Sunday, traditionally set aside for rest, was just that. Most men, unless forced otherwise, spent the entire day in their bunks. Those fortunate enough to possess underwear or socks, would venture to the washrooms to launder their prized articles. There were two so-called washrooms for the entire compound, which meant there was one for every twelve-thousand men.

The washrooms were ludicrous. There was one trickling flow of rotten water in each building. Often it was necessary to stand in line for ten or twelve hours to wash out a pair of soiled underwear.

It was not uncommon for the kapos or block seniors to assemble large groups of prisoners in the freezing air and mud for punishment. This consisted of standing at attention, in any weather, for the entire day. Sometimes men were forced to assume the attention position while kneeling. The freezing cold started at the knees and slowly worked up the body into the brain. Balance was lost. Equilibrium was impossible. If a man wavered or fell to the ground, he was beaten with reckless abandon while wallowing in the mud. Ah yes, Yakoff pondered facetiously. Sunday, the day of rest.

Hanukkah, the Feast of Lights, passed without formal recognition. This deeply troubled most prisoners, since Hanukkah was celebrated to commemorate Israel's first recorded victory in the battle for religious liberty. A small band of Jews fought valiantly to defeat a mighty Syrian army in order to rescue Judaism as a faith and way of life from obliteration. This year the celebration was silent and private. This year no candles were lit or group prayers offered. It was too dangerous and the Nazis, as well as kapos, were watchful for small gatherings of any kind. The punishment for discovery would be swift and severe. The traditions of thousands of years were strained. Questions never before questioned were asked. Beliefs were painfully transferred into doubts. It was a time of trial. The greatest of which was this very place itself.

Christmas Sunday they'll certainly leave us alone. Won't they?

It was early, pitch-black, when the yelling and screaming started. The wish for a real Sunday of rest was another exercise in wasted futility. This Sunday was different. Following the familiar "Raus! Raus!" came a further stipulation; only the Jews were to assemble outside.

"Now what," was a muffled, choir-like response as the Jews dragged their weary bodies from the bunks to the cold dirt floor. They were used to separatism, but this was the most extreme example to date. The gentiles remained peacefully in their bunks, most shrugging off the call with total indifference.

The morning seemed darker, the air colder, the pungent, flesh-like aroma, hung unusually low in the sky... Jews from blocks on either side were heard shuffling in the mud. Yakoff sensed today would be different. It was an ominous foreboding feeling, growing in accuracy with each day of survival.

A rumor factory throughout the compound shared and embellished information among the prisoners. The major news whispered from bunk to bunk during last night's rations, was that the Commandant and all his senior officers would be taking a Christmas holiday. If that's the case, Yakoff wondered, turning up the collar on his shirt, who's left in charge of the camp.

When the columns formed and the neat rows of ten were established, they marched out of their compound towards the main road of the camp. Then they waited.

Sunrise broke through the fog and Yakoff was astonished at the sight unfolding before his eyes. Prisoners from compounds on both sides of the main road were standing in formation at attention. Like the work patrols, the number totaled well into the tens of thousands. It was quiet.

Are all these people Jews, Yakoff asked himself. If given the opportunity to see the upside down triangles under tattoos on every left forearm, the question would have gone unasked. Yes, they were all Jews, prisoners from every country in Europe, the unwilling pawns and participants in Hitler's Final Solution.

A large contingent of SS men and armed guards marched through the main gate, divided themselves into two groups, and took positions spacing themselves evenly on either side of the road. The entire canine patrol was with them and by their vicious and unrelenting snarling, unfed.

This was the first time the men were exposed to this particular formation. They held their ranks, silently wondering what the German captors had in store on this the highest and most holy of Christian holidays.

It didn't take long to find out. From the far right of the column came a thundering which shattered the silence. Yelling, screaming, footsteps, wooden clogs pounding through the mud at full speed. The dogs were barking wildly.

Yakoff stood precariously on his tiptoes, straining, trying to see what was happening. When the pounding noise reached the front of him, the vision was all too clear. Prisoners, an endless, continual line, were running down the center of the road as fast as their weary legs would carry them. Guards, on either side, were beating them with sticks and whips as they ran by. Killer dogs, trained to attack anyone in a striped uniform moving faster than a slow walk, snapped and bit all legs and ankles within striking distance.

Kapos and room seniors moved Yakoff's column to its right, towards the head of the line. Thousands of eyes darted everywhere looking for some possible escape from the upcoming pain. No one tried to run. There was no possible escape, and movement from assigned positions called for certain death.

As the continuous blur of men ran by, they were holding and carrying something. Yakoff couldn't see what it was but it apparently had something to do with the vicious Nazi plan. Whenever anyone dropped what they were carrying, the guards attacked with an abundant degree of violence. When the unfortunate soul bent over to retrieve his precious cargo, Sticks from all directions pummeled him to the ground. Most never got back up. They were dragged to the side of the road and left in a growing pile.

Some were still alive. Their moaning and cries for help created a bizarre counterpoint to the yelling, screaming, and barking which filled the air. Another sound, unfamiliar and out of place, added to the cacophony ringing in Yakoff's ears. It was the sound of laughter. The guards wielding sticks and whips were laughing hysterically at each fallen prisoners, some so hard they were doubled over holding their sides.

Yakoff's column moved closer to the head of the line. A fearful trembling was felt. The Muzzlemen resigned themselves to the fact this was their final day and felt nothing, absolutely nothing. Those who had decided over days, weeks or months they would find their freedom by going to the wires, felt cheated. They were denied the opportunity of spending Nazi bullets. Bullets which would be used on others who could have had a chance to live.

Bodies piled higher at the sides of the road and the sickening laughter shot through the crisp morning air. Legs, arms and faces were ripped open by the well-trained snarling animals. It was beyond ludicrous; the pain and suffering inflicted unnecessarily upon other human beings, the ridiculous, senseless waste of lives. Like everything else, it made no sense. It was completely illogical.

But to the Germans, the Nazis, this particular exercise at the expense of the Jews was considered "sport." It was a part of the planned annihilation. Rid the world of the Jewish race. Kill them all. No matter how, no matter where, just kill them all.

Yakoff's group reached the front of the deadly line and guards, screaming through their laughter, explained the "game" they were playing. Each man was to pick up a load of dirt, rocks, sand or mud, and carry it in his cap or shirt tail to the other end of the road, a thousand yards away.

"If you make it," they laughed, "turn around and try to make it back to the starting point."

Selecting what the guards considered a suitable load was hurried along by swinging sticks. No one was excluded. If you were a Jew, you played.

Yakoff filled his cap, and a sharp blow to the small of his back sent him quickly on his way. Nazis up ahead were swinging at men's kneecaps, trying to break their legs and bring them permanently down. This added to the ease of their execution. Dogs ran wildly beside the prisoners sinking long sharpened teeth into unfortunate thighs and calves. It was an obstacle course with death for the losers.

Yakoff was smashed in the chest and spit up blood. A whip lashed across his shoulders, barely missing his face but somehow he maintained his balance. A dog, flashing teeth, lunged in his direction, but at the last second, decided to take a large bite out of the man to his right. The bite was followed by thuds and whacks from the sticks. There was no reason to look around. He knew the man was dead, another corpse, dragged to the growing pile.

Insanity prevailed. People were dropping like flies. With each pain-inflicted fall came the certainty of a crushed skull. The Nazis were relentless, perverse, enjoying what they were doing. The prisoners kept running, an endless stream of targets, trying desperately to avoid the sticks and dogs, trying to stay on their feet and alive.

Some gave up. They let the first blow take them down and waited with hollow sunken eyes, not even trying to protect themselves. The release from this hell, was their only escape.

Yakoff narrowly avoided another set of snarling fangs, being careful to guard and protect his valuable capful of dirt. His eyes swept from side to side, watching for the Nazis, dancing away from their weapons. It was necessary, every ten feet or so, to run around or jump over a body. Legs, dead-tired and exhausted, were like lead. Clogs slipped and slushed through the gripping mud, even more difficult to traverse with the fresh blood flowing through the ruts. The cuffs of his blue and black striped pants turned a grotesque shade of human red.

He blinked for a second and a leather whip caught him in the stomach. He doubled over and his knees started to give out, but miraculously he didn't fall down. There was no explanation fathomable except for the will to go on, the will to survive.

One thought. One overriding constant thought: to live, to make it through one more day. Maybe tomorrow...maybe somehow... Yakoff could see the end of the road ahead. His goal, the one with the chimneys in the background. The chimneys that would soon reduce to ashes the countless bodies strewn at the side of the road.

The sound of Nazi laughter was the loudest of the noises. It screamed into his ears, pounding relentlessly at his brain. Who are these men? How can anyone do a thing like this? It's Christmas Sunday for God's sake. These men are Christians. Believers. Most of them have wives and children. This morning they went to a church service, praising the birth of their Lord Jesus Christ. They asked for His countenance and blessing; and for what? To march inhumanly into the depths of hell, and murder innocent people unable to defend or protect themselves?

Yakoff was not unfamiliar with the words, he'd heard them before: "And forgive us our trespasses as we forgive those who trespass against us ... and lead us not into temptation..." What, in the name of God and all that's holy can that possibly mean to these people, these mass murderers of women and children. What?!

He arrived at the end of the road, turned around and started back through it all again. More beating, more pain, more laughter-filled violence. The men were thinning out. The piles of death on either side grew at an alarming rate. Step after step, around the bodies, avoiding the sticks and dogs. It went on for hours. An endless, continual cycle. Around and around. How much can a human body take? How much can a soul withstand? It was relentless, but a force unknown and deep inside, pushed Yakoff on.

Finally, as quickly as it began, it stopped. The results of the Nazi "sport" were incomprehensible. The death toll was in the thousands. The remaining prisoners, barely able to stand, were ordered to carry the corpses back into their respective compounds.

Yakoff grabbed a body by the wrists and turned it over. The man's face was nearly chewed away. He was too tired to be sick. He walked backwards, pulled the mangled corpse toward block 14 and saw Leon walking in his direction. Thank God, Yakoff thought. Leon made it. He was carrying a body in his arms and his face was a chalky grey, empty, completely blank.

As he neared, the reason for the look became abhorrently apparent. Leon was carrying his brother Nathan. Yakoff's cousin was dead. His heart cried out to Leon and then sank to new depths. He was empty, a void. Now he, Leon, and their fathers, both in the Sonderkommando and never to be seen again, were the only ones left alive from his family. Yakoff lifted his eyes to the heavens and slowly shook his head from side to side.

Much later that night, lying in his bunk unable to move, the front door of the block burst open, capturing Yakoff's attention. Another transport arrived, a major transport with thousands of fresh prisoners for slave labor.

That was it, Yakoff thought. The reason for thousands of senseless murders today. To make room for the new arrivals. New, fresh bodies, better able to carry rocks from one stupid pile to another.

Four trembling, freshly shaved, freshly tattooed souls crawled into Yakoff's lice-infected bunk. He closed his eyes seeking escape, avoiding their questions. They'd learn soon enough. He shuddered at the combined thoughts of bodies stacked in front of the blocks, and the parents, wives, and children of the new arrivals, marching unsuspectingly towards the west, towards the showers. He shuddered at the mind-wrenching work facing his father. Tonight the chimneys would burn brightly. This would be a Christmas Yakoff would never forget.

The following days were difficult. Punishment from the Christmas run had severely taken its toll. Each morning he'd drag his black and blue body out of the bunk and exist through another twenty-four hours. The only part of the day Yakoff looked forward to was the evening, after the second count, when he'd talk with his father over the brick wall. His father had become his only real friend. The youngster learned how illogical it was to form friendships with other prisoners. They had an unfortunate tendency of disappearing or dying too quickly.

Once this occurred with a bunkmate who went to the latrine one black night and never returned. Another man, also a bunkmate, turned into a Muzzleman in front of Yakoff's eyes. The youngster even tried to share his own food with him but the man refused, growing thinner each passing day.

One night, in whispered silence, he told Yakoff he couldn't go on anymore, he was going to the wires. Yakoff pleaded with his friend to hold on, not to give up, somehow he'd make it. But the man's empty eyes indicated how far gone he actually was. Like so many others, he'd lost his entire family to the Nazis and could find no reason for continuing his own miserable existence.

Repeated pleading was pointless. Yakoff even tried soliciting help from other prisoners to talk his friend out of the suicidal mission.

"Leave him alone," was the universal response. "If he wants to go to the wires, let him."

Before failing into a much needed sleep, Yakoff wrapped his arms around his friend, holding him close to his own body. He could sense the hollow eyes staring into nothingness. "Please, my friend," he whispered in a final attempt, "don't do it..."

When Yakoff awoke to the bell, screaming, yelling and the continuation of the madness... his arms were empty. The man had become another statistic. One less Jew to kill.

Throughout the day Yakoff thought about his friend, about his head being shaved, the gold fillings ripped from his silent mouth, and Pesach, placing his friend's body on a steel slab and rolling it into the white-hot oven. Friendships, and their loss, were too emotionally expensive. They cost too much. Yakoff countered the all too painful experience by becoming a loner.

He'd help someone, whenever possible, especially newcomers, the greenhorns, inexperienced in the ways and rules of survival in Birkenau. This was done to the point of sharing food with others who'd had theirs stolen, which was commonplace.

Yakoff was still receiving small morsels of food from his father so it was possible, on occasion, to offer his portion of the foul tasting soup and crusts of bread to others more needy than he. This deed, in his own mind, was never considered an act of charity. Rather, it was an act of necessity. Watching a fellow human being starve to death while sleeping beside you was far more tormenting and gut-ripping than the planned, well-executed Nazi deaths which were normally swift.

He was assigned to a new work patrol on a semipermanent basis. At first, Yakoff felt being taken off the rock carrying squad was a blessing in disguise. Quite the opposite proved to be true.

He was chosen, with thirty others from his block, to work for an indefinite period of time, inside the women's compound. Both sections, Yakoff's and the women's, were officially designated as compound B-1. The men's being B-1-b and the women's B-1-a. The women's compound was directly to the east, through the double wire fence, fifty yards across the access road, and through another electrified enclosure.

Several prisoners in Yakoff's block expressed the opinion that he'd been lucky in his selection. Because he was working on the women's side, the tasks would be easier, the kapos would be more lenient and perhaps even understanding. His first daily report to the others silenced their accusations.

The work was grueling. The patrol was assigned to dig ditches and lay pipe within the entire area of the women's compound. Ultimately, the result was to provide a source of water, rotten as it was, for the women's latrines and washrooms. Their tools were crude and most of the actual digging was done by hand.

Ditches were dug down the middle of each road in the compound. This provided additional hardships on all the workers, for the roads had a thin top layer of lime. When mixed with the mud and thousands of clogs trudging over them, the footing was impossible to navigate or maintain.

"Schnell!! Schnell!! Faster!! Faster!!" was a constant cry. The kapos in charge of this and similar patrols, were determined to receive an abundance of work from the men in their charge. Each time a prisoner fell, a result of the slippery, lime covered surface, the kapo was instantly on his back, beating and screaming for the man to get to his feet and return to work.

Yakoff noticed the primary source of motivation for the increased violence and hostility. Each time one of the women's kapos was within the immediate vicinity, their own kapo showed an inherent tendency of being much more harsh and cruel. They were performing for their female counterparts; a sick animalistic dance, designed to catch the female's attention and favor.

After each of these momentary sightings and vicious beatings with accompanying verbal abuse and threats, the kapos, both man and woman, would smile at one another. He was seeking her approval in the form of a gratuitous nod or wink.

The perversion of their overt barbarism was sickening. The reality that both kapos involved were prisoners and had absolutely nothing to gain from the senseless acts of violence made it even more so.

Still, logic had no bearing in this place. The beatings were as regular as clockwork, occurring each time a woman and her work patrol walked by. Yakoff was the victim of many of these performances. His chest, legs, and back were permanently discolored. Freedom from pain was little more than a wish, a dream captured briefly during the fleeting night hours of solitude.

It was the end of January when the block senior made the announcement during the morning roll call.

"Who will volunteer," he asked, "for a physical examination? We need people between the ages of eighteen and twenty-five who wouldn't mind missing a full day's work."

The room seniors chuckled at the offbeat humor. Their laughter was the only sound. There were no eager shouts from the prisoners.

"Come on," the senior continued. Not pleading but forceful, "A full day without work. You'll be done with the physical after lunch and can have the afternoon off."

A hand went up on Yakoff's left, then another on his right. The necessary quota was quickly being filled. His mind vividly flashed on the day ahead, grueling backbreaking work and slipping, always followed by incessant, never ending beatings. His ribs and side were sore to the touch. They longed for a day off, a whole day without pain.

Before logic could dispel the "never volunteer for anything" rule, pain took precedence. His right arm shot into the air and he was picked. In the darkness, Yakoff couldn't see the old-timers around him, shaking their heads in a "you'll be sorry" fashion. Advice within the camp was seldom offered. It was impossible, based on the lack of Nazi logic, to ever know if it was accurate or not.

The only thing Yakoff felt as the others marched away to their assigned work patrols was relief. Admittedly, it was based upon a German assurance. but it was better than nothing. For the first time, a day began with hope.

Twenty-five youngsters shuffled back and forth in the freezing mud, waiting tentatively, filled with apprehension about their supposed day off. A man approached the group and announced his name was Doctor Schumann. The prisoners were to follow him. As they marched without guards into the women's section, Yakoff's heart sank. It was another trick, another devious lie intended to build up hope about the smallest of things, then callously snatch it away.

When they marched past the work patrol, the one Yakoff was usually assigned to, he realized his questioning and mental accusations were inaccurate. Several of the workers' faces expressed a look of envy.

The most envious of them all was the man lying on the lime covered road being beaten. Yakoff stole a glance to his right and saw a women's patrol marching the other direction. Their kapo shared a sinister smile with the man wielding the stick.

Women within the camp were not treated with special favor or leniency. They, like the men, were shaved, tattooed, given threadbare rags for clothing, mashed into lice-infected blocks and treated inhumanly.

Women SS members and kapos were as bad as their male counterparts. Often, women were forced to disrobe and stand stark-naked in the freezing weather for hours on end, solely for the amusement of their captors, many of whom were lesbians. Sexual favors were forced and often traded for life.

It was common for an SS man to enter the women's compound, order an entire block to remove their clothing and ridicule and animalistically fondle anyone he desired. Rape, with the promise of instant death as an alternative, was a regularity within the fences of the women's section.

But Yakoff was still a virgin and those earthly pleasures had not yet been experienced. In Sierpc, at the time of his childhood, sex was not something discussed on the street. The father explained it to the son when he was old enough to become engaged.

Yakoff's only exposure to sex had been through conversations with other prisoners in the block. Conversations of remembrance, now bordering fantasy. A fantasy Yakoff knew would have to wait.

The block was like the thirty-five others in the compound, no visible difference to set it apart from the rest. Once inside was a different story. The group immediately noticed the relative cleanliness of the walls as well as the people who worked within. And the building had a floor, the first floor they'd seen since the memorable train ride bringing them to this place of destruction.

There was a familiar smell, but Yakoff couldn't put his finger on exactly what it was. They were ushered into a long narrow waiting room with wooden benches on either side. Another prisoner following the group into the room was considerably different than themselves; he was clean. He wore shoes rather than clogs and had on clean socks. His striped uniform showed no traces of mud or wear. His hair was longer than most, and combed.

From his walk and stance they could tell the man was much better fed than they, and didn't exhibit the cowering ambiance so prevalent among the general prisoner population. The unspoken conclusion; this was a very privileged man.

He carried a clipboard and ordered each of the volunteers to roll up their left sleeve. Then he circled the room, carefully recording the numbers of the tattoos. Following this, he told the group to remove their clothing and wait.

Then Yakoff got it, the smell. It was the same smell he remembered from being in the hospital in Sierpc after his arm was broken on three different occasions. The same distinctive, antiseptic aroma. Of course, he justified. Aren't we here for a physical? Wouldn't this be a medical facility? His justification served to provide only momentary pacification.

The group did as told, sharing facial expressions of "what now?" answered with shrugs of, "beats me." The only thing they knew for sure was none of them were outside in the freezing cold, doing back-breaking work and getting beaten. These three indiscernible points made whatever was going on both palatable and easier to live with.

Doctor Schumann opened a door at the far end of the room and read a five digit number. The man with the corresponding identification mark on his left arm, stood and walked through the door. The rest waited, covering themselves with their hands.

After awhile the man returned and sat back down. He looked alright, nothing appeared to be wrong, no visible or noticeable changes. He shook his head, answering the questioning stares with a "no big deal" look, like nothing of importance had occurred.

Schumann appeared again and a second man followed him out of the room. The prisoners, now alone, leaned closer and whispered, "What happened?"

The man shook his head, offering a look of innocence.

"Nothing. Absolutely nothing."

"What did they do?"

He shrugged, "It was just a physical."

"But did they..."

"Like I said," he replied, cutting short the questions. "A physical. A plain examination. Look,"...he held out his arms, "no scars, no welts, no cuts. They don't even have sticks or whips in there."

The men smiled at that piece of good news and sat back down, a little more at ease. Maybe they were telling the truth. Maybe we will make it through a whole day without getting beaten. It was a pleasant thought but much too impossible to hold for very long. This place was mired in lies and deception and nothing the Nazis said could ever be trusted or believed.

After three more people returned with the same report, it was Yakoff's turn. Tentatively, even with the information received, he followed Schumann into the next room.

It was well-lit by an overhanging lamp. Four other clean looking prisoners, assistants, were in the room. Schumann never touched Yakoff. Instead, he issued clear and distinct orders to his helpers.

First Yakoff's height was measured. He was still 5'5". He stood on a scale and his weight was taken. A prisoner deftly slid the steel bar back and forth until it stopped, balancing at one hundred and ten. He'd lost more than thirty pounds in the six weeks since his arrival. Another quick, fleeting realization, if it weren't for his father, by now he would have wasted away to nothing. Odd, how anyone could feel lucky in a place like this.

But luck, unknown at the time to Yakoff, had a great deal to do with it. Survival, to a large extent, included being at the right place at the right time. Skillful positioning for selection to proper work patrols was necessary for longevity. It was important to be picked for patrols returning to camp with more men walking than carried. Getting to know the work kapo was an integral part of the process. A kapo would never dismiss or let anyone out of a beating, but hopefully during the punishment, a punch or two might be pulled or held back. All this plus food. A secondary, additional source of food was virtually imperative if life was to continue. Those without it, perished.

126

Yakoff was still learning the subtle nuances of the camp, the ins and outs, tricks, things necessary to stay alive.

He walked between two assistants to a large machine facing the far wall. There was a door by the machine with a small window showing a room on the other side. The smaller room had equipment visible and reminded Yakoff of similar devices he'd seen during unpleasant, painful childhood visits to the hospital.

A feeling of uneasiness settled around him. He repeated the message reported by others who recently left this room; nothing happened, nothing hurt, there was no pain. The feeling wouldn't go away. He erased the troublesome questioning with thoughts of what might have been; the cold, the rocks, the mud and the beatings.

The machine was unlike anything Yakoff had ever seen. It was large, a drab green, and stood nearly to the ceiling. It had a pedestal on the near side, like a running-board, with small chrome-covered wheels on both ends. Behind the pedestal was a box-shaped device, three-feet tall, flat, and two-feet square on its top. The covering was plastic.

But the thing on top was what intrigued Yakoff the most. It was a large, upside down pyramid, a cone shaped thing, suspended in the air by a stainless steel post. It looked innocent and ominous at the same time. His open eyes and look of concern gave him away.

"Don't worry," Schumann said, "nothing's going to hurt. Just relax and you'll be out of here in a minute."

Schumann didn't seem like the rest of the Nazis. He wasn't harsh and showed no overt signs of cruelty. Even his voice had a comforting, reassuring tone.

Two assistants held Yakoff's arms and helped him stand on the rubber covered pedestal. Then, turning the chrome wheels, they adjusted its height until the square table was just below waist level.

Another assistant reached forward and placed his hand on Yakoff's penis. The youngster grabbed the man's wrist, pulling it away. His face instantly turned a bright shade of crimson. His heart pounded rapidly.

"Calm down," Schumann said, in the same controlled reassuring tone. "We're not going to hurt you. We just want you to place your penis and testicles on the table in front of you."

Yakoff glared at the man "I can do that...without any help."

"That'll be fine."

Slowly, with much reservation, Yakoff heeded the request. The thought of asking what they were going to do was uppermost in his racing mind, but experience had painfully taught him no questions were ever asked of the SS, the guards, or the kapos.

The plastic was cold. The sense of humiliation was worse. Thank heaven, as if it would have mattered in the least, there were no women in the room.

Schumann: "Would you move your penis to one side..." Yakoff didn't understand but followed the instruction. The doctor pointed at the large green hanging cone and an assistant manually lowered it towards the table. "Don't move," he said.

The bottom tip of the cone was brought as close as possible, without touching, to Yakoff's right testicle. "Don't move," he repeated. Yakoff was too frightened to do anything. Sweat poured from his brow and armpits, the sticky smelly kind, instantly giving away innermost fears.

The assistants moved away from the machine, to the back wall, as far away as possible. Schumann walked into the smaller room and closed the door behind him. When the door slammed shut it exuded a thud of finality. Yakoff could see the doctor through the window, positioning himself in front of one of several pieces of equipment. Schumann reached forward and placed his right hand on an oversized black dial.

A loud "clunk" filled the room when Schumann moved his hand. Yakoff didn't flinch. He was still too frightened. The cone shaped whatever it was, even with Yakoff's eye level, began to emit a low dull hum. It was painless. There was no sensation or feeling at all. Only the cold from the plastic and the hot sticky sweat, still dripping.

Sixty seconds later the "clunk" sound echoed again and the humming ceased. An assistant walked to the machine, moved the cone until it hung ominously over the left testicle and returned to his position at the far side of the room.

"Clunk," followed by the humming. Then it was over.

"You can step down now," Schumann said, reappearing at the doorway, "and rejoin the others."

Yakoff was greeted with the same questioning faces as the ones preceding him. All he could do was shrug his shoulders in a gesture of complete non-understanding.

"It was nothing," he said. "Absolutely nothing."

Chapter XI

"Work Makes Freedom" the sign said.

Bold, block, black German letters spanning the thirty-foot entrance to the new camp. The morning darkness obscured the surroundings during their mile and a half walk so it was understandable none of the prisoners from Birkenau knew where they were. It was cloudy, not even stars were visible.

Much of the walk was through open fields, familiar to some from their outside work patrols. They were heavily guarded and no conversation was allowed, not even when they crossed the railroad tracks which carried them all to this dreaded place.

The morning started the same as any other. The bell, screaming, latrine, rotten water, dragging outside the ones who hadn't made it through the night, standing in freezing, late February air for the count, anticipation of back breaking work and beatings to follow. Normal things, by now ridiculously familiar.

But this morning, before the kapos arrived to handpick their work patrols, the routine was broken. A motorcar drove into the compound and stopped directly in front of the block. A large burly man, a civilian, got out of the car and had a short, hushed conversation with the SS man in charge. Those close enough to see the man were clearly envious. He wore a thick wool overcoat, hanging past his knees, providing more than adequate warmth as the coat was unbuttoned. The vest under his matching suit-jacket was stretched and straining from an abundant and rotund belly. The man looked very German.

Without explanation the well-fed civilian and the SS began marching row by row through the men. They would stop occasionally and the man wearing the long coat would point at one of the shivering survivors, then walk down the row.

When they finished the SS made an announcement; those selected were to go immediately to the main gate of the compound. There were no plans to make, nothing to pack. The men wore everything they owned.

No one had any idea if they'd been chosen for a different work patrol or selected as the next candidates for the gas chamber.

At the gate they were met by a different SS man and a full contingent of guards. Each of their numbers was recorded on the SS clipboard and the silent march through the open fields began.

Now, as the sun was hanging half in the horizon, they could read the words as they marched underneath them..."Work Makes Freedom". And, for the first time in more than eleven weeks of confinement, Yakoff finally realized where he actually was. He just entered AUSCHWITZ.

This camp was considerably different from Birkenau. Blocks were constructed out of red bricks, three stories high, and only separated by fifty feet between each. The roads were much harder, more defined, perhaps a cobblestone or pressed rock. Prisoners, walking without guards to various work patrols, had a more relaxed attitude. And the place was clean, remarkably clean. It was reminiscent of college campuses Yakoff had seen during his class trip to Warsaw; neat rows of dormitories.

It was smaller than what they'd grown accustomed to. As they entered the gate they could actually see the far side of the camp in the distance. When they crossed the first main road, fences were visible to their right and left, clearly defining the interior perimeter of the compound.

For all of its initial differences, the fences remained the same; double barbed wire, ten-feet high, six-feet between each fence, and still singing their constant and never ending song of death.

Yakoff wasn't sure if he was comforted or relieved about Leon and several others he knew also being handpicked for this patrol. Only time would tell. Still no explanation as to why they were moved here. Those things would come, as they had in the past, via discovery.

The column marched straight ahead to the third and last row of blocks, then turned to their left. In single file they entered the building nearest the fence, designated as block 1, the disinfectant area. Barbers shaved each of their heads as quickly as possible, leaving small piles of hair throughout the room. Another prisoner, checked inside each of their mouths to see if anything was being smuggled into the camp.

The armed guards remained outside. Yakoff and the others were back in the custody of prisoners carrying sticks and whips. One, a short German who walked with a limp, ordered the new arrivals to remove their clothing and hang it on hooks on the walls.

Most of the men began to unbutton their overshirts, but one hesitated. The guards, proving they were no different than the ones in

Birkenau, began to savagely beat him. This continued while the others undressed.

Then the man with the limp opened a door leading to a smaller room, also without windows, and ordered the naked mass through.

"You're going to take a shower," he said.

A shower, Yakoff thought, nearly breaking into a full-scale smile. How long has it been? Three months? Four? The thought was little more than a fond remembrance. His mind reached back to happier times, Friday afternoons at the mikvah with his father and little Moishe. The hot steam rising from the public bath and the men, relaxing comfortably while they cleaned themselves, discussing business or current events. As he reminisced, even the scum from other bathers didn't seem that bad.

His attention was recaptured by a wooden stick jabbed sharply into his kidney. A thin man with a stubble of whiskers began to scream in Yakoff's face, "Move, you worthless piece of slime!!" The daydream was over, he was again in the grips of reality.

And it was then Yakoff felt the tension and apprehension in the air. The feeling was the same one felt when walking close to the wires, a hesitancy, a caution, an absolute sense of fear. The only thing missing was the electrified humming.

The youngster didn't understand the reservation expressed by the others. He turned to a man beside him, mouth open, eyes wide, a complete look of terror engulfing his face.

"What?" Yakoff whispered. "What?"

The anguished soul looked deep into Yakoff's eyes. His brows were raised, his veins were protruding, he trembled when he spoke. "The showers..." was all he said.

"The showers..." Yakoff repeated. And finally he understood. The showers. They were marching clean-shaven and mouth inspected into a gas chamber. They would walk inside that room, the guards would lock the door behind them, and they would never come out.

The chill of the thought hit him worse than any blow he'd received. Yakoff was experiencing his last living moment and there was nothing in the world he could do about it. He was marching through that door to his own death.

One of the guards finally realized what was happening and tried to calm the men. "No, no," he said, waving his hand back and forth. "These are showers, real showers, with water, hot water."

Their looks explained their disbelief.

"You'll be clean for the first time in months."

No movement.

The man's voice lowered, becoming demonic..."Into the room." The tone left no question as to the results if the men didn't follow his instructions. They knew without question they would be killed where they stood. To fight would be fruitless, escape was impossible. Slowly, resolved to their fate, they filed into the ten by twenty-foot sealed enclosure.

Looks were exchanged spanning the bridges of uncertainty. Absolution was offered to anyone listening or willing to accept. Prayers were mumbled, mostly in Yiddish and Hebrew. Then the door closed behind them.

There was no panic, no hysterics. Only quiet. The deadliest silence Yakoff ever heard in his life. So this is it, he told himself. This is the last sound I'll ever hear.

There was a sputtering, gurgling sound as a valve was turned on the other side of the wall. Most bowed their heads in silent prayer. What does one feel or think as he enters the last moment of his life? A fleeting, reflective vision of its highlights? To an extent. A glimpse of the blinding white light and future encounters on the other side? No. Understanding or forgiveness for the Nazi bastards who imprisoned them for the last three years and viciously murdered his entire family? Never!

A great rumbling came from inside the walls and the shower nozzles began to shake and tremble. Then, as if it were an unexplained miracle from God, strong steady streams of hot steaming water began to spew forth, dousing the prisoners with warmth as well as joy.

When they returned to the outer room, the only thing remaining was their clogs. Their clothing had been taken somewhere for delousing and would be recycled to other incoming prisoners. This was somewhat despairing to Yakoff since he'd managed to accumulate three layers of clothing. Now, he deduced, he would have to start over again. But the thrill of being clean and the warmth the shower brought displaced that particular worry until another time. The feeling was actually strange. He couldn't remember the last time he'd felt so warm. But, like everything else, the feeling was short-lived.

The group marched, still naked and dripping, to the front door of the block. They were ordered outside and forced to run more than three hundred yards in the freezing weather until they reached block 7. By the time they arrived, the refreshing water had transformed into stinging, painful icicles, burning their skin.

No one was allowed inside the blocks during the day so the men were formed into columns and made to stand at attention in the subzero February weather. They weren't permitted to move for nearly eight solid hours. No breaks were taken and no food was received. If one had to relieve oneself it was done on the spot. Urine froze to legs as it dripped down, serving to intensify the pain and agony.

They heard a familiar, bizarre sound in the distance, a band playing more disgusting German marching tunes. Tubas, trumpets, trombones, even poignant strains from violins, now used to mark time for human destruction and death. It was sick, perverse, but at least it signified the end of the work day and hopefully the end of their own ordeal.

Several newcomers contracted severe hacking coughs coming from deep within their chests. Breathing was strained and difficult, even for those unencumbered by the quick-setting pneumonia. When the residents of block 7 marched past the freezing, naked bodies, they paid little attention. There wasn't much capable of redirecting concentration away from the relative warmth and safety of their blocks and bunks. After a long day of back breaking work, all they cared about was rest.

A prisoner, one of their new room seniors, dismissed the group, directing them inside toward a first floor storage area. They were given a fresh set of clothing. Clean, but only one layer. The warm clothes were hastily donned but the chill, boring its way to the center of their bones, would last for a very long time.

Just as the last man dressed, the door burst open and a menacing figure appeared. It was instantly silent. The man's legs were spread slightly, like an animal ready to pounce at the slightest provocation. He carried a dangling cat-o'-nine-tails, the same type nearly all the men were painfully familiar with. When he spoke, the walls of the room seemed to shake.

"My name is Alfred Olschevsky," the man announced. He slowly went around the room, making eye contact with each of the new, shivering men. "I'm your block senior and what I say..." he paused for a moment letting the emphasis take its full toll..."goes. If you follow the rules, you'll do just fine in here and we'll all get along. If you don't..." he flicked his wrist and the leather ends of the whip danced dangerously. The message had been delivered and was understood. There was no margin for error.

Olschevsky continued, "I have one rule you will all follow. The toilets are on the first floor and you'll be sleeping on the second. If you have to go downstairs during the night, you better make goddamned sure you do it without wearing shoes. 'Cause if you wake me up..." he shook the whip again, leaving the unpleasant repercussions for this violation to their vivid imaginations. He made his point. No hands were raised or questions asked.

Olschevsky weighed more than two-hundred pounds and was stocky. He obviously wasn't eating the normal, regular prisoner rations. But the men all knew the block as well as room seniors ate much better than anyone else incarcerated. Their violence and cruelty was rewarded, among other ways, in the form of additional food. Real food which they prepared themselves in the block.

As quickly as he entered, he left without another word. The new prisoners were now under the control of the remaining room seniors who marched them up a flight of stairs into a large open room, filled with three-tiered bunks. These were markedly different from the ones they'd slept in last night. First, they were individual. Yakoff couldn't believe his own eyes. In his life he'd never had a single bed to himself. Never.

The beds each had a mattress. Crude, but a mattress nonetheless. Something reasonably soft to rest weary bones on. Lastly, each bunk had a blanket. It actually seemed too good to be true.

Caution took over. These bunks certainly couldn't be for us. There's no way. Yakoff continued to think it was a trick of some sort when the room senior assigned him a sleeping place in one of the middle tiers and walked away.

He felt the mattress, tentatively, expecting any moment to wake up from this dream and have his arm broken and fingers crushed. It was the softest thing he remembered touching in a very long time.

"It's yours, go on, get in." The man in the lower bunk accurately sensed Yakoff's apprehension and tried, in his own small way, to help erase it.

Yakoff looked at the old-timer with questioning eyes and the man nodded, "It's okay, go ahead."

Still watchful for the guards, he slowly pulled himself up and then laid down flat on his back. Now he knew it was too good to be true. His own bed, a mattress, a blanket, too impossible to believe.

"You new?" It came from underneath.

Yakoff looked over the edge. "What?"

"Are you new here?" the man repeated.

"No," he answered, shaking his head. "We came in from Birkenau this morning."

"Uh-huh," the man grunted. It was a noncommittal grunt, not really saying anything one way or the other.

"How 'bout you?" Yakoff asked, looking down.

"Been here three weeks, maybe four. Most of the people in this block are pretty fresh. It's a new school they just started."

"What kind?"

"Bricklayer's..."

"For what? I mean..."

"To build new blocks so this goddamned place will hold more prisoners."

How ironic Yakoff thought. Now he's being forced to create housing. It could be worse. He knew that for a fact. He felt the mattress with his left hand, the one replacing the jammed, lice infected, urine stained planks. Oh yes, he knew it could be worse.

"What about this Olschevsky guy?" It was good, whenever possible, to find out everything you could about the kapo or senior directly in charge of your life.

"You gotta watch out for him," the man said. "He's a bad one." Yakoff remained silent, knowing the man was going to continue. He was right.

"They say he killed his wife and parents and children in cold-blood. Tied everybody up and made them all watch until the last one was dead. Went crazy or somethin'. That's why he's here. That's the reason they made him a block senior, 'cause he's so mean."

"Sounds mean."

"Mean don't come close. It doesn't bother him to kill people. Just don't get on his bad side..."

Yakoff rolled over and laid his head back down, staring at the bunk above. He digested the information carefully, silently vowing to heed the unexpected advice.

Rations arrived, the same as before; two small crusts of black bread and lukewarm foul tasting soup. Even this, after the day Yakoff had, was received graciously. For some unexplained reason the soup went down a little easier. He wasn't sure if the water in Auschwitz was less rotten or if he was just getting used to it. To tell the truth, right now it didn't matter.

After the ersatz dinner, there was an hour of free time before curfew. Not knowing anyone in camp, other than those he arrived with, Yakoff stayed and peacefully enjoyed his new-found comfort.

The second floor of the block, technically referred to as 7-A, with B on the first floor, housed one-hundred and twenty of the three-tiered bunks. If that statistic was universal, the twenty-eight blocks composing Auschwitz would hold between twenty and twenty-five thousand prisoners.

Yakoff's compound B-1-b in Birkenau held twenty-five thousand and the women's area, directly to the east, another twenty-five. The rest of Birkenau, which he'd heard referred to as AUSCHWITZ TWO, was capable of confining another two-hundred thousand.

Now came the discovery of AUSCHWITZ ONE, the main camp. The numbers were too staggering, too impossible to begin to comprehend. But he'd seen it with his own eyes and experienced it with his own pain riddled body.

Through mental calculations shot another mind boggling thought. Until this morning, Yakoff wasn't even slightly aware of the existence of AUSCHWITZ ONE. What if, he logically deduced, there were other camps hidden in this same area. What if, they're the same size or even larger. What if, the entire Jewish populations of Poland, Hungary, Austria, Czechoslovakia, Belgium and even Germany had been rounded up, captured and transferred here as prisoners, the eventual fate of all of the...all of us...lying at the base of the chimneys, using our own gold fillings to help finance their own Final Solution, using our own hair to stuff and fill German mattresses...

Yakoff quickly rolled to his side and ripped open the corner of the cloth covering. The contents were straw. His body shivered at the very thought and he emitted a deep sigh of relief.

He could hear other prisoners clopping up the steps. The curfew hour was approaching. There was little conversation which was fine as far as Yakoff was concerned. All he wanted now was sleep. Warm, comfortable, clean sleep.

Which didn't come. Lights were turned out and other than snoring and an occasional moan, the room was quiet. But his mind was active and his thoughts refused to allow rest. There was a noise, then more, coming from the ceiling, but it was more of a minor annoyance than anything else. Coughing, the unexplained kind occurring during steep, was heard from several men he'd spent the day with, standing naked in the cold.

Tonight was the first time in weeks he hadn't been to the wall to visit his father. He missed the comforting words of encouragement and strength flowing over the brick barrier. These were the thoughts creating the constant tossing and turning, lasting deep into the night.

Minor discomfort, lower abdomen, he had to go to the bathroom. Bathroom, repeating mentally, a smile on his face. An inside bathroom. Clean, probably warm. He almost chuckled as he climbed out of the bunk. Not like the old days he thought, way back yesterday.

This is different he reminded himself. Very different. When he reached the floor and leaned over to pick up his wooden clogs an air of confusion came over him. He tried to remember but his mind was blank, a void. Am I supposed to wear my shoes down the stairs and take them off in the bathroom or the other way around? He walked barefooted to the door of the stairway and couldn't remember. It had been a long, painful, trying day. This, added to the frightful realization he might never speak to his father again, left him without the simple answer he so desperately wanted.

His last conscious remembrance, before lights out, was the men returning to the second floor. He remembered hearing clogs on the staircase. That must be it, he thought. On the stairs, off in the bathroom. In any event, he was going to be as quiet as possible.

He eased down the wooden stairs making only the slightest of "ticks" each time his shoe met the floor. Inwardly he was pleased with how well he'd done. And he was right about the bathroom. It was clean and warm. Even the smell, the putrid, sickening aroma from the latrine in Birkenau was missing.

He returned to the top of the stairs after thirty more insignificant "ticks" and turned the corner to enter the room. There was one more step before an ominous figure appeared from the darkness, blocking his path. Moonlight, filtering through a nearby window, cast oblique, frightening shadows on the floor. All Yakoff could see were calf-high laced boots and leather ends of the cat-o-nine- tails suspended menacingly in midair.

The voice was unpleasantly familiar, "You don't learn good, do ya boy?" When Olschevsky stepped from the shadows into the light, there was a bizarre grin of satisfaction covering his face. Brown saliva hung from the left corner of his mouth and he quietly spit out each word. "We got a lesson for ya...one you won't forget." Yakoff's eyes darted protectively between the hateful face of the mass murderer and the deadly, dancing whip at his side. "Upstairs boy... you're gonna' learn Olschevsky's law..."

The entire third floor area was open. This was the classroom for the bricklayer's school. But not tonight. The room was large, windows lining both sides, all open as wide as possible. It was so cold, Olschevsky and his assistants wore heavy coats, buttoned to the neck. Yakoff shivered as he entered the room, seeing more than twenty other prisoners, apparently waiting, just for him.

"I think we have enough to start," Olschevsky hissed. "Everybody spread out and stand behind a stool." Stools were plentiful, the classroom type, three-feet high and constructed from a solid, heavy wood. "Bend your knees and hunch down." The men hunkered over, like Chinese working in a rice paddy. "Up on your toes and balance."

One of the late-night visitors to the bathroom fell over on his side. As he struggled to return to the assigned position, Olschevsky kicked him square in the chest, taking his breath away, knocking him over backwards.

"Stand up," he yelled. Several others followed the order. "Not you, you dummies! Just him!" Slowly the man stood, legs trembling, face filled with fear.

"Bend over!"

The man was familiar with the position. He leaned forward placing his hands on his knees.

"You count..." Olschevsky said, "out loud. If you miss the count or scream, we'll start over." The man clenched his teeth, bracing for the onslaught.

The tails of the whip whistled through the air before thunderously crashing onto the man's back. His knees buckled under the blow and he whispered, "One..."

"What!?" Olschevsky screamed.

"One!" he shouted back.

"Better."

Then it was "Two," then "Three," then "Four, five, six." With each blow the man's legs grew weaker. "Seven, eight, nine." He started to cough, wheezing, blood began to trickle from the corner of his mouth. "Ten, eleven, twelve." His shirt was cut open and the taut skin was ripped and bleeding. "Thirteen, fourteen, fifteen..." the voice was fading, he could barely mutter the numbers. Still he didn't move. "Sixteen... seventeen..." On seventeen, he fell to the cold concrete floor.

"Stand up...we start again."

It took a long time for the man to pull himself back up to a standing position and eight more lashes from the whip before he died in a pool of his own blood. Olschevsky returned his attention to the rest of the men still hunkered down, balancing delicately on their toes.

"See what happens when you fall?" The men nodded. "The same

thing will happen if your heels touch the ground. Reach out and pick up a stool by the bottom of its legs and hold it straight out at arms length." This maneuver impeded the problem of balance. The men were tired, weak, even holding the stool was impossible for some.

Olschevsky responded with his whip, leaving several lifeless bodies around the room. Yakoff was beaten during the tirade, as were all the others, but managed to withstand the grueling pain. His hate for Olschevsky grew with each stroke. There were twenty in all. Tears filled his eyes and he felt warm drops of blood crawling down his back from the open wounds.

The prisoners held the stools straight out in front of them for the better part of an hour. Olschevsky happily busied himself each time one was dropped or a weary body collapsed to the floor. Miraculously, Yakoff was only beaten one time. The inner-strength to take the pain and hold the stool, like so many times before, came from an unknown source. It was welcomed and never questioned.

Finally, Olschevsky grew tired of the game and ordered the prisoners to stand. He had them remove their clothing and assume the attention position. The room was freezing, painfully reminiscent of the naked, day-long ordeal they had just experienced.

The blocks in Auschwitz had running water, even on the third floor. An assistant left Olschevsky's side and returned moments later carrying a bucketful of the cold liquid. The killer issued his order with a flick of the finger and water was poured over the nearest prisoner's head. The muffled shivering cry was silenced by a whip in the face. Olschevsky smiled.

A water-hose was produced, drenching each of the men. When ranks were broken in the form of a sneeze or cough, an agonizing penalty was paid. Each time it appeared the water was drying the men were hosed down again. The ordeal continued throughout the night and the majority of the prisoners who fell down or passed out, never returned to their feet.

Mentally, physically, and statistically it was an awesome evening. Of the twenty-four men, captured and punished for wearing clogs on the stairs, only five remained standing when the bell sounded for the morning roll call.

Standing in neat rows of ten was the same, stacked bodies were the same, morning rations were the same. The major difference was the work patrol. Instead of being selected and marching out of camp for a day's hard labor, he'd be in school learning a trade.

The thought contradicted itself. A trade, a skill, for what? To build more blocks so there'll be more room for more of us? It wasn't right but he had no choice or say-so in the matter.

It was eerie walking back upstairs to the third floor. The room had a different feeling than an hour earlier. The bodies had been removed. By who, or when, Yakoff didn't know. Even the blood-stains on the floor had been washed away. Nothing was ever mentioned, as if the night-long ordeal and the harsh lesson in Olschevsky's law hadn't occurred. Yakoff's arms, rendered nearly worthless from holding the stool, and his back, with continuing stinging pain from the festering wounds, silently cried out the truth.

There were nearly two hundred "students" in the bricklayer's school, separated into two groups approximately the same size. One end of the large open room was designated as a lecture area with stools and a black-board. The other end was for actual practice with bricks and mortar, hence the water supply.

Yakoff was directed to a stool with the other new arrivals and the boring lectures began. His exhaustion was complete, total. The pain he was experiencing served as a catalyst, keeping him awake. Even that, after several hours without movement, began to subside. He fought the much-needed sleep with all his might, knowing firsthand the penalty if he should fall from the stool.

No sleep. Dead tired. Standing naked all day and then all night. Freezing. Back killing. Need rest. Eyelids drooping. Head nodding. He'd blink and shake his head from side to side. He licked his fingers and placed them on his eyes, weaving first one way then the other. Shifting positions. Nothing worked.

A shot of pain exploded throughout his entire body. It was his left shin, on fire, excruciating. Now his eyes were open, wideawake. The man facing him was short, thin, with beady little eyes. He was a Frenchman, one of Olschevsky's assistants who administered the pain via the steel-hard toe from his right boot.

No words were exchanged. None were necessary. The Frenchman's evil smile transcended a "stay awake" warning. It was a message to the newcomer that he was in charge, his word was law; he, as a room senior, could do anything to anybody at anytime he wanted.

Yakoff grimaced, gritting his remaining teeth. He wanted to cry out but logic and a determination to survive silenced his straining vocal cords. God, how it hurt. Oh, my God. He could feel a steady stream of warm blood crawling down the front of his leg and still he refused to scream.

The Frenchman, satisfied with the results as well as response, maintained his callous smirk and strutted away. Yakoff inhaled deeply, close to passing out. Oh, for the opportunity and strength to choke the little son-of-a-bitch to death. He would have done it in a minute with no reservation or remorse whatsoever. The pain was intense, growing by the second. He looked down to the left side of the stool, at the steady rhythmic dripping of his own blood splattering the freshly washed floor.

In the following weeks the pain never went away and the wound didn't heal. It remained open, festering, a constant oozing of foul-smelling pus. Yakoff walked with a limp and the fear of gangrene was constant. The fear of going to the hospital for treatment was worse. What if, he asked, it is gangrene and the leg has to be amputated? There were no prisoners in Auschwitz with one leg. There were no prisoners in Auschwitz who walked on crutches. Discovery of the long-lasting wound could prove terminal, so he learned to live with the pain.

His life, like all the others, was cheap, easily expendable. The Nazis weren't going to feed him if they weren't receiving work in return. The adage hauntingly returned..."If you don't work, you don't live." "Physician heal thyself," was the order of the day, and he tried everything at his disposal to do just that.

He found a discarded piece of paper and created a makeshift bandage which provided little help and no relief. On occasion, during evening rations, the prisoners were given a small portion of margarine with their black bread crusts. Yakoff ground the margarine into his wound, trying to manufacture a protective salve type substance to cut down the seepage. That didn't work either but it was better than nothing. The water, with its foul smell and probable contamination, should not be used. Still he felt the open hole in his leg needed to be cleaned and treated with some form of liquid. Hopefully, if possible, a warm one. Eventually he used his own urine.

With great regularity, daily as well as nightly, he heard the familiar report of machine gun fire, coming from a block at the end of his street. The gunshots were coming from an area between blocks 10 and 11, a place known as "the black wall" or "the wall of death."

It was a brick wall constructed between the two blocks with a huge piece of heavy steel in its middle. Prisoners were taken here for various, assorted reasons. Some for attempting to escape, others for insubordination. Those caught trying to steal food from a block senior or hiding to avoid work patrols, eventually made their way here.

The sick and lame were often seen after being carried here from the hospital. The mentally deranged, having no idea what the hell was going on, stood with their backs to the steel plate. It was a place for execution. It was the designated and official area of Auschwitz where prisoners were lined up against the black, bullet-pocked backdrop and shot down in cold-blood.

The thing most prisoners feared more than the back breaking work, probability of starvation, constant and relentless beatings, or the prospect of going stark raving crazy, was the "selection" process. A high ranking SS man, without notice or forewarning, would enter the camp and randomly select prisoners to be executed. One man, usually a devout Christian, wearing the high peaked military cap with skull and crossbones and a large silver cross hanging from a chain around his neck, could point a finger at anyone. When this happened their moments on this planet were numbered.

The selections could be any time, any place, day, night, at work, during rations. There was no moment of relaxation when the threat to end individual life wasn't prevalent. A flick of a finger and for any reason the selectee was marched to the black wall and murdered. It was the ultimate reality, never out of the prisoners' minds.

There was an area outside the kitchen to the right of the main gate the Nazis kept active and busy. Heavy-duty steel poles were erected in a neat row right on the street itself. It was commonplace at the end of the day when prisoners were returning from outside work patrols for a formation to be called. The assemblage would be forced to watch as an SS man beat a prisoner viciously until he was rendered senseless. Usually this was done to men who tried to escape, or worse, when some-one talked about the possibility to the wrong person.

After the beating, the helpless body was dragged up and onto a wooden platform. Sometimes, a result of weakness, they had to be held up by their arms as a well-worn noose was draped around their neck.

"This will happen to any man who tries to escape!" the SS would scream. "There is no escape from Auschwitz! Anyone attempting it will be shot on the spot or hanged!"

The lever was pulled and the body dropped through a trapdoor. It was quiet enough to hear the neck bones crack. Legs, dangling in mid-air, jerked violently, but only a few times. Then it was still, the lifeless body swaying in the breeze. The men were dismissed to return to the blocks for evening rations.

There were five poles outside the kitchen and multiple executions were common. These bodies, the ones from the wall, men beaten to death in their blocks or on the street, prisoners who'd died from typhus, pneumonia or starvation, and men who went to the wires, were collected twice daily in the large wooden wagons.

Metal wheels, clicking along the pressed rock road, echoed throughout the camp issuing a stern warning to anyone and everyone: this is your fate, this is where you belong, this is where you will all end up. The wagons rolled through the main gate, turned and disappeared from sight. No one ever spoke about the final destination of the wagon or its load. But they knew without a question, the wagon headed northwest to Birkenau, to the crematoriums and the chimneys.

Yakoff missed his father desperately and thought of him often. Especially when he'd see a wagonful of bodies taking their one-way trip. He wondered and hoped with all his heart Pesach was still alive. Several attempts at finding out had been unsuccessful, for there was little communication between the two camps. Still, his father's survival, along with his own, was something he had to believe in. It was the only remaining dream.

Chapter XII

Living together and attending the bricklayer's school created an atmosphere where friendships were formed. Sometimes protectiveness was the motivation and a "buddy system" was established where two or more people looked out for each other.

Yakoff already knew a few people in his block. There was Leon, his cousin, and Isaac Orenstein, who grew up in Sierpc but attended a different school. The group of new friends included Heim Berkovich, Harry Foreman, Yossel Engel and Lulek Solarski. The bonds they shared were strong. They were young, nearly the same age, from the same generalized area of Poland and victims of Nazi perversion. Every one of them lost loved ones or family in the ghettos, the initial selection when the transports arrived, or as a direct result of being in the camp.

Most of the men came to Auschwitz from various Jewish ghettos and had not experienced the filth and slime of Birkenau. Several who were hand-selected by the overweight German civilian and marched to the school seemed vaguely familiar to Yakoff.

There was David Levin, Herschel Novedvor, and Martin Klein. All Jewish, all victims, and all familiar faces. The familiarity, they later determined, stemmed from a chance meeting they'd experienced while incarcerated in Birkenau.

Of course, Yakoff thought, finally remembering. We met briefly, without really talking, the day we took the physical examination and managed to spend a full ten hours without work or getting beaten.

Auschwitz was a model concentration camp; used by the Germans as a showcase whenever the Red Cross wanted to inspect facilities and determine prisoners were being treated fairly and according to the terms of the Geneva Convention. Hence the cleanliness and constant insistence on neatness.

Prisoners were forced to remain relatively clean-shaven and have short haircuts. Cold water was available in each block and once a month they marched in unison to the disinfectant area for a hot shower. Soap was at a premium, only those fortunate or clever enough to obtain it themselves enjoyed that luxury. Fresh uniforms were distributed once a month. All this served to convince visitors from international organizations that the prisoners of war were well taken care of.

The Nazis knew well in advance of upcoming visits or inspections. They instructed prisoners clearly and forcefully how to answer any questions put forward:

"Yes, I'm getting plenty of good food and rest."

"No, I'm not being overworked or treated unfairly."

"No, I have no concern or fear my life is in danger."

"Yes, the Nazis are taking good care of me!"

Questions posed to the prisoners were always in the presence of an SS man or guard. Failure to follow Nazi instructions to the letter resulted in instant executions the moment the visitor left the camp. This was clearly understood.

The cleanliness observed, and responses to questions by interviewers, resulted in written reports filled with glowing superlatives about the place and the people. It's unlikely any of these visitors were remotely aware of the existence of Birkenau, with the constant burning ovens, less than two miles away. Still, it seemed someone would notice or question or even investigate the smoke and ashes in the northwest, belching upwards, blackening the sky. It would also seem someone would ask the rather apparent question, "Where are all the European Jews disappearing to?"

Block 18 was directly across the street from Yakoff's block 7. Almost every night, following the evening rations, great throngs of prisoners would gather between 18 and 19 and "conduct business." The first night Yakoff walked over there he was shocked, he couldn't believe his eyes.

Nearly everything imaginable was available in this place. Socks, underwear, clean and pressed uniforms, belts, soap, straight razors, scissors, food of all types and varieties, playing cards, blankets, paper and pencils, eyeglasses, watches (both pocket and wrist type), currency from different nations, cigarettes, even liquor. This was the Auschwitz black market and anything one could possibly want or need was obtainable here. Anything except freedom.

Since Auschwitz had no currency system of its own, the prisoners would trade and barter with one another for various items. Food was the most often used coin of the realm since it was the most commonly available. Other items were brought here as a result of someone's ability to organize or procure. An organizer was a person who could obtain something of value he wasn't supposed to have. This included anything and everything not issued directly by the guards or kapos. Some of the organizers were highly proficient.

Yakoff saw his first American ten dollar bill along with a rare twenty dollar gold piece. There were whole loaves of bread and full bottles of whiskey and vodka. Men shouted out what they had to trade or wanted to obtain.

"Clean socks! New uniform! Bread for cigarettes! Need a razor!"

It was all here. On occasion, special, privileged prisoners even traded valuable passes to the German bordello.

The bordello was just outside the main gate and down the street. Security was high and the much sought after passes had to be authenticated before the holder was admitted. This was to prevent Jews, Russians or Gypsies from frequenting what they referred to as the pleasure palace. These three groups, out of all the different nationalities in the entire camp, were absolutely not allowed.

The others however, kapos, seniors, German or Polish political prisoners, and men with exemplary work records or a history of supporting the Nazi cause, were rewarded with occasional visits to the whore house.

The women forced to perform sexual favors were mostly chosen from incoming transports and nearly always against their will. They were offered an option: prostitution or death. Refusal to submit to the obscene Nazi wishes, provided a one-way ticket up the chimneys. Jewesses weren't chosen for this duty, for a true Nazi of mind and heart, would never lower himself to physical contact with a Jew. While this was the spoken and written opinion, quite the opposite was true. Jewish women, composing the majority of incoming prisoners, were raped and sexually violated at an alarming rate by SS men and German guards. Following the animalistic and brutal sex, the unfortunate victims were sent directly to the gas chambers for purposes the Nazis casually referred to as "security."

Yakoff and the rest of the group attended school during the day and visited the black market at night. Olschevsky's activities and whereabouts were constantly reported between them and their tight-knit communicative network kept them out of his way and out of trouble.

Constant hunger continued to be a pressing matter even though the thin soup didn't taste quite as bad and the food was a little more abundant than in Birkenau. Sometimes on Sundays, the Auschwitz prisoners received a thin slice of salami. On rare occasions they were given small amounts of marmalade for their black bread. The food was measured carefully, just enough to keep a man alive but never enough to provide any degree of strength, or erase the painful gripping void in the pit of a stomach.

The school was boring and repetitive. Day after day they'd listen to the same monotone lecture. Then they'd practice over and over the exact placement of brick on brick, side by side. Mortar was never used, only dry bricks. Great detailed care was given to the instruction of how to properly and correctly build a long-lasting chimney.

The man with the straining buttons on his vest, the German who'd selected Yakoff and the others; could usually be found in the third floor kapo's office. He and the kapo in charge would sit there most every day, cooking on a small potbellied stove and eating. The rotund civilian seemed to be the one with the final say-so in matters pertaining to the school, but it was never explained nor was he ever introduced to the students.

For the most part the school provided a haven of relative safety. Prisoners were seldom bothered by the kapo and never by the civilian. Even Olschevsky had no jurisdiction over the students during the day. The assistants, however, were another story. They had to be watched out for, especially the short Frenchman with the boots. But those who stayed awake and pretended to be paying attention were generally left alone.

Being bored was a small price to pay in exchange for escaping cruel, vicious kapos and backbreaking work outside in the freezing weather. There were few complainers.

Late in the spring, before the ground thawed, Isaac, a good friend, had an opportunity to transfer to a better job. He moved to the laundry where the building was warm and the work was soft. Even so, Yakoff and he maintained close contact.

The weather finally turned and one day the kapo addressed the entire group of students. "Tomorrow morning after rations, instead of coming up here, you're to report in formation in front of the block."

No further explanation was offered. Announcements like this usually served to put the prisoners even more on edge than normal. The rest of the day was filled with a flurry of "what ifs" and guarded apprehension. After months of a false sense of security they were reminded that their own fate was still definitely in the hands of others.

When they formed ranks for the morning count, a noticeable chill was prevalent. This, added to the uncertainty the men were experiencing, extended the waiting moments.

The bricklayers grouped in lines of five and marched, as a separate unit, among the thousands of others toward the front gate. The groups, the lines and the men were counted and noted on clipboards at the guardhouse. Their destination and fate was completely in question. The journey was short, well within the outer perimeter of the camp. It was a large construction site, cleared, staked, and ready to go. Tools, equipment and supplies were there and waiting. They were divided into smaller work crews and assigned to experienced bricklayers and builders. The students would act as apprentices and helpers until they became proficient in practical application.

Assistance, in this case, meant hauling loads of bricks and mortar to the craftsmen constructing exterior walls of additional blocks intended to house new, incoming prisoners. Yakoff was amused at the turn of events. The Nazis' mentality was confusing as well as warped. To think, Yakoff pondered, they'd keep us locked inside that school for literally months of incessant practice, and then assign us to push loaded wheelbarrows from one place to another. Like everything else, it made little sense.

It felt good to be outdoors in the sunshine. Even though the work was strenuous and the hours long, it was strangely refreshing, almost therapeutic, after the grey winter season and restrictive confinement. As the walls grew higher, the scaffolding followed and the apprentices learned to maneuver their heavy loads through mud and then up steep inclines on the narrow planks.

This too became highly repetitive and was broken only when a full load would slip from the bouncing boards and crash resoundingly below. Cries of "Look out!" were shouted, followed by bodies scurrying in all directions. The first time this occurred the responsible party mentally prepared himself for an onslaught of physical abuse.

The kapo, a stocky, square-shouldered man with fiery red hair, ran up the scaffolding waving his arms in the air. He reached the unfortunate perpetrator, screaming at the top of his voice. All work ceased, the balance of the prisoners expecting to witness another extremity in violence and cruelty. They were as much surprised as the man without the wheelbarrow when the kapo continued to rant and rave.

He threatened this, that and the other. Beatings, solitary confinement, even death if it ever happened again. "These bricks cost money, etc., etc., etc..." He waved his stick menacingly above the prisoner's head, poised, ready to crash down violently at any second...but it never happened. He just continued to scream. And then, satisfied his threats had been dutifully received, walked down from the scaffolding, and work resumed.

Could it be, the men asked themselves, they actually had a kapo who retained an ounce of compassion in his heart, one who wouldn't render them senseless, lifeless shells without provocation, let alone validity of reason? Based on what they'd witnessed, that seemed to be the case; but one tree does not a forest make. Time, as always, would be the eventual as well as judgmental factor in determining the makeup and character of their new boss.

That time, over the next few weeks, leaned toward and in favor of the prisoners. After several spills and opportunities to prove otherwise, the kapo traditionally exhibited his bark was far worse than his bite. Oh, he'd yell and continue to scream. He did that a lot, but his stick, for some unknown but highly respected reason, was held in check.

The men plodded through the motions, doing what was expected but never exerting themselves. The exception among the entire group was Lulek. He seemed to possess a passion for laying bricks. No one, including himself, could explain why. At every opportunity, he'd badger the stocky redheaded man with requests to be promoted from apprentice to a full-fledged bricklayer.

Finally his request was granted and he proudly took his position at the wall. With an uncanny deftness and expertise gleaned over the months, he troweled and mortared the bricks more rapidly than any seasoned veteran. Perhaps it was Lulek's own personal form of mental escape, to throw himself completely into his work so nothing else would register. No one knew.

What they did know was the speed at which he was laying the bricks. Everyone else on the crew was forced to pick up their pace and work much harder. This, from one of their own, was highly unpalatable. A short, to-the-point meeting among the group during the midday break, quickly convinced Lulek of the unintentioned error of his ways. After sincere apologies, he returned to the wall and worked at a much more acceptable pace.

The days began to meld, one into another, and a new routine was established. Sunshine lasted a little longer and several attempts at trying to discover if his father was still alive were unsuccessful. There was no real news about the war raging throughout Europe, other than bits and pieces from guards' conversations, concerning how well the Nazis were doing. The German forces sounded invincible, and according to the firsthand knowledge Yakoff possessed, they were.

It was early and the men were standing in front of their block, unanxious to return to the wheelbarrows. Olschevsky raised his voice and growled, "The following men will remain here today." Then he read off a list of numbers. "80629" was among them.

As the majority marched away towards the construction site, Yakoff and the men whose numbers had been called, looked unknowingly at one another. They transferred the same look of confusion in the direction of Olschevsky.

"Someone will be by to pick you up,' was all he said, and disappeared into the block.

They waited for five minutes before another prisoner approached the small group. He was distinctly different from the rest, wearing a plain white overshirt rather than a striped one. This indicated, clearly and unpleasantly, the man was an orderly from the hospital ward.

Carrying an ever-present clipboard, he read off numbers, confirming the waiting men were the ones he wanted. When questioned about what was going on and why they'd been selected, he shrugged his shoulders replying he had no idea. He was just there to take them to the hospital.

Block 28, the hospital block, was in the extreme southeast corner of the camp. Not isolated, but clearly the most removed from the others. Its reputation of being an unsafe place to attend was well-known within the confines of the singing wires. Still, Yakoff and the others singled out for the visit had no idea why or what they'd been chosen for. There was some consolation. A few close friends were along.

David Levin was among the six walking through camp. So were Herschel Novedvor and Martin Klein. Other than forming friendships and being residents of the bricklayer's school, the only thing they had in common was the chance meeting they'd experienced while captives in Birkenau; the meeting occurring when they volunteered to trade a day off for a harmless, painless, physical examination.

It was the first time Yakoff or any of them had been inside the hospital block. The walls were dull white, actually more of a washed-out grey, and there was a musty antiseptic aroma. Men wearing white jackets moved throughout the halls in no particular hurry. They seemed to have places to go and people to see. Little attention was paid to the new arrivals, which was fine as far as they were concerned.

The man who picked them up in front of their block ushered the six into a waiting room. Yakoff was pleasantly surprised, then instantly suspicious to find another friend, Isaac Orenstein, along with two others. The suspicion rose from the fact all nine men had undergone the same physical examination with the large, green, cone shaped machine in Birkenau that cold January day over six months ago.

Other than whispered conversation about how Isaac was doing in the laundry, the room was quiet. The uncertainty created an uncomfortableness which was deeply felt by all nine. The wait grew into an eternity. It was one of the men waiting with Isaac who broke the stifling silence with a matter-of-fact comment, the kind of idle chitchat everyone is expected to know.

"Guess you all heard about what they did to us over in Birkenau..."

Several pairs of eyes opened wide. It was obvious the captive audience hadn't heard. Heads shook from side to side but Yakoff was the first to respond.

"No," he whispered. "What did they do?"

The man looked both ways, confirming their aloneness. "Remember that machine? The big green one with the cone thing on top?"

The men nodded they did, but were still uncertain as to the direction of the conversation.

"It was an x-ray machine," he finally said. "Don't you get it?"

They didn't. None of them had seen or even heard of an x-ray machine before. The man was noticeably surprised that he was the only one aware of what transpired.

"An x-ray machine," he whispered again. "We were all sterilized."

The impact of the statement was unfelt. The word, like x-ray, was foreign. It had no bearing or meaning to the eight attentive listeners.

"You really don't get it do ya?"

This time there was no head shaking. The men stared with quizzical looks covering their faces. The man spoke slowly, this time to himself rather than the others, an exclamation one makes when wishing   desperately for a retraction.

"Oh, my God." The words were evenly spaced and drawn out. Then, with reverence they were repeated, "Oh...my..God..."

There was still no recognition to the consequence of the statement and the man felt obligated to further his explanation.

"What that means," he started slowly, "is none of us will ever be able to bear children ... we can never be fathers." He hung his head and stared at the floor.

How can that be, the others thought in unison. Nothing was really done to us, no pain was inflicted. It was understandable their comprehension was impossible. They were virile young men looking forward to having wives and raising children. A simple "clunk" from a switch and a momentary buzzing from a cone shaped machine couldn't have stripped that possibility from their lives. Could it?

Of course not. It was unfathomable, unthinkable! There was no reason or logic to condone anything that bizarre and cruel. The thought was replaced with the fact of where they were, the atrocities they'd seen, the things they'd been inhumanly forced to do. Their losses and trials, intermingled with a hundred other confusing thoughts, made the prospect of what was just reported seem strangely but remotely possible. But how? And why? Sterilized...no...too difficult to imagine, too far removed from any concept of reality or understanding to believe. It had to be a rumor, another sick Nazi rumor to wear us down, steal our minds, make us give up.

Another prisoner in a white coat entered the room and read off a number. One of the two men waiting with Isaac slowly followed and the others remained in silence, delicately pondering the information just imparted. If it were true, Yakoff thought, he didn't believe he wanted to hear anymore, akin to the concept of what you don't know can't hurt you.

Yakoff's entire life was totally oriented toward the family. It was the mainstream unit from which everything else stemmed. The thought and dream of eventual release and having a family of his own was one of the things that kept him going. No! his mind screamed. They can't take that away too.

Another number was called and Herschel Novedvor walked away. Remembrance of the physical they'd succumbed to flashed through his racing mind. This time was different than the last. The first man didn't return to the room. Asking questions or seeking information was a futile as well as dangerous exercise, so the room remained quiet, except for the electricity emanating from the seven remaining bodies.

One by one they left the room in half-hour intervals. Then the door opened and the voice calmly said "Eight, zero, six, two, nine." Yakoff stood, obediently following the other prisoner. He was alone now, completely alone.

What if the other man was right? What if he really was unable to ever be a father and carry on the family name? He was the last and only surviving Skurnik. The realistic concept of all the "what ifs" conjured and released vast throngs of grotesque demons ripping at his senses, playing havoc with his mind.

But the havoc was carried out in silence. The demons, echoing obscenities across his brain, couldn't be responded to. To question, object or fight, meant to die. Life was still cheap. Death still came swiftly and easily. Yakoff held his tongue while his mind nearly exploded. In silence, he would adhere to the Nazi requests. To do anything contrary would absolutely and certainly place him among a hundred other corpses on the large wooden wagon ago for the one-way trip to Birkenau.

The room was small. A flat table the size of a single bed was in the center, and three smaller tables were against the walls. They held test tubes and objects reminding Yakoff of surgical instruments he'd seen in the hospital in Sierpc. Tables were made of wood and nothing appeared to be particularly clean. There were no windows, only one overhead light. Three white-coated prisoners in the room had no unusual characteristics other than they appeared to be better fed than most and all spoke German. Their draw in the Nazi game of life was a good one. They were deliberate about their business and put on a confident air, knowing what they were doing, mixed carefully with a detachment from everything going on.

Yakoff was ordered to strip. Logic was superseded by a clear understanding of the alternative and with controlled hesitation he followed the instruction while the others watched.

"Get up on the table on your hands and knees." There was no suggestion it might have been a question. It was a hard statement with an unspoken implication that if Yakoff didn't wish to go along with the plan, assistance would be provided.

Slowly the youngster crawled onto the table and positioned himself as told. One of the prisoners stood behind him. The other two, both much larger, stood on either side. A new level of fear ripped at his heart and stomach. He was completely vulnerable with no possible means of escape. Profound dialogue or begging for one's life was worthless, a waste of time and breath. He'd seen how well that worked for others in the past.

The two men on either side gripped his arms with large dirty hands. Circulation was cut off. He could feel his fingers going numb.

"Don't try to move," one said gruffly, "or we'll break your arms." It was a matter-of-fact statement without emotion. The man standing behind spread Yakoff's legs as far apart as the table would allow.

Then, a huge left hand grabbed and squeezed the youngster's buttocks.

The pain was intense-unlike and worse than anything he'd known or experienced. Worse than ripping his own teeth out, worse than standing naked in the freezing cold, worse than any of the beatings or the ever present sense of starvation. It was white-hot, like raging coals, then freezing, like the coldest imaginable piece of ice. Then hot, then cold, then both at the same time. He could feel his skin being ripped apart and the insides of his body being scraped as if with a brick or sandpaper. Hot, cold. Hot, cold. The pain was unbearable. Finally he screamed out.

"Shut up you fucking Jew!" the man on his left shouted. "Shut up or we'll kill you right here on the spot!"

Yakoff knew without question they would, and gritted his remaining teeth, biting the inside of his cheeks until his own blood dripped on the table underneath him.

The pain continued, growing. The man standing behind was jamming a blunt, large instrument into Yakoff's rectum. Hard, and deep, ripping the skin. The thing, whatever the hell it was, was huge. Oh my God, the pain. Hot, cold. The men on either side held his arms tighter.

The purpose of the exercise was to create an erection. It was completely successful. As the instrument or broom handle or whatever was jammed ruthlessly further inside Yakoff's body, it created an involuntary ejaculation, the results of which were captured on a large piece of glass.

As soon as the sperm was released, the man standing behind, callously jerked the long, thick thing out. Yakoff collapsed on his stomach, gasping for breath. His insides felt like they were going to fall out. The pain, though subsiding considerably, certainly didn't go away. His body was shaking, reacting to its violation.

The piece of glass holding his sperm was taken from the room and analyzed for a potency count. The results were never shared with Yakoff but apparently, from the sequence of events which followed, were positive.

A fourth man, another prisoner, entered the room and nodded to the others, a signal. Yakoff was still flat on his stomach, unable to move. He was surrounded as the new man walked to one of the tables and picked up a shiny instrument. It was selected at random from a pile of several like it and there was no evidence of any sterilization equipment.

With great effort, Yakoff turned his head to see what was creating the metal tinkling noises to his left. He didn't like what he saw. The fourth man was holding a large syringe, eight-inches long with a three-inch needle. His vision was blurred, unsteady, a result of the continuing pain. The needle was covered with a dark brown substance, perhaps red. Blood, Yakoff questioned, from the man before me? There was no way of knowing.

"Doctor Doering's ready," the man holding the syringe said. The other three pushed Yakoff's body down flat and repeated the order not to move with the same seriousness and intensity. The man with the syringe walked to the table and stood there for a second. Yakoff couldn't see what was happening. The second doubled, then redoubled. Which was worse? The pain ripping through his body or anticipation of what was coming?

A cold clammy hand rested on the middle of his back, just below his waist. It gripped the skin, squeezing it firmly and methodically together. He felt the tip of the needle, slow, cold, being pushed deep into his arching back. He pressed his eyelids together, but tears still found their way through the slits. Deeper and deeper. He was writhing.

"Don't move, you asshole, or the needle will break off." The chuckles following, indicated this was not an uncommon occurrence. It was impossible for Yakoff to conceive how other human beings could enjoy inflicting such pain. He wanted to pass out, he wanted to die, he just wanted it over.

His back grew white-hot as the contents of the syringe were released. Time stood still, all he could do was wait. It took forever as the six burly hands continued holding him flat to the table.

Then a strange tingling feeling started and the pain began to subside. He felt less and less and then couldn't feel anything. Not his back, legs, feet, toes, nothing. He couldn't even feel it when the man pulled the needle out of his back. It was the first time he could remember some part of his body wasn't experiencing massive pain. The release was quick, certainly unexpected.

But the pleasure only lasted a second. Just until the realization he was paralyzed from the waist down.

He didn't speak or cry out, choosing to pile the new layer of fear on top of the others. Motionless, unable to move, the table was wheeled into another room, equally stark as the first. The two men pushing, positioned the table in the center of the room and turned to leave. "Don't try to move or get off the table or you'll be shot." They walked out, leaving him alone.

Yakoff tried without success. There was still no feeling or movement in the lower half of his body. The best he could do would be to roll off the table, onto the floor, then make a getaway by crawling. His only prospect, at best, was impossible. There was no other choice but to lie there naked and wait.

Two men reentered the room and Yakoff's heart nearly stopped. They were dressed in white from head to foot and their faces covered by surgical masks, pure business, no idle conversation. They approached the table and looked down at the boy as if selecting a piece of meat in a butcher shop window. One of them, with a needle, jabbed Yakoff in the side, just below his rib cage. The process was completely visible but fortunately there was no pain. A small drop of blood came out of Yakoff's skin and trickled down. The man with the needle spoke to the other one: "Tell Doctor Doering he's ready."

Who's ready, Yakoff thought. Me? Him? Who? And for what? Tiny beads of perspiration formed on his forehead and scalp. One slid slowly across the bridge of his nose and into his left eye, creating a salty stinging sensation. That was good news, he still had some feeling left. He wanted to rub his eye and relieve the pain but was afraid to make any movement while the man in the mask was still staring down.

The person who'd just left and a third man, also wearing a surgical mask and gown reentered the room. The gown was covered with bloodstains and he carried a scalpel.

"Doctor Doering," one of the men said, "the next patient just had his spinal."

Doering nodded and stared at Yakoff's groin. "This won't take long." The voice was authoritative, strong, in complete command and control. It was also emotionless, void of feeling. His face was covered. All Yakoff could see were his eyes. They were cold, distant, calculating. Doering nodded several times, as if mentally counting something.

Bodies, Yakoff thought to himself. Victims? Is my number on some Nazi clipboard about to have a line drawn through it? He swallowed hard and the gulp was noticeably audible.

"What's the matter Jew boy?" Doering said. "You afraid?" The sides of Doering's mask raised slightly, covering a cruel, devious, sinister smile. His eyes sparkled and danced, flashing a particular contempt, a hate for the naked, helpless youngster in front of him.

The look was obvious but the question was too large to begin to comprehend. Was the hate in his eyes for Yakoff? One, single, young Jewish soul? Or was it for an entire race? An entire religious sect that Hilter himself had vowed to exterminate? No one knew.

As Doering raised the knife over Yakoff's body, the question became incredibly irrelevant. When the sharp, cold steel met the skin, there was no feeling or sensation. Nothing. The incision was just over two inches long and dead center between the middle of his stomach and the tip of his right pelvic bone. Blood oozed from the opening and the assistants dabbed it away with rags which were thrown on the floor. When the outer skin was broken, Doering quickly started to work cutting through the fatty tissue underneath. It was odd for Yakoff to watch with full consciousness as someone cut a large hole in his side. It was frightening as well as fascinating. The fact there was no feeling or pain attached, served to remove the youngster from the actual operation, as if he were little more than an interested but objective observer to the procedure.

But something went wrong, desperately wrong. As Doering was slicing away, and the other two mopping up blood, Yakoff felt a tingling sensation in his side. It was small at first, more curious than anything else. Then the feeling grew and intensified at an alarming rate. It was pain. He was feeling pain. He could feel each mechanical whack Doering was making in his body.

He wanted to scream but was too afraid. Fear created from watching this man with the hateful eyes as he cut him wide open gripped his vocal cords, rendering them helpless. What if he could scream... they wouldn't stop, they didn't care. They'd just keep doing whatever they were doing. His fingers wrapped around the edges of the table and squeezed until his knuckles turned white. He grimaced with each butcher-like stab Doering made in his side. Slicing, slicing, wiping the blood away.

When the knife broke through the fatty tissue and opened a hole to the interior stomach wall a great gush of air was released. Yakoff groaned loudly and his torso twitched involuntarily reacting to the new and colder air as it rushed back into his body. Doering turned and stared menacingly at the boy's face.

"Shut up," he whispered, "and don't move." The threat was well-taken. One of the assistants spoke, "The spinal didn't take..."

"So..."

"At least not completely..."

Doering exhaled, shaking his head, more annoyed than anything else. "It doesn't matter. He's just another Jew."

That's what it got down to, the bottom line, the common denominator. Yakoff was just another Jew. A nonhuman being to be practiced on, experimented with, cut open, shot, gassed, burned, forgotten.

He felt Doering's fingers probing deep inside his body, reaching for something, grasping veins, tubes and arteries. Squeezing, looking blindly for a particular and certain one. The pain returned. He could feel it all, every insensitive mash of the butcher's fingers. Still he suppressed the scream.

As Doering pressed his thumb and forefinger together, Yakoff felt an agonizing barrage emanating directly and specifically from his right testicle. Doering felt the twinge and noticed the grimace on Yakoff's face. With satisfaction in his eyes, the sides of his surgical mask raised slightly once again.

The doctor placed his other hand on the testicle and squeezed, hard. "This might sting a little bit," came from behind the mask and a sarcastic, muffled chuckling followed. Yakoff's head was flat on the table and he couldn't see what was being done, but he certainly could feel it. The testicle was being pushed, a half inch at a time, through a tube and into his lower stomach wall. His body reacted to each callous and brutal squeeze Doering made, and one of the assistants placed his own hand, palm down on Yakoff's chest, trying to restrain his movement.

"Hold still, Jew, or we'll cut it off."

Cut what off, Yakoff questioned. He actually had no idea what Doering and the others were doing. None. At this moment the pain was all consuming, unpleasantly reminiscent of the time in Sierpc, when he was very young, and a friend borrowed a bicycle.

They were teaching Yakoff to ride and started his journey at the top of a long steep hill. They balanced him, holding either side and pushed with all their might.

As the bicycle and its inexperienced operator careened down the hill out of control, the friends rolled on the grass in hysterics. For a few seconds it was the funniest thing they'd ever seen. Yakoff was terrified, going from side to side, trying to balance, trying to steer, afraid to fall but afraid to keep going. Inertia took care of that.

When he ran into the large tree at the bottom of the hill, the impact threw him from the seat and onto the crossbar between his legs. His groin, with the full weight on top, was pushed down as it hit the metal, bringing a long series of stars dancing before his eyes as he doubled over holding himself.

More vivid stars reappeared as he felt Doering's hand, again squeezing. A fourth man, dressed in white, entered the room. He was different. He wasn't wearing a surgical mask and was also strangely familiar. It was a face Yakoff had seen before but couldn't quite place. Each time he tried to concentrate, the pain ripped through him, interrupting the process. The man's eyes were set close to his nose, narrow, piercing. The jaw was square, strong, clean-shaven, and his hair was jet-black and straight. He moved around the room in the goose step cadence indigenous to the Nazis. He stood at attention with hands clasped behind his back. It was clear this was the man who was in charge. Yakoff blinked, he knew he'd seen the man before.

"How much longer?" the man asked in perfect German. Now Yakoff had two of his senses exploring. The voice was also familiar. How can that be? From three words you could recognize a voice?

"We'll be closing in a few minutes," Doering said. Yakoff was hoping for a reply, another sentence, another word. Something to help him identify the stranger who seemed so familiar. But the man only nodded at Doering and continued to watch.

The pain, in half-inch intervals, continued to keep Yakoff from the concentration he was trying so desperately to obtain. Who is this man? Where have I seen him? Each time he got close to an answer, a squeeze would jolt him back to the reality at hand. Something was being shaved or pulled or pushed at an agonizingly slow pace through the inside of his lower stomach.

The light in here is all wrong, Yakoff thought, trying to escape the misery. It's too bright in here. I've seen this man in different light. Yes, that's it. It was darkness and shadows and then bright beams of intense light...spotlights. Then it came to him and it was all too clear.

It was the December night Yakoff's transport arrived. The spotlights were flashed on the innocent Jewish victims as they were forced off the train and herded like cattle at gunpoint to the hard red ground. Families were separated with the women, children and old ones on one side, and the men who could perform the senseless work on the other.

This man, the one looking down with the square jaw and straight black hair was there that night. He marched through the throng of terrified people with an armed SS man on either side pointing his finger this way and that. Each time he pointed, the recipient of the gesture was moved, sometimes bodily, to the women's side. From there, the black beast trucks hauled the moaning, praying passengers to the raging ovens.

He was there, Yakoff's mind screamed. He was there. Pointing the finger of death and extermination. Even the mere sound of the voice was the same, a haunting echo he heard in his nightmares of the man's voice as he pointed and ordered, "You, you, you..."

But why, why, why? Dear God what is happening to me? Why have you allowed this to occur?

A door behind Yakoff creaked open and an unseen voice broke the silence. "Doctor Mengele, they need you in the other operating room." The man without the mask nodded and walked away.

So that was him. The infamous Doctor Josef Mengele. The one responsible for the first selection as the transports arrived, the one who initiated the bizarre experimental surgery designed to annihilate the entire Jewish race, the one they called the Angel of Death, the man initially and morally responsible for the deaths of more fellow human beings than any other person in the recorded history of the world...so that was him.

More pain, more squeezing, he was weak. He tried but couldn't lift his head from the table. All he could see was his own chest, heaving up and down from the increased heartbeat.

"Scalpel," Doering said coldly

One of the assistants handed him another piece of steel. Yakoff could see the shiny object moving toward his stomach, but then lost sight of it. He was being cut again, this time inside. The pain was sharp and quick. He felt another great surge of blood released as one of Doering's assistants shoved a rag into the open wound.

The half-inch at a time squeezing continued for another few agonizing seconds. Then it stopped. Not the pain, just the squeezing.

"It's out," Doering announced. "Suture..." He was handed a long string attached to a needle and returned his attention to the youngster's stomach. Yakoff was gasping for breath, trying to maintain consciousness but losing the battle.

At first his fingers and hands had a tingly feeling. It was difficult to move anything. Then they started to get cold, icy-cold and numb. He stared at the single light hanging above the table and it appeared to be moving slightly from side to side, then in tiny concentric circles. The background, ceiling and walls faded into a dull, flat blackness with no beginning or end. Doering and the others were speaking but he couldn't make out their words.

One seemed to ask something like, "Should we save it?" But the answer was garbled, unintelligible, like the man's mouth was full of stones or dirt. Yakoff's arms were cold, freezing, then they seemed to be removed as if no longer attached, floating.

The room began to spin with the light. So did Doering and his assistants. Around and around, laughing grotesquely each time they passed Yakoff's face, pointing strange, bizarre, unknown fingers of hateful accusation and abuse at the helpless youngster.

A swirling, foggy mist formed over his eyes, engulfing everything within his line of vision. He squinted and strained all the muscles in his face, still feeling the fiery pain shooting through the bottom of his stomach. It felt like a giant faucet was jammed into his right side, then turned on full, releasing everything within.

The laughter, real or imagined, resounded and reverberated through his brain, then echoed in the far-off distance to a hollow nothingness. The room spun faster, hurtling the faces and fingers into a continuous blur of streaky grey light, almost wispy and cloud-like. He was sinking. Falling down and down...

Chapter XIII

Yakoff was dizzy, surrounded by a loud buzzing. Focusing was still difficult. The first clear thought with any logic attached was whether or not he was actually alive.

The question was answered as he painfully turned his head to one side and saw a roomful of occupied beds. When he tried to lift himself up he unpleasantly discovered he couldn't. He was being restrained but there were no straps holding him to the bed. He was simply too weak.

"Don't try to move." It was a voice from the far side of the bed. Slowly, amid much agony, he turned and saw a man standing, looking down. It was a hospital orderly, another prisoner. "If you do, you'll rip out your stitches."

At the mention of the word, the pain which had never really gone away, returned in full force. Yakoff flashed a grimace, blinking several times. The orderly showed no compassion or feeling.

"Do you have anything...you could give me...for the pain...?"

The whispered request brought a response of a low guttural laugh. The insensitivity and lack of caring from a fellow prisoner seemed to hurt nearly as much as the burning in his lower stomach. It was as if the orderly were announcing to the world and Yakoff in particular, "I've got mine and the hell with you." The orderly was obviously pleased with his relative position of authority. "You're lucky to be alive," he announced with a smile. "Stay in bed and don't move."

As he strolled away Yakoff perused the rest of the room. Experience told him he was on the second floor of one of the blocks, most likely block 28. He saw familiar faces lying in nearby bunks. Isaac was there along with David Levin and Martin Klein. Even Herschel Novedvor. They'd all managed to make it through the ordeal. Yakoff was the last to regain consciousness. The other two men waiting with Isaac when they all arrived at the hospital, weren't in sight.

The room held close to sixty beds, each one filled with its own horror story of pain and mutilation. There were amputations and

162

macabre experimental surgery cases of every imaginable sort. Massive doses of exposure to x-rays turned bodies a charred and crispy black, eyes had been removed, chests and stomachs had been cut open for no apparent reason. The true Nazi sickness under the watchful eyes of Doctors Mengele and Doering rose to disproportionate heights.

Rations were delivered, the same thin smelly water and crusts of black bread. With every ounce of energy, Yakoff lifted his head to pour the brown liquid into his mouth. At least it was lukewarm and helped relieve the numbness in his arms and hands. There was no one to assist in the feeding process because no one cared.

That night after the lights were extinguished, Yakoff learned the truth about what transpired. While in the makeshift operating room, earlier that day, he'd had his right testicle surgically removed. He also heard a new word used for the first time in his life...castration.

He responded to the whispered report with stunned silence, the silence and look following something impossible to believe, as if your own ears were playing grandiose tricks. He moved his right hand under the covers, not wishing to rustle the sheets and announce his disbelief to the others. Slowly he slid his hand down his side until he reached the area of the incision. It was oozing with a warm pus, caked, hard, but still sticky to the touch.

There was a hesitation, a wanting to know counterbalance with not wanting to know. But he had to. The area was tender, sensitive, white-hot with pain. Gritting, clenching, mashing his teeth together he reached for his right testicle.

He emitted a low, very personal grunt, discernible throughout the quiet room. Through the stillness, a voice from a distant bed drifted across the space between and rested on Yakoff's ears. It was compassionate, understanding, clearly from someone who shared a very uncommon bond. "See..." was all the voice said.

Even by feeling, he couldn't believe the truth of it, and was personally forced to repeat the painful process. Once again, he touched his thumb and forefinger to the now empty and loose hanging skin between his legs.

They remained on the second floor of block 28 for four days and nights. During the entire recovery period, they never again saw Doering or any other "qualified" physician. The second day they were allowed out of their beds to use the bathroom. The minimum tasteless rations remained the same. Yakoff's stitches continued to ooze the sticky pus as well as the still open and unhealed wound on his right leg, the one from the Frenchman.

From talking with other recovering patients in the ward, Yakoff determined complaint of any kind or degree was unwise as well as dangerous. Too many times he'd seen people wheeled away who never returned. Their largest and most constant fear was being selected for the gas chamber. Stories with foundation were related about Mengele or others who would walk into the ward and clear it with a wave of their finger, sending sixty sick and mutilated men to the ovens.

A terror would grip Yakoff's entire being each time an orderly entered the room. In younger days he developed an understandable and uncontrollable fear of the unknown. Now the fear was clear, certain, well-defined. It was the fear of someone, anyone, walking into the room and pointing a finger or reading the number on your arm from a clipboard. These selections were always met by silence, acceptance, then a prayerful trip to destruction.

Night time was the worst. Yakoff's eyes sprang open each time he heard footsteps in the long wooden hall outside their door. What he needed was rest and sleep but there was little of either. The pain continued at a steady pace, never dissipating in the slightest. And he never complained to anyone.

On the eve of the fourth day, Yakoff and his friends were released from the hospital and instructed to return to their own blocks. The five of them never saw the other men who underwent the same painful operation. It was believed they perished during the surgery. Or, perhaps they were part of a selection. No one ever knew.

Walking down the steps of block 28 was nearly as bad as walking up the steps of block 7. There was no assistance of any kind and no sympathy was outwardly shown. The latter was much appreciated.

Upon their return, they were warmly received by Harry, Yossel, Heim, Lulek and the others. It was a homecoming few of them imagined would ever take place. Bread and saved rations were shared with the weak returnees along with stories about what the bricklayers had been doing. The communication network within the camp was swift and generally accurate. This allowed Harry and the others to be aware of what their friends had just experienced. Yakoff was relieved, even in his friends' knowledge of the travesty; not one word about the surgery was ever spoken.

Each step was like an electric prod, jolting his body into gritting, spasmodic pain. He could feel the stitches pull and give every time he lifted his right leg and then put it down. The march to the work site seemed ten times as far as he'd remembered. Then there was the picking up of wheelbarrows full of bricks, trying to push them up ribbon-thin boards, and tightrope across creaking, swaying scaffolding.

The stitches gave with each exertion extended. He could feel the hole in his stomach reopening. The redheaded kapo was unsympathetic but did reassign the scrunched over youngster to a job mixing mortar. At least he could remain on the ground.

Bags, a hundred pounds at a time, were dumped into the large flat mixing tub. Then buckets of water were added until the texture and consistency were correct. Back and forth, back and forth. Yakoff wielded the long handled shovel through the thick gooey substance until his arms were ready to fall off. The ooze flowed through the stitches until the outside of his trousers were stained. The misty fog, remembered from the operating table, returned to his eyes and he stumbled to one knee, ripping his skin even more.

One of Yakoff's friends, seeing what was happening, quickly helped him to his feet. "Let your shovel follow mine," he said. "You won't have any resistance and it'll still look like you're working."

Yakoff nodded, gasping for breath, trying to shake away cobwebs and maintain consciousness. To fall down on the job meant you couldn't work. And if you couldn't work...

He collapsed into his bunk that night, some of the others had to help feed him. On the way up the steps, Olschevsky had given him one of his patented evil eyes, but nothing more came of it. Nothing more than the perpetual and continual fear deepening every day.

The pain continued through the night, increasing the following day at the work site. Yakoff knew his time was short. He couldn't keep up this pace much longer. The small group of friends did whatever they could to cover for and protect one another against Olschevsky, the guards, and the work itself, but there was only so much they could do.

Weak, totally exhausted, and still unhealed, Yakoff made a slow painful trek to the laundry to visit his friend Isaac, who had cleverly manipulated his way up the ranks and into a position of total authority over the entire washateria operation. Isaac had a kapo who left him completely alone in exchange for being well-fed. The work was warm and most of the time easy to the extent it wasn't the normal back-breaking hard labor.

Isaac, having undergone the same grotesque operation, could feel a degree of empathy for Yakoff few others could begin to comprehend. Their bond was strong. By virtue of his working environment, he'd had time to heal and was actually in pretty good shape. He was deeply saddened by the unchanging grimace of pain and limp his friend had developed.

Before the question was asked, Isaac offered Yakoff a job, taking him away from the daily killing routine of the bricklaying patrol. "But," he continued, his voice filled with understanding and compassion, "it'll have to be on the night shift."

That was fine with Yakoff. That was perfect. Isaac's kapo prepared the necessary transfer request and the next day the half-dead youngster moved out of the bricklayer's school, and into block 5. Later that night he limped to his new job.

The laundry facility itself was not assigned a block number, even though it was nearly as large as all the other buildings within the camp. It was on the far east side, directly across the street from the hospital block. On the other side of the street and behind the laundry, was the equally infamous block 11, the one attached to the wall of death. This was the prison within the prison where men were tortured until their brains as well as bodies turned to mush. Then they were dragged outside, usually half conscious, stood up, and shot in the head. This practice was utilized by the Nazis as a cost-saving device so the uniforms could be saved and recycled among incoming prisoners.

When Yakoff arrived, Isaac waved a hand indicating for the pain riddled youngster to sit. It was apparent he was half starved. Without being asked, Isaac offered food. Yakoff's mouth fell open in disbelief. Was he really seeing what was placed in front of him? It was a potato, a whole potato. But more than that, it was cooked. Steaming hot, bursting with mouth-watering aroma. He ravished the food, out of his mind with pleasure.

"Slow down," Isaac said, "there's more."

More, Yakoff thought...how can that be possible? But the very thought filled him with a renewal of hope. With food you could sustain. With food you could survive.

There was a steaming machine in the laundry and when you placed a potato, which was organized or procured from the black market, inside the machine, it would cook completely in less than five minutes. It was an amazing device, unlike anything Yakoff had ever seen. But right now, the only thing he cared about was stuffing his mouth and stomach with hot food. It had an anesthetic effect, even better than the spinal at the hospital. His pain, for only a moment, seemed to subside. The laundry was responsible for cleaning all the prisoner uniforms, blankets and underwear. It also pressed various uniforms for some of the privileged few. These mostly included kapos and seniors. The SS had its own facility outside the fences and clothing between the two was never mixed.

Yakoff's job, while not easy, was considerably softer than the ones he'd had since his arrival. The laundry had no equipment for drying, so his assignment was to string the wet clothing and blankets on long clothes lines. This he accomplished by loading the freshly washed uniforms on a wooden wagon which he pulled from one end of the camp to the other. Then he'd hand-carry the load up three flights of stairs to the mezzanine of block 22 and hang them up to dry.

Since he was working during the late night and early morning hours, there was little if any activity throughout the streets of the camp. He had the opportunity to work at his own pace. There were no quotas, time clocks or kapos to contend with. And, even though the loads were heavy and the work strenuous, he was out from under the thumb of someone constantly threatening to beat or kill him at any given moment. This, combined with the regularity of food, good hot food, enabled Yakoff to regain most of his strength, as well as a modicum of energy, within the next few weeks.

Uninterrupted sleep was also a blessing in disguise. Yakoff would return to his block as nearly everyone else was going off to work. It was quiet inside the camp during the day, and since everyone knew he was working the graveyard shift, he was generally left alone. To a slight extent there was even a feeling of a relative degree of safety.

After much needed rest, certainly an integral part of the healing process, he'd arise as the others would return from their various work patrols. By now he was eating well enough at the laundry that he no longer wanted or needed the rancid camp rations. However Yakoff would still stand in line as the soup and black bread crusts were doled out. Then he would give his portion to the weakest or most hungry. Pesach's lessons to an adolescent Yakoff were still more deeply embellished than the hate, contempt and mistrust being forced by the Nazis.

After rations, Yakoff and several of the others would stroll over to the area between blocks 18 and 19, the black market. But these days, the trip was never made before Yakoff first stuffed an indistinguishable bundle of something inside the waist of his trousers and then covered it with his shirt.

The black market actually resembled a stock market in progress on a heavy trading day. Hundreds of prisoners would be milling about, each hoping to trade something they had for something they wanted. Sometimes the trading and bartering process became very complex and difficult. The value of a potato today could be considerably different than what it was yesterday. It was all a matter of supply and demand; how much people were willing to pay, or in this case give, for what they wanted.

What Yakoff wanted today was dinner. He was after food for his evening meal. Slowly, as if methodically stalking, he mixed among the throng. Most of them were shouting and screaming the items they possessed or desired, but Yakoff remained silent, his ears perked and listening. There was a bizarre game to it all. Deadly, to be sure. But a game nonetheless.

Yakoff was becoming known as a trader among the regulars in attendance, just as he had as a youngster in the open-air, fresh fruit market in Sierpc.

"I got some German marks," a tall emaciated man whispered.

The youngster shook his head, continuing through the crowd. He'd even gleaned the nickname of "the Gypsy" from most of the others. His inherent ability to collect, upgrade, and exchange goods, was earning him quite a reputation. If someone wanted something badly enough, it was becoming known within the small circle of insiders, Yakoff was one of only a handful who could arrange it. It was a position he fully enjoyed but seldom took advantage of.

"Hey Gypsy..." Yakoff turned toward the voice, "you lookin' for dinner?" The man smiled, knowing full well the youngster's objective. He was shorter than most, with high cheekbones and only one eye. The other, a blackened hollow pit, had been removed by the end of a Nazi rifle barrel, a result of not taking off his cap quickly enough in the presence of an SS officer.

"What'a you got?" Yakoff whispered.

The scene now became very private, very serious. It was just between the two of them. The noises and screaming in the background seemed to fade to barely a dull murmur.

"I got an onion, a whole onion...and a carrot."

Yakoff studied the man, sizing him up. He stared at the one blood-shot eye, then shook his head and started to walk away.

"Two carrots, Gypsy. I'll make it two."

They all knew where Yakoff worked and more than likely what he had to trade. Generally it was clothing. Clean, warm clothing. Another thing they all knew was his trading was fair. He bargained and negotiated hard but he was fair. The clothing he traded, quite naturally and obviously, was stolen from the laundry. It was a relatively simple process most of the time since he was generally left to work on his own. He had ample opportunity to put on two sets of the best available uniforms he could find, or stuff various smaller articles down the front of his pants.

When he stopped and turned back towards the man there was a good chance a deal would be consummated on the spot. The man looked both ways then spoke again, parroting Yakoff's own words, "What you got?"

"Underwear, one pair and socks."

"Clean?"

Yakoff rolled his eyes upwards. Of course they were clean. The man once again checked their privacy and then reached into his own pants pockets producing the food as promised. Yakoff slowly raised his shirt tail and took out the small bundle which he'd placed there earlier.

They exchanged merchandise and drifted away from one another, each happier for the encounter. It was like that. Day after day and night after night. A new pattern was formed, a new routine. The consistency always hanging in the air, like a dark cloud of foreboding doom, was the fear. It never ever went away. The daytime, nighttime, all the time fear someone was going to beat you to death with a club, a whip, or end your life and very existence with the mere pointing of a finger.

Yakoff, or the Gypsy as he was becoming known, was transferred from the night to the day shift and resettled into a life of relative normalcy. At least as far as that word could be used in Auschwitz. Sometimes he'd be assigned to go down to block 28 and retrieve the clothing hung there to dry the night before. Sometimes he'd stay in the laundry and help work the machines. He had some freedom of choice, which was rare, and he liked that a lot.

Because of his access to trading materials, extra food was seldom a problem. Things were always available if you were able to pay the price. Everyone including the kapos and seniors had things they wanted but were unobtainable. Yakoff, with his ears perked sharply, listened closely to conversations like these and used them to his advantage.

He overheard his block senior in 5 tell another man he'd obtained a much desired pass to the camp brothel. But, the story continued, the senior wanted to take the young lady a present of some sort to leave in return for her services. The trap was set and the plan was in motion. For the next four evenings in a row, Yakoff went to the black market to obtain the item he desired. Walking around, listening and asking the right questions of the right people, he found a man who had in his possession a pair of frilly, black lace panties. The man said he would only trade them for a new pair of shoes.

So, Yakoff found a man with shoes, but he in turn insisted he would only exchange them for two bars of soap. The man with the soap was trying to obtain margarine and wanted nothing else. The Gypsy searched until he found an acquaintance who worked in the camp kitchen and the first trade was entered into. The kitchen helper was in need of a fresh clean uniform, pressed of course. Yakoff was in business.

They agreed to meet the following evening and the exchange was consummated, the uniform for the margarine. Then he patiently and persistently looked until he found the next man and so on. The margarine for the soap, the soap for the shoes, and the shoes for the black lace panties.

When he returned to the block and walked past the senior's room he stopped and casually stuck his head inside the door.

"What'a you want, Jew?" It was shouted in a gruff authoritative tone.

"Nothin," Yakoff answered. He reached inside his pocket and pulled out the prized, sought after possession. The senior's scowl disappeared as the youngster offered them to him. "Here," he said, "thought you might be able to use these."

The senior took them with a quizzical look on his face. "Why?" This time the tone was different. Not nice by any stretch of the imagination, just different.

"No reason," Yakoff lied, "I just heard you had a pass." They both understood what he was talking about. "That's all..."

The man nodded, not a smile or a "thanks", just a nod. Yakoff left the room and returned to his bunk, mission accomplished.

Bribery was a way of life within the camp and everyone who had the nerve or opportunity did so. Sometimes it worked and sometimes it didn't. It was impossible to tell, going in, which would be which. It was always a crapshoot so you simply did what you could and hoped for the best.

In this case the best, or the hopeful reward, would come in the form of leniency if Yakoff was ever caught doing anything construed as wrong. The senior owed him, they both knew that. Whether or not a payoff would ever occur was quite simply a matter of time. And there was never any guarantee it would. The realistic philosophy was your odds of survival were increased if those in any position superior to your own owed you favors. Many lives were spared in exchange for the parenthetical loaf of bread or jug of wine.

Guards were also highly included on everyone's list of whom to bribe. The town of Auschwitz, a direct result of the camps, was isolated and many items which would normally fall into the category of personal interest or necessity were difficult if not impossible to obtain. Ironically these same items were generally available on the black market and proved beneficial to prisoners who could organize or procure them.

Hands were always out, palm up, wide open, ready and willing to be greased with even the smallest token from any prisoner who had the nerve to approach and initiate a contact. The payoffs, in whatever form or shape they took, were in exchange for hoped-for protection. Maybe not today and maybe not tomorrow. Maybe never. The guards as well as kapos and seniors were totally and completely unpredictable. They could never be trusted.

Trust among most of the prisoners themselves was a foreign thing. The men were from all over Europe and beyond. There was a multitude of nationalities which made mass communication difficult at best. The language barriers created situations which kept most of them among their own kind. The language one learned quickly, if one was to survive, was German. The rule still very much in effect was if you didn't understand the language, the stick or whip would clearly translate for you.

It was not uncommon for prisoners to report on or turn in other prisoners for the slightest discrepancy or deviation of the stoic and overly strict rules. This too was done to gain favor with superiors. These despicable acts of treachery could come from anywhere or anyone. The result was the majority of the men kept to themselves for the most part and trusted only small groups of close friends who had earned each other's respect.

Fall of '43 came and the trees seen on the far side of the fences began to change their colors. The oranges, golds and crimsons outside the double wires brought little beauty to Auschwitz. This was a place of death, destruction and human degradation.

The advantage of the falling temperature created a higher value on the black market for the extra uniforms and warm underwear Yakoff had to trade. Meticulously and by design he had done things and acquired items for the majority of the guards and others who were directly responsible for his life. He became adept at organizing just about anything he or anyone else wanted.

But each trade was a risk, for it was being transacted with something which was stolen from the Germans. To be caught would mean instant death. No explanation would have been accepted. The youngster felt the risk was commensurate with the rewards.

One of the rewards was a certain degree of respect which actually came in two forms. One was the reputation he'd earned for procuring things and favors. The other was derived by nature of the very number on his arm. The men still alive who had tattoos in the high seventies or low eighties were few and far between.

When an unknown guard, usually a new one, stopped Yakoff on the street to harass or ridicule, the "80629" permanently inked on his body would normally reduce a mindless beating to a high-pitched reprimand. He had survived nearly a full year in this place and that, in and of itself, seemed to bring an unspoken sense of respect.

The laundry was a relatively decent work patrol. In addition to food and other items of necessity the trading provided, it was also a warm place to be. This was becoming increasingly important as the harsh winter months set in. Other inside jobs like the maintenance crews, the electricians, the tailors, the shoe cobblers and anything at all in the kitchen, were much desired by most of the general prisoner population. These positions however, were normally filled by old-timers, men who'd been there awhile and had proven their ability to survive. The men not fortunate enough to obtain or hold these jobs worked on construction crews outside the main area of the camp.

The days were long, twelve hour shifts, the food was minimal, barely enough to stay alive. The work itself still amounted to backbreaking hard labor. Each evening, six nights a week, as the orchestra played the same German marching tunes over and over, the work patrols would return to the camp marching under the "Work Makes Freedom" sign. Each time they returned, they came back with far fewer than they left with at sunrise.

By the following day, each of the missing had been replaced with a new, unwilling, terrified soul. The transports with boxcars jammed full of people continued to arrive. The stockpile of humanity to feed the insatiable Nazi hunger for destruction was endless. The fully loaded wagons continued to roll towards Birkenau and the ashen-filled skies.

It was a chilly morning. Frost would have covered the grass if there was any. Instead, it blanketed the surrounding mud and dirt. Even the pressed rock streets were slippery, making marching hazardous. Winter had set in and would be there for awhile.

Yakoff was having coffee, real coffee, with Isaac and Leon, who'd also transferred to the laundry, and a few others on the crew. The machines were working at full speed, creating a warmth which was much appreciated. Something caught their attention, a thud of some sort, bringing an immediate halt to their conversation. Then another thud, this one followed by a groan of pain. The sound was all too familiar.

Without thinking, Yakoff quickly walked behind one of the nearby machines, toward the direction of the noise. The situation he discovered was completely apparent. Their normally docile and reasonably passive kapo found one of the other prisoners asleep on a pile of clothing. To show his displeasure he was beating the man's head and back with his ever-present club. The man was trying, with little success, to protect himself with his arms, but the blows kept coming.

"Sir.." Yakoff said without hesitation. He spoke loudly, above the noise of the machines. The kapo spun, his face in a rage, clearly annoyed at the interruption.

"What!" Odd, how in anger a question can sound like a statement.

"Sir..." he repeated, "I know this man made a mistake..."

Yakoff spoke quietly, forcing the kapo to lean towards him if he was to hear. The device, simple as it seemed, was intentional, designed to transfer the kapo's attention and hopefully get his mind off the planned destruction.

"What about it?" The voice was still stern, gruff.

"Well, sir..."

Yakoff's demeanor was akin to a child who'd just broken a window and was trying to explain his innocence to the homeowner. He stared at the floor moving slowly from side to side, his face filled with remorse.

"...You see, this man's my cousin..."

The kapo lowered his stick, exhaling a deep sigh.

"...And if you could see clear to let him go, I'll make sure it never happens again."

The kapo paused as if contemplating the request. What he was actually contemplating was the food Yakoff had provided for him in the past and the possibility of losing that supply in the future if he continued the senseless beating. He maintained his posture and stuck out his chest, a face- saving device.

"You're lucky this time," he snarled at the man on the floor. "Don't let it happen again." With that he walked away.

The other prisoner slowly drew himself to a standing position, wincing with each move. A large bluish welt formed over his left eye, nearly closing it. He nodded at Yakoff, a sincere gesture of thanks and appreciation. The fact the two were not related, and barely acquaintances, was at this moment of minor importance to either of them.

"You okay?"

The man nodded again, wondering why Yakoff had done such a thing. Kindness or generosity in any form was a rarity.

"Stay away from him," Yakoff said. "And try to take it easy today. The rest of us'll cover for you."

Once again the bribery paid off. This time it worked. Next time could be an altogether different story.

And try as he might, Yakoff still couldn't get any word or information from the Sonderkommando about the status or fate of his father.

Chapter XIV

It was literally a cold day in hell when the block senior stopped Yakoff and Isaac on their way to work. Snow was falling as the senior dispassionately told them someone would be by to escort them to where they would spend the day. That was all he knew, there were no other details. Even subtly trying to cash in chips owed wouldn't budge the man from his story.

They waited nervously without speaking, each carefully avoiding the other's eyes, as if they both knew but really couldn't bear to accept it. Their worst suspicions and fears were realized as a hospital orderly approached their block and read their tattoo numbers off a clipboard.

They walked in silence through the camp, the only sound was the freshly fallen snow crunching under their feet. Soft at first, then crescendoing into a deafening roar, drum-like, beating them back towards the dreaded hospital.

The room was the same, the smell was the same, the nondescript faces moving to and fro were the same. Everything, most unfortunately, was the same. They were joined by David Levin, Martin Klein, Herschel Novedvor and another familiar face. Their number had diminished to six and the quiet continued until it was broken by the creaking of the door on the far wall.

Then, even the routine was the same. Their numbers, one by one, were called and they followed the orderly into the adjoining room. The shooting pain from the unseen instrument brutally jammed into their rectums was expected this time, but still hurt just as much. The humiliation and degradation was at the same level if not increased from the time before. The long, unsterilized needle stabbed into their lower backs brought the same silent tears. The callous and serious threats of death were shouted at each involuntary movement. Doering was there, hiding cowardly behind his mask. Even Mengele drifted in and out of the rooms, supervising and overseeing his perverse madness.

The cutting open of the flesh was the same, as was the agony emitting from the inside of the lower stomach, as Doering probed and grabbed without concern or compassion for his unwilling patients.

The mist returned, just as before. The haze. The room turned a milky grey, swirling, then it started to spin.

When Yakoff regained consciousness on the second floor of the hospital and was able to clear his head enough to think through the excruciating anguish, he recalled the rules and procedures: "Don't try to move, don't get out of your bed till tomorrow."

Isaac was there, so was David and the rest. The ward was full, every single bed filled with unnecessary suffering at the hands of sadists who had absolutely no regard for human life. It was all the same.

With one exception. The pain which before burned so brightly inside his lower right side now came from the left. And again, just as before, he had to find out. He had to be sure. The discovery was the sick and gripping reality of what he expected. The Nazi surgeons, this time, removed his left testicle. Yakoff had been completely, totally castrated.

In performing this incredible atrocity, the Nazis not only stripped a caring and innocent youngster of his manhood, they also implanted a misery which would continue to plague Yakoff and the others for the rest of their lives.

The four day recovery period was the same as the previous operation but this time the resulting pain was considerably more severe and longer lasting. Once again the stitches came loose and the sticky pus oozed through.

Walking was difficult, nearly impossible, sapping their strength, leaving them weak and breathless. Again Yakoff slumped into his own bunk and again someone had to help feed him. The pain was far beyond physical. This time it cut psychological cords of bondage, severing them neatly and trimly to such an extent they could never be rejoined. He'd been deformed. Defiled. Now there was the certainty; even if he should somehow miraculously manage to live through this ordeal, he would never be able to father children and rebuild the family that was stolen from him.

Via the grapevine, the rest of the laundry was aware of what Yakoff, Isaac, and the others had just experienced. Their understanding faces spoke the words their mouths couldn't. Like the first operation, this verbal omission was deeply appreciated. There was an uncomfortable moment of strained silence the first morning Yakoff and Isaac returned to work. Then an acquaintance of theirs cautiously approached.

He seemed to be the unappointed spokesman for the rest of the group. He cleared his throat and started slowly. The words came out soft, almost embarrassed, as he stared at the floor refusing to make eye contact.

"You guys try to take it easy today." You could hear the emotion creeping into his voice. "The rest of us'll cover for you."

It was the man Yakoff befriended and saved from the stick of the kapo.

That year Auschwitz had a particularly brutal winter. Countless prisoners lost their lives in the subzero temperatures. For them, the warmth the ovens provided came much too late. Bodies, blue with desperate eyes wide open, hard and stiff as boards, were loaded on wagon after wagon for their last freezing ride over the icy road to Birkenau. Even though it was readily available, no warm clothing was ever provided. Fingers and toes, frostbitten from day after day of non-interrupted exposure, would fall off in the snow and frozen mud. It was too cold to bleed. Transports continued to arrive with fresh bodies to constantly replace the stiff ones in the wagons. Even the orchestra continued to play their daily song of death, blowing eerie frozen air through their trumpets and trombones. There was no escape from Auschwitz.

Recovery for Yakoff was slow and painful. Had it not been for the others in the laundry who helped lighten his load, recovery would have been unlikely. Had he been forced to work outside in the killing weather, recovery would have been impossible. He knew that and felt a deep-seated debt of gratitude to his friends.

The operation was never talked about, not by anyone at any time. There was no point. Retrospective sorrow or hours of clinical discussion couldn't change what Doering and the others had done. No treaty, victory, defeat or miracle could ever return Yakoff's manhood. As psychologically damaging and humanistically demeaning as it was, it was something which had to be accepted. At least for the time being. Right now all energy, strength and hope had to be directed towards one singular objective: survival.

Some of the others lacked the will to live, which was inbred in Yakoff's heart. It was something that could be seen in their eyes and heard in their voices. Seldom overt, but always there. Always gnawing and eating away at their insides, each time their minds consciously reflected on the void between their legs.

Martin Klein was one of the others. He'd become distant, removed, reticent. His eye-sockets were deepening and he usually had a glazed, faraway stare that never really looked at anything. Just space. It was three months after the operation when it happened. It was the middle of the night and Martin was lying on his bunk, sunken eyes examining nothingness. It was quiet and his thoughts returned, as they had constantly for the last ninety days, to the personal butchery and shell of his own life that remained.

Slowly, without sound or fanfare, he sat on the edge of his bed. He was not alone in his hate for this place. He was not alone in despising the Nazis and everything they represented. But still, this night, he felt completely alone and totally isolated, wrapped and ribboned in his own personal tragedy.

Quietly, without forethought or intention, he walked out of the room and down the narrow stairway. Martin Klein was seventeen and his life was over. He was going to the wires.

Harry Foreman, one of the close-knit group of friends and confidants, shared the same block as Martin. For some unknown reason, Harry woke up from a sound sleep just as the boy walked out of the room. The rest of the group had been keeping a distant but watchful eye on Martin, concerned about his withdrawal as well as refusal to communicate. They watched as the youngster turned slowly into a nonspeaking recluse.

The camp was silent without any movement or activity. Snow still covered the frozen ground as Martin turned to his right and headed toward the northernmost perimeter. Harry, wanting at least one backup, stopped in block 5 and arose a sleeping Yakoff.

No one ever ran inside the camp. It was more than likely the Nazis would shoot down anyone they saw running, so the two of them walked as quickly as possible without breaking their stride. The moon was full and they could see Martin clearly up ahead. He walked with determination, "a knowing where he was going and nothing was going to stop him" kind of walk. Yakoff and Harry picked up their pace.

Auschwitz, like Birkenau, was surrounded on the outside with free standing guard towers. The fences were well-lit during the entire night and the towers were also equipped with large, high-beam spotlights. Billowy, slow-moving clouds cast eerie shadows on the crispy snow.

There was a line, invisible, but known by every prisoner who wore the striped uniform. It was thirty feet from the fence and if you crossed the line, with or without a reason, you'd be shot on the spot. There were no exceptions. Martin was heading directly towards the line and the fence beyond it.

The two friends following were afraid to scream for fear of waking guards or kapos. Their shouts were whispered, ringing with futility, laced with a certain desperateness.

"Martin! Martin! Come back before it's too late!"

He had to hear, but still kept walking. Closer and closer to the invisible line.

"Martin, stop!"

Nothing, no response or reaction, only muted footsteps in the snow. He was nearly there and nothing in the world Yakoff and Harry could possibly do was going to stop him.

Thirty feet from the fence a giant blinding beam of light covered them all. The three stopped dead in their tracks. Martin, because he temporarily couldn't see, and Yakoff and Harry from fear for the certainty of the locked and loaded machine gun on the other side of the light.

It was very quiet, only the humming of the wires. No one moved.

"Turn around and return to your block!"

It was a shout from the guard tower, obviously in German. The unseen voice sounded young, immature, almost like a teenager trying to imitate an adult. That observation was beyond irrelevant. His actual age mattered little considering the deathly firepower he controlled.

"Turn around now! And leave!" No one moved, "I don't want to shoot you but I will!"

Could Yakoff and Harry believe their ears? Martin, according to all the illogical rules of this place, should have been dead seconds ago. He was clearly beyond the line and by all rights should be lying in a pool of his own blood, lifeless, another statistic.

Martin, bathed in the light, was transfixed. He was frozen, unable to move even if he wanted to. Yakoff and Harry didn't cross the line but held their place, not able to help or assist in any way. To move would have surely brought a finger down on the trigger, ending all of their lives.

There was a long moment of silence and the guard spoke again.

"Do you two know this man?"

They both replied they did.

"Then come and get him and take him away," the voice lowered and vocal pretense of adulthood seemed to fade and diminish. "I don't want to shoot anybody."

Martin was young and looked even younger. Maybe that was it. Maybe the guard didn't want to mow down a person who'd recently completed his childhood. Maybe the guard was the same age and could relate or feel something for the terrified youngster. And maybe it was all another sick Nazi trick to get Yakoff and Harry to cross the invisible line and sign their own death certificates.

They turned to face each other. The last maybe was the most likely of the possibilities. Rules were hard, fast, and incredibly clear-cut: cross the line and you die.

"Come on," the guard said. It sounded like he was pleading. But what if they were wrong. What if he was tempting, seducing them to take that one final step, only to fulfill his own personal sadistic tendencies.

Staring into the light and without verbalization they decided the risk must be taken. Martin was a friend. Stomachs tightened and hearts pounded with each step they took, waiting for the blast and blare of the machine gun fire. But the night remained quiet.

"Martin," Yakoff whispered, taking his arm. "We're going back now."

The boy's face was blank, a void, as if he didn't know who or even where he was. He didn't respond or acknowledge the comment. Just the same empty, hollow staring.

Harry took his other arm and the three of them turned, crunching snow, and headed back toward their blocks. As they walked back through the invisible line, the spotlight behind them turned off, leaving only the moonlight to guide their path.

The snow melted and the mud thawed but little else changed. Transports kept arriving and work patrols would return to the camp each night dragging or carrying twenty-five percent of the men.

Martin withdrew even deeper within himself until he was little more than a hollow shell. But at least his overt suicidal tendencies seemed thwarted. Even so, the group continued to keep an eye on him. Yakoff, Harry, Yossel and the others would meet regularly in the evenings for a card game or two. It was actually something to do while they reflectively talked about the old days, the days of childhood, the days of growing up, the days of food, family and loved ones. The days before all this.

There was little if any conversation about the future. It was too uncertain and impossible to plan ahead. All they had was the fact they'd managed to make it through another long, painfilled day. The realistic conception of freedom was a fading thing, confused and clouded in the destructive reality which surrounded them. News from the outside was sparse and never promising. Daily survival was the only thing which really mattered.

As the meetings and card games went on, Yakoff started to notice something different about his friends. It was subtle at first and impossible for him to accurately define, but something was certainly there. Finally it occurred to him: it was their skin. It was getting darker, tan, a result of working outdoors in the sunshine.

His realization brought back fond memories. Memories of a childhood spent at a wide spot in the creek in Sierpc, "the swimming hole" they called it. That memory segued softly into fantasies of whole summers working barefooted in the warm earth of the orchards. They were happy times, his youth, with the family together. Bright times, hot and sweaty. He remembered how each summer he'd turn a golden shade of brown, as if the sun returned his affection.

He stared at his pale white hands and was envious, jealous of his friends' pink faces and tan-lines. They all looked so healthy. And he, well, his skin looked like chalk, a pale milky shade, eroding away by the constant exposure to moisture.

The machines which only months before provided life-sustaining warmth were now hot, stifling, making breathing difficult. The entire laundry crew would stumble through their daily routine, sweat by the bucket coming through every pore. Sometimes the steam and moisture inside the room was so thick vision was impossible. It offered a good and safe place to rest but who could rest when you couldn't breathe.

The air inside the camp was never fresh. That was impossible with more than twenty-thousand sweaty men packed so tightly. But outside, where the construction still continued, was a different story. Out there the air was clean and at least semi-fresh. And the glorious golden sun shown down. Auschwitz, for some God-forsaken reason, was constantly covered with a hazy grey cloud, as if a Higher Being was so embarrassed by the inhumanity perpetrated there, He chose to cover it up and erase it from His vision.

There was also something else. Yakoff had heard from friends working on the outside about the presence of women prisoners at the construction sites. Women were assigned cleanup duty which would allow the bricklayers less time to rest and more time for heavy work. It was reported however, that during the midday rations, men and women were close enough to talk with one another. Never to touch, just to talk.

It'd been over a year since Yakoff had even seen a woman and the prospect was intriguing. How would he react? What, if anything, would he feel? Having never had relations with a woman before created muddled and confused impressions. His only real concepts came from talk, mostly cheap and crude, from other prisoners. It was a disgusting sort of schooling but better than nothing.

And what about the operation? He listened quietly to the others' stories and wondered and questioned if he himself would be able to sexually perform when and if they ever got out of this place. The fact fatherhood had been stolen was psychologically damaging enough. Now came the more disturbing question as to whether or not he could perform the very act itself.

Chronologically, and by nature of his experience, he was an adult in all but the sense of the word: sexual. He longed for the look and sound of a woman. He longed for the true meaning of the word manhood. The frustration which developed had to be pushed aside, buried but never fully covered, dealt with but not on an immediate basis. Survival ... that was the priority.

When he told Isaac he was going to transfer back to the bricklayer patrol, his friend shook his head, clearly not understanding. Why anyone would volunteer to return to hard-labor made absolutely no sense to him. Isaac even kidded him with, "At least we'll finally be able to keep some uniforms around here." Yakoff gained a reputation with his ability to remove clothing and other laundry items under the most scrutinous eye. He became known as a master thief and even when closely watched, managed to obtain and remove valuable trading articles.

These articles, in addition to providing food for himself and others, also hopefully purchased future favors from an abundance of people. What that meant, at the very least, was decent black market food could be obtained for a reasonable period of time. Available food was important in the decision-making process.

The transfer was concluded with relative ease due to both unwritten IOU's and Yakoff's extensive schooling in masonry. It was good to be back with the majority of the group again and the summer sun beating down on his shirtless back felt wonderful. With minor mental adjustments for the obvious, he even started to feel healthy for the first time in years. Color, a dark brown, came quickly and unlike most of the others, the lifting and loading seemed to improve both his strength and vigor.

The construction site was directly across from the main gate. It was large, nearly two-thirds as big as Auschwitz itself. A few of the new blocks were open and housed women prisoners. The majority however were under various stages of completion, anywhere between the laying of foundations and the actual finishing-out process. When it was done, this new addition would house another fifteen-thousand prisoners.

Yakoff was assigned as a helper in building interior walls. Roofing was yet to be added which meant he was constantly exposed to the warm shining sun, a position he dearly enjoyed. However, when it rained, the footing and scaffolding became dangerous, even treacherous. Many times men trying to maneuver loaded wheelbarrows across the thin creaky lumber would tumble to the cement below. If the fall created broken bones, especially in a leg or two, the men simply disappeared. They were hauled away, hypothetically to the hospital for treatment, but their pleading faces were never again seen.

Marsha was attractive with high rounded cheekbones and dark eyes which still had their shine. She was on the women's work patrol doing cleanup duty in the block where Yakoff was building walls. Like all the other women she wore a torn, tattered scarf, procured from somewhere to protect her shaved head. The protection was twofold: both from the blazing sun as well as the never ending sense of embarrassment any woman would feel after her hair had been completely sheared away.

The attraction was mutual. It began when their eyes met. The first morning seemed abnormally long. Yakoff searched, anxiously anticipating the arrival of rations and hopefully the opportunity to talk with her. The reports had been better than accurate. Not only were there women nearby but now there was one particular woman who seemed to be returning his casual but constant glances.

Whatever the Nazis had taken away, their butcherous knives didn't get it all. Seeing Marsha return his staring created a feeling he'd never before experienced. Was that really his heart beating a little faster at the prospect of actually meeting and talking with her? Seemed illogical, improbable at best. But nonetheless, a different emotion was beginning to burn down deep within his chest.

Finally the men from the kitchen arrived. Work was halted and the prisoners formed separate lines to receive their rations. Even in the line, Yakoff couldn't take his eyes away from her. She was small in stature but stood tall, still proud. He thought one time he even caught a glimpse of a smile. What if, he asked himself prematurely, then just as quickly let it go.

The prisoners sat on the ground while consuming the warm watery substance. There was a subtle but distinct shuffling for position as some of the men maneuvered themselves as close as safely possible to the women. The groups were separated by at least ten feet of empty space and to venture into no-man's-land would have resulted in a severe beating if not a bullet in the back of the head. Even so, to be close enough to a woman to speak in hushed whispers was a treat Yakoff never expected.

She was Jewish, from Grodno, a small town in northeast Poland. They spoke in Hebrew. Others had vied for her attention but she avoided them, pretending not to hear, until Yakoff found a space across the way. He could see clearly without question, the smile had not been a hopeful figment of his imagination. It was there and seemed to be reserved solely for him. It was politely returned.

The first day's conversation was little more than pleasantries. Who they were, where they were from, how long they'd been here, things expected in any normal first confrontation with the opposite sex. The normalcy, even in this most unlikely of places, ended when the talk accidentally turned to family.

She sighed heavily, biting her lip, staring down at the cement.

"We all came here together," she said. "I'm the only one left."

Yakoff was truly sorry he'd asked but it was a question which would inevitably come up anyway. It had to be dealt with and he was glad the unpleasantry was over. He understood completely how she felt and explained why. They were both, for all practical purposes, the last remaining members of their families.

Marsha was young, seventeen, and there was an instant, relaxed ease between the two. The kinship they felt was pleasant and immediate. They'd just decided to talk again the following day when the whistle blew, alerting the prisoners to return to work.

"Tomorrow..." Yakoff whispered.

"Tomorrow..." she replied, nodding slowly in a positive manner.

He picked up the wheelbarrow and for some unknown reason it felt much lighter than usual. All afternoon he could feel her eyes on him, following, watching. It was a feeling he enjoyed very much. The rest of the day flew by without effort or strain. Even the evening whistle seemed to sound early.

The groups formed their two different ranks with columns of five, and began to march away in opposite directions. In the background they could hear the orchestra at the main gate. When they finally lost sight of one another, Yakoff felt a sudden intense sense of urgency about himself, Marsha, and everything else.

He was feeling something very special and different about her, a new feeling, indescribable. He liked her, that was for sure. But the urgency eroding his emotions had to do with the clear and certain possibility he might never see her again. She might work somewhere else tomorrow. So might he...

As he walked underneath the sign proclaiming "Work Makes Freedom", and the compelling reality returned to his conscious mind and screamed out like the brass instruments blaring to his immediate left. By nature of the fact they were both Jewish prisoners in a Nazi concentration camp, there was always the distinct and ever present possibility neither one of them would be alive tomorrow.

Chapter XV

People on this and similar work patrols, where women were close enough for any kind of contact, often became known to the others and even considered themselves as boyfriend and girlfriend. Relationships were formed quickly over hushed, choppy, midday exchanges, series of longing glances, or what would appear to the untrained eye to be little more than a causal or flirtatious wink. People in striped uniforms with shaved heads fell in love without the benefit of extended conversation, privacy, or the opportunity to touch in even the slightest manner.

Among the prisoners it was common knowledge about whom was involved with whom. It was also interesting that there was little if any competition between the men for the attention of a particular female. If it was established a boy and a girl liked each other and considered themselves a couple, their feelings were respected and they were left alone. Jealousy, as it's commonly referred to, was at a minimum. It was supplanted with a sincere sense of relief that even in this pit of hell there was still the slightest degree of hope one could hold on to.

Yakoff could hardly wait that night for the black market to open and the trading and bartering to begin. He'd created open accounts with people by giving them items they wanted in the past in exchange for items he might want or need in the future. For Yakoff the future was now.

As always, he was greeted with the perpetual, "Hey Gypsy, what'a ya want?" He moved through the market with confidence and ease. He'd been responsible for helping many of these men stay warm enough to survive the bone-chilling winter and was accorded due respect by his contemporaries. In whispers and with suspicious looks in all directions an overdue IOU was collected and a small item changed hands.

He had trouble sleeping but for the first time in years it was a pleasant kind of trouble. Marsha, without question, was solidly in his mind and heart. He recounted every word they'd spoken in finite detail.

The phrasing, the breathing, the way her mouth moved, the sparkle in her eyes, the way she seemed to smile when she said her name for the first time.

He had thoughts of telling her about his operation. Then he had second thoughts. Logic, shaded by emotion, deduced there was little if any reason to share that burden with her at this particular time. She'd been through enough. He decided there was nothing for either of them to gain by Marsha knowing what had been done to him and ultimately feeling even more sorrow and despair.

She was there. An integral part of the same work crew as yesterday. Yakoff smiled down from the scaffolding and exhaled a great sigh of relief. Even from this distance he could see the sparkle in her dark brown eyes. More sparkle than yesterday? So it appeared.

Rations arrived and they positioned themselves across from one another. At first they just smiled, happy to be together, happy to be alive, thankful for a reason to go on. Muted conversation was normal: How was your day? How was your night? How are you feeling. It was also normal by the standards set in Auschwitz. How long have you been on this patrol? How may people in your block? How bad is your kapo and the seniors who control your life?

They were learning about each other, trying to understand. The feeling and direct sense of urgency about their knowing was prevalent and made each word seem as if it were spoken in capital letters and followed by exclamation marks. They had fifteen minutes, twenty at the most, for total discovery about a fellow human being. After that, and the distant smiles the afternoon would bring, they had no guarantee or promise they'd ever see each other again. Only hope.

He longed desperately to touch her, just her hand, her skin. He could see it was rough, red, calloused, raw, but to Yakoff it most certainly would have felt like the finest and most expensive silk ever manufactured.

The whistle blew and an unnatural sense of despair covered both their faces. It was the not-knowing that was so perpetually devastating.

"Marsha," he whispered, more urgent than ever.

"I know," she said, smiling. "Tomorrow."

"Something else..." She gave him a quizzical look. "On the ground. By my right hand. Underneath this box ... I brought something for you."

As they returned to work Yakoff didn't see if she'd had a chance to look or not.

When they returned to the construction site the following morning, his fourteen-hour question was solidly answered. The torn, tattered rag which previously adorned Marsha's head was replaced by a fresh, white, clean scarf, the one Yakoff obtained from the black market.

With this humble, simple gesture, the relationship was bonded. Yakoff and Marsha were a couple. Midday rations would be secondary to the private, guarded conversations concerning their pasts and presents. As was the unwritten rule, the future was seldom discussed. Occasionally it came up and a hope or dream would surface. But those words, at this point little more than idle wishes, had a painful tendency of drifting into unfinished sentences, leaving looks of remorse on both their faces.

The bringing and giving of gifts continued. Outside the singing fences of Auschwitz these items would be considered small, insignificant, unimportant. But inside, even the tiniest gesture brought hope, strength, belief and in some cases even life itself. Usually the gifts were in the form of food, the commodity everyone needed the most. A turnip, onion or extra slice of bread could potentially provide the sustenance to stay alive for just one more day.

The sharing of anything construed as "extra" was vital, important, and commonplace. The subtle exchanges of goods and materials occurred under the noses of Nazis and SS guards who were always present. The tradition of sharing among the Jewish faith wasn't new. It'd transpired out of necessity to perpetuate their feelings and beliefs for thousands of years and wasn't about to stop on the order of a madman in Berlin.

Lulek, Yossel, Heim and the others were all pleased with Yakoff's new found sense of happiness. In any degree or form, it was a rare and unusual emotion, seldom found or seen. There was a shared sense of the momentary pleasure their friend was feeling. It too, offered them a sense of hope, not only for tomorrow but for the tomorrow following that. In the contaminated world of creeping madness in which they found themselves, there was little to be thankful for or happy about. One of their own finding solace from hushed whispers with a female prisoner was cause for celebration. Yakoff's feelings and emotions were passed around and shared among his friends.

There was a feeling of desperation as the block neared completion. Now what would happen? What if the men's and women's work patrols were separated? The fifteen or twenty minutes a day, six days a week, for three weeks, had created in Yakoff the best feeling he'd ever had. Even better than what he felt the day before the Nazi occupation, or the joyous news from his father that he was actually going to attend the

Hebrew university in Warsaw.

In his mind, Yakoff created a fantasy of a life with Marsha. It was like a film he replayed over and over each night in his bunk. They had a house, small but comfortable, and a yard filled with bright blooming flowers. The reds, greens and violets had to be recalled from memory for there was no color here. He had a job, highly respected, probably as a teacher. He'd come home each night to Marsha's waiting and open arms. They'd embrace, happy to be together, thrilled to be alive. Then he'd hear a tiny happy sound in the distance. It was a voice, laughing. Then soft footsteps running toward him. It was a child, an infant, a son running towards his father's extended arms. Every single time he had the dream, his son would disappear just as they were about to touch. He'd vanish like a desert mirage into thin wispy air, leaving the father alone and empty.

Then the morning alarm would sound, blasting eardrums, brain cells, and Yakoff would awake in a cold sweat, realizing again and again he could never be the father of his own child.

There was an incredible sense of relief when the men's and women's crews were rejoined at the next construction site. The distinct possibility of never seeing a friend, girlfriend or loved one, added heavily to the psychological toll already being taken.

The kapos and guards didn't seem to mind or appear to be bothered by the relationships that formed. They were mildly amused by them. They'd watch the couples during the midday break, desperate to touch, desperate to be together, but separated by the worst of all possible fences, an invisible one. Knowing the additional frustration they were inflicting brought many smiles of sadistic satisfaction to the Germans in charge.

Seeing Marsha each day gave Yakoff a reason to want to go to work. Their togetherness deepened and talk of the future remained at a minimum. Like the card games, they'd talk about the old days, their youth, their growing up, their freedom. There wasn't a single day, in the following two months, they didn't each have to face the realistic possibility of never seeing one another again.

And then it happened. It was right after they'd completed one block and had moved on to a new one. When the women's s clean up patrol arrived it was different-all new faces, all new people. Yakoff was stunned, crushed beyond his own imagination. Friends provided sympathetic consolation but it helped little in the mending of his broken heart.

Through the grapevine he learned she was still alive and working on

189

another building not far from where he was. That made it even worse, knowing she was close, probably within shouting distance, and also knowing there was no way he could get to her, see her, talk with her. His life and existence returned to the same miserableness he'd known prior to their meeting.

Letters, messages and notes were smuggled back and forth between them, and for all practical and intrinsic purposes they remained a couple, faithful in their feelings and their dedication. Time dragged slowly. The work became harder and much more tedious. His motivation was gone and his spirit was slowly following. The possibilities of seeing Marsha again were somewhere between slim and none.

There was an opening on a different work patrol and because of Yakoff's longevity as well as favors owed by the kapo in charge, he made the transition. It was referred to by the majority of envious prisoners as the Canada Squad, so named because the European prisoner population of the camp viewed Canada as a land of plenty, a land of vast wealth and riches, a land of easy pickings and easy living.

Based on their generalized impression of the country, their viewpoint of the patrol was accurate. The Canada Squad, or Kommando, was responsible for sifting through and sorting all the luggage and material goods stolen from the incoming transport trains. When the newly arriving prisoners were herded out of the cattle-cars, they were ordered to leave behind all the possessions they carried with them. To avoid anything from a minor-disturbance to a full-scale riot, the Nazis always lied and told the new mass of slave labor their goods would be returned after they'd been processed.

Once the bodies passed through the first selection with Doctor Mengele choosing the immediate candidates for the gas chambers, the Canada Squad moved in. Luggage, trunks, and everything else imaginable was heaped in great piles, small mountains usually reaching as high as the tops of the boxcars themselves. The no-longer personal possessions were loaded by the squad into wagon after wagon and transported to one of three huge warehouses.

Yakoff was absolutely shocked the first day on his new job when he saw the incredible volume of stolen materials. There were clothes of every size, shape and variety. Massive piles of boots and shoes, men's and women's, filled an entire corner of the building. Stockpiles, ten, twelve, fifteen feet high of food, both canned and fresh. There were areas designated and filled to overflowing with wines and liquors. Countless shelves were covered with various brands of beer from throughout

Europe. Soaps, razors and shampoos spilled out of bin after countless bin. Small items of furniture, antiques, family heirlooms, paintings and art objects created their own rows of space. Sewing machines, tools from various other trades and small exotic pieces of equipment were everywhere.

Inside this building was a veritable wonderland. There was abundance everywhere. Nearly anything and everything conceivable was locked and stored within these walls. The building was well-lit and heated to prevent spoilage of any kind. The massive thievery taking place was awesome.

Yakoff blended unobtrusively with the rest of the workers. He was assigned the job of opening and emptying suitcases as they were unloaded from the endless streams of wagons. Often they'd be securely locked and had to be broken into with hammers and chisels. Once opened, the precious cargo would be separated, categorized, and stored with items of a similar nature.

It was during the first midday break on the job when part of the truth of the matter came to rest on young Yakoff's ears. European refugees, mostly Jews forced out of their homes, were told by the Nazi occupationists they were being resettled to a safer, less war-torn part of the country. It was only temporary, they lied, but even so, the displaced families should take anything of value with them along with tools or equipment to perpetuate their occupations.

It was common that the alleged flight to safety and freedom was actually sold, serving only to blatantly steal even more money. Families by the thousands waited in line and then bought and paid for passage to Auschwitz and their own destruction. This information only solidified the incredible security the Nazis had managed to maintain.

On rare occasion word would slip to the outside world, news of the existence of a death camp where tens of thousands of people were being murdered. The stories, limited in scope and detail, were generally received with a raised eyebrow by individuals as well as various countries alike. Heads would shake and statements like "Impossible" would follow. "The world and especially the Germans are too civilized. A thing like that could never happen." Explanations of the travesties and mass injustices were fruitless and fell on deaf ears. After all, hadn't the Red Cross and various other agencies personally visited and examined Auschwitz? Didn't they find, on a regularly scheduled basis, the prisoners themselves had little if anything to complain about? That was the written report which was accepted. The saddest part about the truth was the truth itself. It actually was impossible to conceive that many people being viciously and callously murdered, when conversely, the Jewish population as a race or religion posed absolutely no threat whatsoever to Hitler or his armies.

The break ended and Yakoff returned to work sorting and sifting through people's personal belongings. There were children's clothing and underwear, tiny stuffed animals, and dolls with yellow braided hair. It was a gripping experience giving him pause for reflection, especially when he realized the owners of these things, by now had been reduced to ashes and released to the sky.

A kapo's stick across his shoulder blades brought him back to the reality of the moment as well as the work at hand.

"If you're gonna work here, you're gonna work!" the kapo snarled.

Yakoff nodded understanding and quickly returned to the task in front of him. It was unpleasant and distasteful but nowhere near the wrenching agony he was forced to go through and experience on his work patrol in Birkenau: collecting dead bodies from throughout the compound.

The job, like most, had a breaking-in period, a learning to know your way around. Who could be trusted and who couldn't, how much or how little you could get away with, angles, sidetracks, places to safely hide and rest during the day--all integral pieces in the process and nearly unsolvable puzzle known as survival.

Yakoff worked hard at his new job and earned a reputation of being industrious as well as highly organized. Within a short period of time he had eight other men working for him. He taught each of them the ropes necessary to cling to if they were to stay alive. Those fortunate enough to gain positions on the Canada Squad and clever enough to avoid capture in their covert activities had opportunities and advantages few others in the camp experienced.

The warehouses were a gold mine. Nearly anything anyone wanted could be found there and existence was softened to an extent, if only for a short while. The men of the Canada knew their days, like every other prisoner in captivity, were limited. It was merely a matter of time before their own number would hauntingly and finally be called.

Yakoff and Marsha continued to stay in touch. Each of their letters and notes closed with how much they missed one another. Somehow, someway, Yakoff told himself, he was going to see her again. At the time the wish seemed impossible but he honestly felt his will was stronger than any double row of electrified barbed wires.

Along with the authority and responsibility of leading a crew of eight other men came a small but certain amount of additional freedom. With his access to the goods and materials in the storage area, he could generally walk the camp feeling almost a sense of safety. Most of the guards knew Yakoff, or Gypsy, by name, and also knew the potential good he could provide in the form of food.

It was the fall of 'Forty-four and for some unexplained reason, the guards who before ate like kings and princes, had their own rations cutback severely. In truth, they weren't eating much better than the prisoners, just more.

The massive piles of food stolen from the incoming transports were all supposed to be sorted, boxed and shipped to the fatherland for Germans more directly involved in the war. The only food which wasn't shipped was that which was stolen by either the guards or the workers on the Canada.

"Yakoff! Yakoff!" There was an urgency in the voice but of a different variety. For a pleasant change, it actually sounded happy.

"Quiet down," Yakoff said, placing his forefinger to his own lips. "You'll get the guards all excited."

He was working in front of the warehouse supervising the unloading of wagons. It was a clear, cloudless day and his mind was consumed with devising a plan to see Marsha.

"It's your father...," the words faded and the informant stood with open eyes and mouth, his face filled with anticipation.

A dryness grabbed Yakoff's throat making it difficult to speak. He tried to swallow but couldn't. Finally, softly, "What about my father?"

"Pesach," the man said. "He's alive."

Impossible was the first thought. It couldn't be. But the wonderment of even the possibility was overwhelming, all consuming. The response was quick, "How do you know? What have you heard?"

"He's alive," the man repeated. "I saw him. This morning."

It was impossible. Yakoff had given up. Every single time he'd tried to bribe information about his father had been hopeless, worthless. It'd been over eighteen months since he'd spoken to his father across that brick wall and two months more since he'd seen him. It was impossible. There was no way it could be. But even in a place such as this, where everything dies eventually, hope seemed to be the thing which died the slowest death of all.

"Where? How? Are you sure?"

The man held up his hand, trying to calm the excited youngster.

"I don't know why and I don't know what for, but this morning the Sonderkommando squad from Birkenau marched down that street right there, " The man pointed to a street barely a block away. "I couldn't believe my eyes when I saw him, but he was there Yakoff. It was him."

Yakoff was speechless, dumfounded, but his friend wouldn't lie. No one would lie about such a thing.

The friend continued. "I talked to my kapo and he told me the squad will be returning, marching back through here this afternoon." They both stared at each other for a long second. "You'll get to see him Yakoff. You'll get to see him."

The morning seemed like it was a month long, maybe more. A million things could go wrong. His friend could have been mistaken. Yakoff spoke to his own kapo during the midday break.

"Sir, there's a patrol that's going to be marching up the street over there this afternoon..."

"So..."

"My father's in that patrol and I haven't seen him for nearly two years."

The kapo just looked, noncommittal.

"Would it be alright if when they come by I just sort of drifted over in that direction? Maybe even have a word with him? Or at least just to see him?"

The kapo picked his teeth with a long black fingernail and didn't say anything. Nothing at all. He just looked and then walked away. Yakoff had no choice but to take it as a positive response. He hadn't exactly said yes but then on the other hand he absolutely hadn't said no.

The afternoon was another month of waiting which seemed like a lifetime. Minutes took days, seconds took hours. What if? What would he find? What would he be like? Would he look the same? Yakoff would blink and his mind flashed childhood visions, memories: riding in his father's carriage with the harness jingling. Sitting at every evening meal watching his father fold his arms across his stocky chest asking each of the children what they'd learned today. Sliding down the great hill in the sled his father helped him build. The mikvah on Friday afternoons and the laughter when Pesach poured water over Moishe's head. Summers in the orchards. The tender and shameless embrace they shared when he went on the class trip to Warsaw. Then the black vision returned as it always did; the cold December night when the family was forced off the train and carted away to their death. For a year and a half he'd thought he was the only one left. Now, thank God, thank the heavens above and all that is holy, there's the possibility his father is still alive.

Footsteps, marching, coming up the street. Sounded like forty or fifty pairs of clogs. Yakoff looked for his kapo but he must have gone inside. The youngster had no choice, he had to take the chance. He had to.

Heart pounding, mind racing, hope swelling, he wanted to run but knew the consequence. He grabbed an empty box, hoisted it on his shoulder and began walking down the street as if he were on a delivery mission. Along the way he nodded politely to guards and kapos. The column was in sight, marching at the same cadence the orchestra usually pounded out. Eyes searching, vision straining, studying each face, scrutinizing for an semblance of recognition, believing more as each man passed.

Then he saw him, middle of the column, second man in. When their eyes locked on one another it wasn't at all the feeling he'd expected. There was joy from within based on the knowledge of his existence but it was mixed with despair and deep sorrow.

Pesach had grown old. He was no longer the young, vibrant, strong man Yakoff wanted so desperately to remember. The stocky barrel chest was gone and his once mighty arms hung thin and limp at his sides. His eyes had gone the direction of thousands if not millions of others: deep-set, dark, hollow, empty.

Yakoff, now the stronger of the two, wanted to embrace his father, to hold him in his arms and somehow reassure him everything was going to be alright, just the way his father had done countless times with him. He knew that option wasn't available. To walk into the column of men would have meant certain and instant death for both of them. Instead, and still at great personal risk, he fell in line and walked alongside the group.

He looked to his left, facing his father. Neither spoke for several steps. Nor were there any smiles. The time and job forced on Pesach had taken its toll. Every second from the first night of their arrival and his selection for the Sonderkommando had been pure agonizing hell. Yakoff choked audibly at the very thought.

They continued to walk, unbothered by the kapos and guards who marched with the squad. Pesach cleared his once deep throat and the sound seemed tinny, unused, as if speaking itself were a rarity. The words came out in a monotone, mechanical, seemingly without emotion or feeling.

"I hear you've been spayed..."

195

Yakoff's knees buckled slightly, disbelieving these were the first precious words he'd hear from his father's mouth. He blinked back tears. "Is that true?"

He tried to speak but his voice betrayed him. All he could do was nod confirmation to the painful question. He was drifting too far away from his own work patrol and he knew it. A few more steps and he'd have to stop and let the column go on. He wanted to explain but couldn't.

He stopped, stood, and watched until the column had marched completely out of sight. After a heavy sigh came a realization from deep within his heart; this would be the last time he would ever see his father.

Yakoff felt hurt and cheated by both the content as well as context of their non-conversation. They were small-town people, simple people, and "spayed" was the only word Pesach knew to describe the terrible and inhuman thing which had been done to his son. He'd never heard the word castration as it applied to human beings. The thought itself was unthinkable, unimaginable.

In his dreams, the son cried out to talk with his father just one more time, to tell him the butcherous operation hadn't bothered him, everything was going to be alright, he was really quite fine, normal, unaffected. And each morning following the dream, he'd wake up and face the reality of the void between his two legs, and know the dream and all it contained was a dark and sinister lie.

Chapter XVI

The SS finally clamped down and tightened their security on the Canada warehouses. Men were searched as they left the buildings and returned to the main camp. Smuggling became difficult. Lifestyles were altered drastically without valuable trading materials and extra food. It was still possible to wear two sets of clothing back into the camp and sometimes smaller articles, flat, folded or concealable. The punishment for being caught with contraband was swift and severe. It was generally carried out in public and the Nazi point was well made. The risk-takers diminished and only the bravest or most clever continued to operate.

Yakoff fell squarely into the latter category. After a long dry spell where little of importance was smuggled into the camp, he devised a workable plan. First he had to find and establish a partner he could trust who worked in the kitchen. That was easy once the plan was explained and his new partner understood Yakoff was the one taking all the risk.

There was an extreme shortage of gasoline at the time since most of it was being used at the front to keep German tanks and other essential military vehicles moving. As a result, the majority of the trucks at Auschwitz were converted to run on steam. The steam was provided by boilers propelled by wood-burning stoves in the bed of each truck. It was crude, but since there was no necessity for speed of any consequence, the device worked effectively.

Each day the flat bed, fire burning trucks would roll away from the kitchen and out the main gate to deliver soup to various work patrols. At each stop, a fifty gallon drum and several boxes containing bread were off-loaded and replaced with empties from the previous day. Yakoff's plan was simple. He'd managed to obtain the additional chore of being the man responsible for loading the empty drum and boxes back onto the truck.

In the morning, before the midday rations arrived, he'd fill the empty drum with food, clothing, and whatever else he could procure. Then, when the truck arrived, he'd help unload the full one and position himself in the bed of the truck. They knew the drums were inspected before they were returned to the kitchen and Yakoff also figured that out. While the guards were busying themselves with lunch and idle conversation, he'd hide the food and other items in the bottom of the bin which held the wood for the fire.

Once back inside the camp, at the kitchen, his partner obtained the job of unloading all the returning drums. He'd empty the catch from the wood storage area, place it in a covered box and innocently carry it into the kitchen. His risk was minimal in that his defense was innocence. "I didn't know it was there. I found it by accident." If caught, the guards would most likely split the booty among themselves and leave the kitchen worker alone.

Even though the risk for this particular enterprise was not on parity, Yakoff chose to split whatever profits accrued on a fifty-fifty basis. When the food, clothing, or miscellaneous items were safely inside the kitchen area, it was relatively easy to transport them anywhere within the camp.

He was transferred to block 5 for no particular or clearly defined reason. Perhaps because the majority of prisoners were old-timers and had been there awhile. The conditions were much the same as in the past with the exception that this block had lockers. For a price paid to the senior, one could be obtained and used. Now for the first time Yakoff had a place where personal items could be stored and kept in relative safety. Included in the bribery-fee was the condition the senior would stay in the block all day, watching and protecting the unknown contents of the lockers.

Perhaps the senior went to the bathroom or perhaps he fell asleep. No real reason was ever offered to explain his absence on the day the lockers were broken into and various items of importance stolen. It couldn't have been the SS or a guard, they never entered the blocks. It had to be one of their own, a fact which was most disturbing.

Yakoff had risked his very life for the missing food and articles of clothing. It was replaceable but that wasn't the point. The point was that an unwritten but strong principle, a trust, had been violated. The prisoners, especially those considered survivors, had a code traveling far beyond ethics. It was a code of life, of existence itself. And one of their own had violated it.

Finding the perpetrator wasn't difficult, not in quarters this cramped. Food and other items were easily recognizable and difficult if not impossible to hide. Prisoner justice was swift but not nearly as severe as the Nazis'. The lesson extended was as much for the rest of the prisoners as it was for the thief himself. While the Nazis would have murdered the man for a crime that extreme, the prisoners still realized and respected the value and importance of life. They broke one of his arms. Nothing else was ever stolen within the block.

Yakoff continued to send packages and exchange messages with Marsha. In distance his heart grew fonder. At work he became more of a leader and was usually consulted on items of importance. This normally happened when one of his work crew found something of real value and wasn't sure exactly what to do with it.

Money, gold, silver or gems were sewn into the lining of clothing or hidden beneath false-bottoms in suitcases and trunks. The misplaced refugees, expecting to never again see their homes, sold belongings and transferred their wealth, no matter how small or great, into currency or stones that could easily be exchanged wherever they ended up.

When discoveries of this sort were made they were usually reported to Yakoff for his assistance and advice as to how the find should be handled. It was common for the finder to keep part of it, and some, if not the rest, was innocently and supposedly naively turned over to the kapo in charge. Yakoff was not exhibiting stupidity in this gesture, he was buying protection for himself as well as the rest of his men.

Once, when one of the workers was caught red-handed pocketing valuable gold coins, Yakoff interceded, explaining the soon-to-be-corpse was a relative. Because of the apparent honesty as well as generosity the Gypsy had exhibited in the past, the guard in charge had little interest in losing his favor. The man was released with a reprimand and somewhat humorously, Yakoff was assigned the task of keeping a closer eye on him. Such events, when warranted and justified, were the norm rather than the case. The mistaken generosity was often the catalyst which prevented many bone-breaking beatings and public executions with the well-used rope of the gallows. Bribery was essential, deception paid off, lying could work well in your favor.

It was the early morning roll call and the entire group was assembled outside block 5, waiting for the boring and ever tedious count to finish so they could relax before starting their work day. Seeing the black uniformed SS men within the compound was a rarity. Their only function in life was inflicting pain on their innocent victims. Their uniforms were a part of their body and flesh, sadists with the skulls and crossbones burned deeply into their black hearts.

Their mission certainly wasn't one of mercy. That'd never been the case and as long as the black uniform existed, it never would. They rounded the corner and goose stepped their way towards the front of block 5. An ominous feeling of doom, quick and instant doom, came over Yakoff. It wasn't that he was psychic, but he knew these SS men were here for the sole and specific purpose of making a selection. They were here to point their polished fingernails and handpick as many men as they so desired to be marched at gunpoint to the gas chambers.

A rush came over him, an understandable fear, gripping his heart, refusing to let go. In that fleeting second he knew without explanation or verification he was going to be selected. He'd been through it a hundred times, starting with the very first night he got off that damnable train. He'd beaten the weather and starvation, survived the massacre of the Christmas run, lived through naked, freezing days and nights, countless beatings and mass humiliation...even had his very manhood sliced away from his own body.

Now, with the casual pointing of a finger because they needed another bunk for a fresh, new slave laborer, he was going to be selected to take the last shower of his life. Not without a fight, he thought. Not without a struggle.

The SS men and seniors stood at the front of the group. Yakoff was near the rear, indistinguishable in the early morning haze, one of thousands of look-alikes in the striped uniforms. There was no logic to the move, his only consideration was staying alive. He broke ranks and started running to his left, towards the end of the block.

At first there was no thought about where he was going or where he might hide. He only knew he had to get away. It'd been nearly two years since he'd run anywhere for anything, but his legs deftly responded to the command from the brain. There was a commotion behind him, shouting, growing louder with each stolen step. Then there were footsteps, chasing, sounding like they were closing. He didn't dare look back to see who or how many were after him.

He headed for the far side of block 6. He didn't know why and there was no particular reason, it just was there. So was a formation of prisoners. An instant thought: blend in with them. Instant answer: no. If they've already taken their count he'd be easy to find. Past 6 and towards the rear of 7. He knew 7 like the back of his hand, every nook, cranny and possible hiding place. If he could only make it inside without being seen... He thought he could hear heavy breathing behind him.

Around the corner. Good. Their count was over and there were only a few men standing around. He was flying now, taking a wide turn.

It looked like he could make it to the door before his pursuers turned the corner. Then he might have a chance. Barely three steps from the door he saw him...his heart stopped cold. It was Olschevsky. The butcher Olschevsky, smiling his sadistic little smile as Yakoff flew past and inside.

It was over. There was no possible place to hide. He was trapped without any ways or means of escape. The driving footsteps pounded closer until they were just outside the front door. By now it sounded like an entire squad of men were in pursuit. The miracle which followed was certainly unexpected. The men ran past the door to the end of the block and out of sight.

Yakoff waited a few moments assuring what safety he could, nearly afraid to breathe and inadvertently announce his whereabouts. Cautiously he stuck his head through the door almost expecting to find a patrol of armed guards waiting. The coast, to his more than pleasant surprise, was clear. The chasers were gone, out of both sight and ear-shot.

The only thing Yakoff found was Olschevsky, still smiling. The reason or motivation behind the one singular moment of compassion in the butcherer's life would never be known. The two men recognized each other but neither spoke. Perhaps Olschevsky carried a degree of respect for Yakoff, knowing full-well what the youngster had been through and managed to survive. Perhaps it was a repayment for various, assorted favors the clever prisoner had provided for his block senior, the one who nearly killed him the first night they met.

Reasons didn't matter. Olschevsky kept his mouth shut and Yakoff was still alive. He thanked the older man with his eyes, not a smile or handshake, and still no words were spoken. As he walked away, back towards the formation area for the Canada Squad, the worst of all possible thoughts attacked his mind. What if he'd been selected and forced to march to the gas chambers and ovens of Birkenau? The thought of his own father closing the door of life behind him was worse than the death the gas itself would bring.

The transports slowed down and the mountainous piles of stolen possessions began to dwindle and diminish. Workers were taken off the Canada and transferred to other patrols. Incoming information was still at a premium so no one knew for sure exactly what was happening. The only thing clear and certain was less and less new prisoners were arriving. The lessening influx was viewed primarily as a hopeful omen.

Yakoff, knowing his days on the Canada were numbered, stepped up his smuggling activities in order to build his own personal stockpile of tradeable items within the camp. By now he knew or was known by nearly everyone there. It was a relatively simple task to approach a kapo from a different work patrol and request a job. Like always, for a price, nearly anything was available.

He transferred, just as the last of the Canada was being disbanded, to a new and better job on the water patrol. Its primary function was delivering distilled water on a daily basis to the homes of all high ranking German officials. There were only four people on the patrol: a Pole, a Yugoslav, Yakoff, and a teamster who drove the horses and never seemed to talk. He minded his own business and never got involved, one way or the other, with anyone else.

The patrol would meet each morning before dawn in a wooded area outside the main camp. Previous patrols, with various and assorted extra construction materials, had built a small but sturdy shed to protect themselves from the elements during the harsh winters. The shelter had some makeshift chairs and a small stove for warmth as well as cooking. It was never explained, but for some unknown reason the guards for the patrol didn't enter the shed unless the prisoners invited them.

Yakoff and the other two would wait inside while the teamster and one of the guards went to a nearby stable to get the horses. The attitude and environment was very relaxed compared to anything he'd experienced to date. The kapo, along with the rotating guards, exhibited no overt cruelty or even outward hostility towards the small crew. Being there was simply a matter-of-fact for them all and they seemed to accept it.

When the horses returned they were hitched to a wagon carrying a two-hundred gallon water tank. The still, rotten water in Auschwitz provided the reasoning behind the luxury afforded to the commandant and his high ranking underlings. Once the hitching process was completed, the rounds began.

The work crew stopped at an average of twenty houses per day, obviously the finest houses in town. When the Germans occupied Auschwitz and forced all the residents out, the top officers picked the homes they would live in as well as the furnishings to accompany them.

As the wagon rolled to a house, Yakoff and the other two would hand carry buckets of fresh water inside to be used for drinking, cooking and bathing. Nothing but the best for the German officers, they'd laugh under their breath. The work itself wasn't hard or backbreaking and he even had the forced opportunity to experience limited female companionship again.

The majority of their contact was with maids, housekeepers and wives of the officers. For the most part, the women reacted to Yakoff in a positive nature, sensing his willingness to work hard and assist in any way possible. The reality was they were all prisoners; the prisoners themselves, the maids, the housekeepers, even the wives and children. They were all either stuck or captured in this place and had no immediate hope or means of escape or release.

For the wives and families, it was a different kind of capture. Their only other option was for their husbands to be transferred to the Russian front. For them a fate worse than death. What they couldn't possibly comprehend was the survivors interpretation of that statement. For a survivor, there was absolutely, positively, no fate worse than death.

Casual but cautionary friendships were formed with the maids and housekeepers and occasionally words were exchanged. Usually only instructions as to how many buckets to deliver and where. Sometimes it went beyond that. Sometimes they'd talk in whispered bursts about their lives, existence, or absolute longing for freedom.

The coworkers were plain, bland, dull, uncreative. Yakoff saw an opportunity and set about to seize it. They'd finished their delivery and had a minute or two before they had to leave. The maid was in the kitchen overseeing their activities. The girl was young, probably mid-twenties and had a kind face, the sort sometimes interpreted as understanding. She was also attractive in a hard, indefinable manner. Yakoff reached inside his pocket and produced a pair of silk stockings, virtually impossible to obtain in town or anywhere other than the camp black market. At first she hesitated. In a short time a small smile began to form.

"What are these for?"

Yakoff did his classic shuffling routine and forced an ever so slight return smile.

"Nothing," he said. "I just thought you might be able to use them."

Tentatively she reached forward, palm up, wondering what the catch was, but hating to miss this golden opportunity. She took them with another smile, knowing a price would have to be paid in return. That was the way it was in this place, even within the confines of the officers' homes.

The following day when Yakoff returned with more buckets of water, the maid was wearing the stockings. He nodded and smiled again, expressing subtle admiration. There was no need to say anything. When the other two helpers returned to the wagon, leaving them momentarily alone, the maid opened the well-stocked ice box and with a sweeping hand gesture, offered its contents to her new friend.

"Are you sure?" Yakoff asked, feigning a naive innocence.

"Anything you want," she said, understanding fully the relationship which had been established.

"Well," Yakoff purposefully stuttered. "There are a couple things my friends and I sure haven't tasted in a long time."

When the water patrol returned to their shed that afternoon, the clever youngster had an unexpected surprise for his fellow workers. Their day was normally shorter than the rest of the prisoners so they'd wait in the shelter and heat-up bits of food they'd managed to scavenge or bring to work with them. It was a warm, quiet, peaceful way to spend the afternoon until the whistle blew and the rest of the men returned to the camp interior.

The small stove was lit and one of the men produced a few thin slices of salami. It wasn't much but it was a welcome supplement to the camp rations. The others had noticed Yakoff limping and walking somewhat tenderly most of the afternoon but no one said anything, figuring if he wanted to talk, he would. The reason for his slow moving carefulness was explained as he cautiously reached into both of his shirt pockets and showed the other men four unbroken eggs. It literally had been years since any of them had seen or eaten an egg.

There were smiles in the shed which hadn't been seen for so long none of them could remember. The salami was sliced, the eggs were scrambled, and the following feast created warm remembrances to truly last all their lives.

A regular trading route was established among all the German homes. The patrol, led by Yakoff, cleverly arranged their schedule so it coincided most often with times the wives were out of the houses. The maids and housekeepers were eager as well as receptive to the under-the-table offers of scarves, stockings and lingerie. For their efforts, the water patrol had good hot food, both mornings and afternoons on a daily basis.

Their guards, experiencing a worsening food shortage themselves, were regularly invited into the shed to share the meals. It was interesting at the time because the guards were replaceable if they were unliked or unpleasant to the crew. If one of them exhibited the cruelty they were used to dishing out, having him removed from the position posed little if any problem.

Yakoff, well-liked by the employees as well as wives in the houses, would simply spill some water on just the right kitchen floor and then begin a magnanimous display of apology. Close to tears, he'd explain how hard he worked so everything would be just right and how hard he tried to be neat and clean because he respected his superiors. Then, just as his eager audience, which always included a wife of a ranking officer, was in place and receptive, he'd carefully and methodically explain they had a new and overly cruel guard who was working them all too hard, preventing them from doing their oh so important job as effectively and efficiently as possible. The guard, Yakoff would explain, was the reason the water spilled.

The youngster's overacting was effective. Following every performance the accused guard was mysteriously replaced. After three or four such actions, each new guard was informed by the kapo of Yakoff's deviousness and the simple but recognizable fact: a challenge of any manner would result in a losing effort and more than likely a transfer.

As a result, the guards while never becoming friends, relaxed their camp-like tendencies and expressed a "you do your thing, I'll do mine" leniency which proved beneficial for them all. Their relaxed attitudes were rewarded in the form of warmth and shelter from the December weather and tasty, hot, well-prepared food which they all knew had been organized from the homes of their superiors. No one complained on a full stomach.

Often Yakoff would sit in the late afternoon and talk with the German guards. He heard voices laced with despair, explaining the beatings Hilter's armies were taking. The fronts were moving closer and the Nazis were suffering heavy, irreplaceable losses to both the Americans and Russians. There was a tonal quality filled with an unspoken resolve: it was over, the war had been lost, it was only a matter of time.

Only a matter of time, Yakoff reflected. Only a matter of time. More than two years of his life along with his manhood had been viciously, brutally stolen from him. Only a matter of time. His entire family had been murdered and burned. Only a matter of time. Friends, more than he could count, had been shot and beaten to death. Only a matter of time. Planned, well-executed starvation and disease had taken thousands and thousands of lives. Only a matter of time.

He listened to the German's words and longed, deep in his heart, to personally watch the demise and destruction of the Third Reich. He wished with a fervor and passion he could see Naziism collectively and individually die a slow, painfilled, agonizing death. He prayed to God for a massive and miraculous roll-reversal; to applaud as the black uniformed, skulled and crossboned killers marched in stream after endless stream into their own ovens.

The feeling as well as news of the impending defeat brought a different reaction than one might have expected. It was suggested, rumored, and commonly accepted, that if and when the war should end, the atrocities of this place would forever remain a closely guarded secret among its perpetrators. The price for maintaining this secrecy, the well-founded rumor continued, was that the entire prisoner population of all the surrounding camps, now numbering nearly two hundred thousand in the Auschwitz compound alone, would be disposed of, mass murdered by whatever means available. Yakoff emitted a deep and heavy sigh. He knew there was truth wrapped tightly in the rumor. The Nazi secret would be kept from the free world. It was only a matter of time.

There was a controlled sense of desperation to see Marsha before the unknown but eventual atrocity and he finally put his well-rehearsed plan into action. Yakoff knew the kapo in charge of maintenance in the women's blocks, and also knew the kapo had a particular weakness as well as fondness for whiskey. The item had experienced such popularity that it was rare and difficult to obtain.

Several trips to the black market were necessary. Trades were made and various deals were consummated. The bartering was complicated and took longer than expected. Yakoff exchanged stockings, clothing, food, even gold before he actually possessed the valuable liquid. Once that was accomplished, the next phase of the plan began.

He "accidentally" ran into the maintenance kapo and "suggested" with just the right smile as well as vocal inflection there was a burnt-out fuse in one of the women's blocks. At first the kapo was unmoved and unimpressed, but Yakoff patiently persisted. He insinuated, with an unmistaken quality of subtleness, if such an assignment should be undertaken it could be more than worthwhile for the kapo issuing the order.

The next line was the ever familiar, "What'a you got?" The price was right and a deal was struck. Now further arrangements had to be made. The exact time and meeting place had to be established and messages with confirmations had to be exchanged. The complex plan called for the assistance of many people who all proved to be more than cooperative.

Then came the day, it was time. The kapo, with the promise of a full bottle of whiskey in exchange for a successful mission, marched Yakoff, carrying a workmen's tool box into the women's compound. He was doing it. He was actually going to pull it off. He was really going to see her and be alone.

She was wearing the scarf Yakoff had given her the second time they'd talked and her hair was finally starting to grow out. She looked radiant, alive, wonderful. It'd been months since they'd seen one another but the feelings were unmistakable. They were stronger than ever. Eyes reflected emotions which didn't need to be spoken. They were alone, no guards or kapos or fifty other prisoners. Just the two of them.

They held hands, touching for the first time, and looked deeply into one another's souls. The rumor of the probable mass execution was widespread by this time so talk of the future was something that didn't occur. It was the moment, this one singular moment of happiness that mattered.

Yakoff squeezed her hands slightly and whispered, "Out of this dough ...bread will come..." Tears, now a rarity from all they'd seen and experienced, began to form in the corners of Marsha's eyes. She smiled, nodding slowly, knowing the improbability of ever seeing the young man she loved again.

There was a cough in the distance, a prearranged signal someone was coming. Discovery meant death so the two released their hold on one another. No further words were spoken, no kiss, no embrace, just a dream of togetherness and of life itself.

Another Hanukkah came and went without celebration or ritual. It was the middle of another freezing, killing winter. Christmas, scorned as a child due to the hateful screams of..."You're a Jew!...You killed Jesus!...You murderer!"...brought an unexpected treat. At nearly every house where the patrol delivered water that Christmas eve, the maids or cooks had prepared delicacies which for years had only been fond remembrances. Yakoff and the crew were presented with cookies, pastries, and even pies. The water wagon was heaped with gastronomic delights.

There was much anticipation for the feast that was soon to be by the warm cookstove in the shed. That's where all the food had to be consumed. The men were searched before reentering the camp, so taking any of it back inside was an impossibility which was truly unfortunate.

They had far more than they could ever consume themselves.

The very last stop of the day provided the greatest surprise. It was the Hess household, Commandant Hess, the man in charge and complete control of all of Auschwitz. Yakoff had seen Mrs. Hess before but they'd never spoken. She was in the kitchen with the cook when they entered carrying their buckets of water.

"Merry Christmas, boys," she said rather brightly. Merry Christmas indeed. What a stupidly insidious remark for her to be saying to a group of prisoners.

"Merry Christmas to you ma'am," Yakoff answered, nearly choking on the lie.

"I have a little something for you," she announced. "I prepared it myself and I hope you enjoy it." She opened the ice box and gave them a three tiered cake covered with creamy, thick, white icing. She was still smiling as she handed it over and appeared to be sincere.

Yakoff was struck with a sudden surge of bravery and a clever idea all at the same time. Why not? he deduced. What can I lose?

"Mrs. Hess," he said slowly, checking her reaction. "We sure do appreciate this and there's so much of it," he pointed at the cake, "would you mind if we shared it with some of the other men?"

"Of course not," she beamed, apparently thrilled with the idea. "Take it on back to your block and you can all have some of it."

That was it, just what Yakoff hoped to hear.

"Well ma'am, we have kind of a problem with that..."

"What kind of a problem?"

"We're not allowed to take anything, especially food, back inside the camp."

She thought for a second and then picked up the phone and called the main guardhouse.

"This is Mrs. Hess," she said authoritatively. "When the men from the water patrol return to camp this evening, they have my permission to carry food inside with them.

The others were afraid it wouldn't work but Yakoff was convinced otherwise. As such, he volunteered his services to once again take all the risk involved. The whistle blew and the inward march began. The Gypsy walked confidently past the guardhouse carrying a huge sack full of pies, cookies, pastries and even Mrs. Hess' German chocolate cake. That night, unlike any before, the prisoners in block 5 went to sleep with full and satisfied stomachs.

208

The New Year was fraught with even more tension, but now it was collective rather than individual. The entire camp felt as if it was walking on a thin layer of ice, waiting for the warm spring weather to melt away their temporary safety, consuming and drowning everyone at precisely the same time.

Both guards and kapos seemed to lighten-up on the prisoners. Beatings and general harassment, without explanation, ceased to exist. It was an overnight occurrence. Rumor had it the Russian front had moved to within twenty miles of the camp and more ground was being lost each day. The constant thunder which droned and echoed through the once peaceful and sleepy countryside, wasn't thunder at all. It was shelling, heavy artillery, pounding the German army and forcing them back.

Most of the work patrols were kept inside the camp, freeing the majority of the guards and in some cases even the kapos to move unwillingly to the front line and fight to protect their precious fatherland. Even Olschevsky was selected for the honor and glory of dying for Germany.

Early one morning a squadron of planes appeared on the horizon. Their altitude was such that their country of origin was indefinable. Closer they came, and louder, buzzing toward the area like a great swarm of killer bees. When they were directly overhead their bellies opened up and their insides spilled out, raining down on Auschwitz to obliterate the place and all its inhabitants, erasing forever what had been done here.

But every single one of the huge bombs missed their mark, if in fact Auschwitz or any of the surrounding camps were the designated targets. Instead, the explosions encircled the camps, almost interpretable as a warning, as if each bomb carried an Allied message: "We know you're there and we're coming. It's only a matter of time."

Expressions of joy were subdued. The previous rumor about the mass execution was uppermost on each of the prisoners' minds. They knew the remaining Nazis weren't about to release them to share the horrible secret which had been kept for so long.

Yakoff's job was necessary so the water patrol continued to function. Each day on their appointed rounds they'd find more and more houses empty. Officers were evacuating their families, they were on the run. The railroad-siding, relatively quiet for the past several months, was once again a flurry of activity,

Boxcars recently stuffed and jammed full of innocent Nazi victims were now filled to capacity with household furnishings, antiques, art objects, paintings. The irony was, the majority of the precious German cargo being swept back towards Berlin had been stolen from those same

209

victims and arrived on those same trains of death only a short time ago. The work days became short. Cut in half and then in half again. They'd spend their days sitting in the warmth of the shed, wondering when the final order for all their deaths was going to be issued. Escape was a thought but never conversation. They'd each concluded there was still no safe or secure place to escape to. Any uprising would certainly have been suicidal. Acceptance of their fate was simply a painfilled matter of fact.

Less than seventy-two hours after the bombing raid, and well before the sun came up, Yakoff was inside the shelter involved in preparing a hot and hearty breakfast. In their rush to leave the houses, the Germans left behind great caches of food and supplies. The water patrol was eating like royalty.

The sound came from the northwest, gurgling, rumbling, close to but not quite shaking the ground itself. It sounded like more bombs landing in the general vicinity of Birkenau. The following moments, filled with anxiety, were spent in silence, waiting. It was too dark to see but certainly quiet enough to hear any planes approaching in the grey, cloud-filled sky. The silence continued, the vast space above remained still and empty.

Within two hours the truth of the matter had crawled its way across the bloodstained fields and into the main camp. The Nazis themselves had purposefully, willfully and intentionally set massive charges of dynamite and blown up their own gas chambers and crematoriums. Their haste to eliminate the awesome evidence of the worst crimes in history created a renewed sense of hope in each of the prisoners. They weren't going to be gassed. They weren't going to be burned. There was a universal feeling of reincarnation.

The reasons and motivation behind the action, as far as Yakoff and the others were concerned, was irrelevant. They had been spared and that's all that counted or mattered. They had been given a new lease on life and the Russians were moving closer each day.

In actuality, Hitler's great plan and Final Solution was thwarted by an overconfident and massive error in timing. His sick and perverse desire to annihilate the entire Jewish race fell short and failed to reach completion due to his own horrendous greed and avarice. The simple fact was that the gas chambers couldn't kill and the ovens couldn't burn fast enough to eliminate the entire prisoner population before the camp was overrun and overtaken by the enemy. There were too many people and not enough time.

Still, the prisoners would not be allowed the luxury of life. An order filtered down from the high command to move all those still incarcerated. March them, at whatever cost, within the boundaries of Germany for their own safety and subsequent execution. Guards who should have been kept at the front were assigned to the great march. Supplies and weapons were issued, to keep the mass exodus moving, no matter what.

One of Hitler's final vows before disappearing into his bunker was all the Jews in Europe would be killed. He was highly fanatical in that regard and more than willing to sacrifice German occupied land, equipment, supplies, and even the rest of his army if necessary, in order to make his demented wish a reality.

Chaos covered the camp like the Black Plague. All work patrols ceased and mass disorganization was the unwritten order of the day. Word of the upcoming forced march leaked and Yakoff was one of the first to hear about it. With nothing to lose he approached one of the remaining guards, one who over a period of time owed him several favors.

"About the march..."

"Yes, yes. What about it?" The guard exhibited characteristics of frenzy. It was obvious he was anxious to begin the evacuation.

"Would it be alright," Yakoff asked, "if my friends and I took a wagon along with us? We'll be responsible for it and won't let anything happen."

"Yes, yes. Whatever. That'll be fine. You have my permission." The guard was noticeably preoccupied, which was understandable, since the now constant shelling was coming closer by the hour. Yakoff seized the opportunity by the throat, organizing like never before. It was time to call in all past due IOU'S.

Rations were issued in the form of two full loaves of bread for each man, not nearly enough to stay alive during the journey they were facing. Storage lockers were emptied, beds were stripped, additional food was stolen from the unprotected kitchen, uniforms, blankets, even civilian clothing was procured from the laundry. While panic and fear settled into the minds and hearts of the majority, Yakoff was working, planning, preparing. He wasn't going to die, not after what he'd been through.

An attempt was made to roundup the group and keep them as close together as possible. Most everyone went along with Yakoff's plan and pooled their possessions into the wagon. Working together and in shifts, they could move it with relative ease and everyone's chance for survival was greatly increased.

Harry didn't exactly disavow the plan but chose rather to follow his own instincts. His idea, he said, was to inconspicuously work his way over to the hospital and pretend to have contracted some disease, preferably infectious. The Germans, he guessed, wouldn't have or take the time to haul bedridden patients along with them. Hopefully, in the confusion to empty the camp, the Nazis would realize the futility in shooting people who were going to die anyway. If he was fortunate enough to make it over that first hurdle, the Russians would break through in a day or two at most and he'd be a free man, liberated.

With precious time slipping by, Yakoff reasoned against the plan, but to no avail. Harry was going to stay and take his chances.

Predawn. Black as coal. Shells exploding in the background. Always closer.

The column, marching five across, was over twenty-thousand strong, an endless sea of striped uniforms without the wildest idea of where they were going. Yakoff's group, along with a few other industrious souls, pushed wagons and carts they'd managed to procure, filled with anything they could find that was edible or might help keep them warm. Armed guards, every ten yards, walked on both sides of the column, fully prepared to shoot down any prisoner who looked like he was going to try to escape.

The shriek of a high pitched whistle blew. The gate was opened for the very last time and the mass of humanity moved forward. There was no orchestra, only the strains of a thousand emotions exploding at once as Yakoff walked under the "Work Makes Freedom" sign.

It was January the fifteenth, nineteen hundred and forty-five, and much was being left behind: family, friends, a lover and twenty-six months of his life. There was a sense of completion, a finality, it was over. But as each step took them further away, Yakoff realistically understood it was only the beginning.

Chapter XVII

The march provided little relief and absolutely no time to relax. There was one scheduled rest-stop in the middle of the day when the men were supposed to eat their rations. But these men, for the most part, had been nearly starved to death. When provided with two full loaves of bread at the same time, the temptation, for the majority, was to eat it all in one sitting.

Stomachs shrunken by deprivation and time couldn't take it. Bodily systems reacted adversely. Men were sick: choking, retching, vomiting. When added to the emaciation most of them were already experiencing, the weakened, rail-thin bodies grew even more so. Each step was a drudgery, keeping up with the column became impossible. But keep up they must, for the Nazis were going to leave no live witnesses in their wake.

Sometimes friends on either side would help hold up and support the agonized victims of too much bread. When they couldn't, the souls would drift, sometimes crawling to the side of the road. They'd fall to their knees and spit-up, coughing, hacking, trying to catch their breath. The action was their last. The two long lines of guards, prodding the men forward, would turn and shoot the prisoner in the back. There was no reason, need or justification to conserve uniforms now. As the day wore on the ditches on either side of the road became filled with bodies: a long, vast, uncovered grave.

Those were the sounds of the march: the thousands of clogs plodding along the road, the coughing and throwing up, the German bullets ending the lives of stragglers, and the Russian heavy artillery in the distance, growing softer and softer with each step taken.

Yakoff and the group kept up the pace with the others. Working in prearranged shifts posed little problem with pulling and pushing the wagon, even with the additional weight of a rider. A friend of theirs had broken his right ankle, a compound fracture with a bone sticking through the skin. By placing him in the wagon they clearly and absolutely saved his life. The machine gun and rifle firing to the front, sides and rear was commonplace by noon the first day. It occurred with such regularity the prisoners grew used to it. After awhile they didn't even look or react. Their eyes stayed forward, looking down the long road, fixed on the eventual but improbable dream of freedom.

The first day, the column covered thirty miles by sundown. The cadence was swift and the death toll heavy. The men made a logical guess that fully twenty percent of their comrades were left in the ditches. Without consideration, without burial. The march was a repetition and continuation of the long line of German blood baths. The Nazi feelings for the human spirit or condition was nonexistent.

The dwindling group was sequestered for the night at a well-preserved and deserted farm outside a small village. Stars indicated they were heading due west, toward the German border. No one was surprised. The farm selected for the short but much needed rest was situated at the top of a fair-sized hill, essential for the Nazi's security purposes. The prisoners were forced to the top of the hill and guards formed a cordon all the way around it, insuring the impossibility of escape.

Yakoff, the group and their wagon, found their way into a small shed near the main barn where they ate and slept in shifts to protect their possessions. Others, on the outside and not as well prepared as they, rummaged through garbage, eating old rotten vegetables. Many ate grass, the first they'd seen in months or even years. Some ate stale, moldy, leftover hay from the barn. A few even ate dirt, anything to fill their starving stomachs.

The men were packed and jammed inside every available shelter to avoid the rapidly dropping mid-January temperature. Room was at a premium and most were left outside to sleep without cover on the hard, frozen ground. When the whistles blew before sunrise the next morning, several of those men didn't respond. They were stiff, covered with frost, dead. Their bodies would be left covering the countryside for an unknown eventuality.

During the night, Yakoff sifted through the extra clothing in the wagon and found a civilian suit with matching coat and trousers which he put on underneath his uniform. The fit was poor but that didn't matter. He'd concluded by day's end the march would probably leave few if any survivors. Based on the current attrition rate, the odds were virtually impossible any of them would live to see their ultimate destination. Hitler's Final Solution was working at full-speed.

They heard whistles, loud screaming and gunshots fired into the air.

The second day began and shortly thereafter, many of those who had eaten the bug-infested vegetables, damp moldy hay, and dirt, began to get sick. The routine was the same; if they couldn't keep up they were shot and left by the side of the road.

Escape, for the first time since his earliest capture, seemed to provide the only available solution. Yakoff had no money, no idea where he was and no possible aid or assistance from anyone. Still he knew, without a question, each step he took carried him two and a half feet closer to his own grave. He had to break away.

As the column plodded forward Yakoff cautiously removed both the shirt and pants of his striped uniform. Accomplishing this while still maintaining the pace was no small feat. Now he was marching in the midst of this sameness wearing civilian clothing and stood out like a sore thumb. For a few steps all seemed to be going well, then...

"Hey! You! Jewboy!"

He'd been spotted by a guard, waving him over. He was trapped with nowhere to go and no alternative but to follow the order shouted by the soldier in the grey uniform. Without options, Yakoff eased himself through the ranks until he was standing alone beside the man holding the submachine gun.

"You must think you're cute," the soldier said, raising his weapon toward Yakoff's chest. Just then a man about three rows ahead began to cough violently. He drifted a few steps away from the column, to the side of the road and fell to his knees hacking uncontrollably, throwing up. The guard was momentarily diverted and flashed a sinister, sadistic smile of satisfaction as he pulled back his finger releasing a two-second burst of death.

In the confusion and noise which lasted no more than five seconds, Yakoff dashed back inside the column of men. He wound his way to the center of the group and hunched down so his unusual clothing couldn't be seen from the sides. The guard was incensed and stomped up and down, checking each row. Other prisoners bunched around, forming a protective shield, blocking the guard's line of sight. Slowly and carefully Yakoff eased his way forward, line by line, until he rejoined the rest of his friends.

Concealment for any length of time was unlikely. The low-profile stature had been abandoned and he was truly a man alone. Discovery was a certainty. He had to try and it had to be now. Up ahead there were local people, Polish civilians, waiting on either side of a small dirt crossroad for the unexpected parade to pass. The opportunity was too good to miss.

There were hushed "good-byes" and "good-lucks." When the group reached the crossroad it was time to take the gamble and make his move. Yakoff straightened himself up to his full height, a far different carriage than the normal, slumped over prisoner posture, and walked confidently past the two men on his right, directly toward a guard. The timing was exact. It appeared he was one of the civilians from the other side of the road, who for whatever reason couldn't wait until the entire processional passed. The guard stared and Yakoff stared right back. He showed absolutely no sign of hesitation and kept moving straight ahead.

There was an incredible moment of tension when it appeared, for a second, the guard was going to open his mouth and say something, to ask for papers or local identification. But the column, the guard, and Yakoff kept on walking in their own respective directions. The youngster could feel the beady German eyes piercing their way toward the back of his own head. The urge to turn around and look was far less than the will to live, to make it safely to the forest and whatever unknown lay beyond.

The thousands of footsteps, one after the other, and the constant barrage of bullets grew softer and softer. His eyes were fixed, straight ahead, never looking back. At a turn in the road he stepped behind a large leafless tree and watched silently as the end of the column marched out of sight.

Run! Everything in his brain and body said, "Run!" The request was unconsciously heeded. Where? Away! Away from here, away from them, away from the eventual promise of death. No thought, no logic, just run. And he did. As fast and as far as possible. Through dense forests, across snow-covered ground, avoiding roads and fences that looked like they might belong to a farm. It had to be at least three miles, maybe further, when he finally slowed to catch his breath. He was walking, rotten branches and last fall's leaves crunching beneath his feet.

"Yakoff..." It was a whisper. Then a familiar face on top of a striped uniform stepped from behind a nearby tree. It was Isaac, his friend from the laundry, one of the group.

The two embraced warmly, neither actually believing what was happening. What were the odds of them both escaping and then finding one another out here in the middle of nowhere?

Four other men, also escapees, appeared from behind various other trees. They were strangers who Yakoff didn't know and were traveling together with Isaac as their unofficial leader. They'd managed to slip away from the column before daybreak and had been on the run ever since.

After handshakes and hurried, first-name introductions, a lookout was posted and a makeshift meeting began. Isaac wanted to head southwest, toward Czechoslovakia and away from the retreating Germans. Yakoff disagreed. He felt their chances for freedom would be better traveling northeast in the direction of Katovitz and the ever-nearing Russian front. Isaac's plan called for running from the Germans while Yakoff's was to slip through them. It was considerably more of a calculated risk but if they pulled it off their safety and freedom would be much quicker.

A compromise couldn't be reached and the group traveling with Isaac was also split on their decision as to whom to follow. Time was against them and they couldn't stay where they were any longer. After another sincere embrace they split up, each going their respective way and each trailed by two of the other prisoners.

As sundown approached the group ventured too near a working farm in order to steal some food. The sequence was simple; they were spotted by a German civilian riding a bicycle who reported them to the local police. The police surrounded the three, arrested them and turned them over to the Gestapo. The Gestapo transferred them by train to Gliawitz, another smaller concentration camp just west of Krakow for interrogation.

The Gestapo in charge was portly with a bald spot on top of his head and cackled when he spoke. At first it was routine: "Who are you, what are you doing here, where are you going, where have you come from... have you escaped from one of our prisons?"

Of course they denied everything, explaining they were Polish factory workers whose plant had been bombed and were seeking new employment. The questions seemed too easy, like the man didn't have anything better to do and was toying with them. Yakoff couldn't understand why the Gestapo didn't simply ask to see their forearms.

Then, as if the rotund German had been reading Yakoff's mind... "Roll up your sleeve." That was it, it was over. "Your right one." Yakoff didn't flinch or hesitate. He showed no reaction to the wrong choice of arms and quickly offered a clean right forearm for inspection. Apparently they'd been exonerated. No further comment was made. Instead they were taken, without explanation, to the basement of the Gestapo headquarters and locked inside a small damp cell.

For ninety minutes they danced wondrously with the illusion that release and then freedom was the next step. And that's all it was...an illusion.

They were taken back upstairs to the office and the smiling German officer ordered them to roll up their left sleeves. Slowly and with a sense of deep satisfaction he noted the tattoo numbers on a clipboard. Then the beatings began.

For a quarter of an hour they were punched, kicked and knocked around the room. In the process Yakoff lost another two teeth. When the Nazi sport was over and the three were miraculously still alive, it turned out to be a small price to pay.

They were stripped naked and marched outside into the rapidly falling January temperature. For a moment the frosty air was refreshing on the bruises and stinging welts. Ice-cold gun barrels were poked into their sides and backs as they were forced toward the singing wire fences. The electricity was turned off and a gate was opened.

Yakoff and the other two walked inside, between the double wires and waited. The gate was closed and the electricity was turned back on. "Stand at attention!" a guard shouted. "If you move you'll be shot." The warning was somewhat redundant due to the proximity of the fences themselves. At Auschwitz there was nearly six feet between the double wires. Here there was only three. If they fell from exhaustion or moved more than six inches to either side, the charge would be instant and permanent: a blackened, skin charred death, a rotten way to finish a journey lasting this long.

There was no sense of freedom felt during the half-day Yakoff was on his own. Even running through the woods he remained a prisoner. The night was freezing but no worse than others he'd experienced. The stereo humming from the killer wires brought a new dimension to his incarceration. Hour after hour exposure to the subzero temperatures and wind, which never seemed to stop, brought a wave of sensations to the skin, now a pale shade of blue in the glaring, watchful floodlights.

First there was the pain: constant, driving, clear to the center of every single bone. Then there was a tingling, a numbness, irritating, with alternating rushes of discomfort in the arms, legs, chest. Finally came the nothingness, no feeling or sensation at all. This was the feeling most feared because it was the first sign of extreme frostbite, which would certainly be followed by death at the hands of either nature or the Nazis. There is no escape.

Limited by the incredibly close deadly wires, the three shuffled bare feet on the frozen ground, moving fingers, shaking legs, wrapping their arms around themselves and squeezing. Anything to avoid that final, fatal, feeling of nothingness.

Before dawn the humming stopped and the gate was opened by two guards. Miraculously all three prisoners managed to make it through the night. Clothes were returned and Yakoff was handed the civilian suit he'd worn, only now the jacket and pants had been painted with wide red stripes. Within minutes the morning whistle blew and other prisoners began to exit nearby blocks, forming their ranks for the count.

It was still dark. Size, proximity and numbers were impossible to guess. Orders were shouted in German and a great thundering began as thousands of clogs started to move all at once. Yakoff's suit, left outside all night, did little to erase the numbing chill. Rifle barrels in their backs dangerously pointed them toward the direction of the marching sounds. Once there, they joined the slow moving throng, passing through the main gate of the camp and ending at a nearby railroad siding.

The train, with open boxcar doors, was waiting like a giant sleeping serpent, prepared to devour all who dared venture too near. As the prisoners were forced inside they were given individual rations in the form of three loaves of bread. As always no destination was announced or explanation given.

Even in seeing these new guards for only a momentary flash, Yakoff could sense and detect a degree of futility, that all was lost. He questioned why they continued this mindless, mass execution. If the war and the Third Reich, for all practical purposes were over, what have they to gain? Historically and unfortunately, the answer would never be known.

The doors to the boxcar were slammed shut and padlocked. The prisoners were packed so tightly it was impossible to sit. Most, nearly starved, eagerly devoured their black bread until they were overcome by sickness. People passed out but remained vertical, there wasn't room to fall down. The effects of the overcrowded condition were more than likely lifesaving as far as Yakoff was concerned.

It'd been nearly three days since he was in any situation which provided warmth. Now, packed body to body, the heat from other human beings, strangers, worked as a form of insulation. Feeling, thought to be lost forever, slowly returned.

Light filtered through cracks in the walls, the sun was coming up. There was neither insulation nor ventilation in the boxcar and the temperature rose considerably. For some, they collapsed from heat exhaustion. For Yakoff and his two followers, it was an unexpected blessing. They waited through the majority of the day hearing only indefinable sounds from outside. Then there were footsteps on the roof, lots. They logically deduced the guards were taking positions up there, an indication they'd be leaving soon.

Yakoff noticed a window of sorts, sealed shut but a window nonetheless, at the side and on the far end of the car. Inch by inch, with much difficulty, the three wove their way toward the small opening. They discovered the window was about a foot high and two feet wide, with boards nailed over it from the inside. The opening was nearly seven feet off the floor but reachable from their hard-earned vantage point. They waited impatiently without discussion. Each one knew what the other two were thinking.

There was no fanfare, no pre-departure whistle, just a sudden, violent jerk as the train began to move. The clackety-clack of the massive steel wheels increased their speed and the straining engine, far down the line, could be heard. The composite feeling was like a cloud, hanging low within the confines of the boxcar. This was going to be their last ride, ever.

When the train reached its maximum speed and the car settled into a rhythmic, side to side swaying, the three went to work. Fingers and brute strength, drawn from a deep personal well of survival, were their only tools. The rest of the unwilling passengers watched, their faces filled with horror. What are these madmen doing? They'll get us all killed.

Thoughts turned to whispered denials and shoving occurred. Yakoff knew what was waiting at the end of the ride. He and the other two continued to pull at the boards, loosening them from the window, providing a passage for escape. Those nearby protested, some heatedly. They were momentarily pacified, as had always been the case, by bribery. Their silence and lack of interference was exchanged for several loaves of bread. The perspective and viewpoint was relative. Fellow prisoners felt Yakoff was merely trying to escape from the boxcar while Yakoff knew he was trying to escape a nearby gas chamber.

The boards were free and fresh air was finally theirs. Snow-covered trees and poles holding telephone wires flashed by. Darkness had fallen providing a much needed camouflage for the exit. The others watched in subdued silence, not believing anyone could actually be so brave...or so stupid. Shuffling occurred, providing a few precious and necessary inches for movement. Yakoff and one of the other men held hands, providing a foundation, lifting the third to the window. He crawled through head first until he was balancing on the window sill by his waist.

There was a massive thud and the snap of a hundred bones breaking all at once. The body was ripped instantly from the opening. The man had escaped the gas chamber only to be executed by a telephone pole. There was no scream, only train sounds and an increased shuffling from above. The guards also heard the noise and were looking to see what had happened.

Yakoff held his own hands together, stirrup-like, and boosted Yosel Reicholz, the second man, up. Yosel stuck his head through the small opening, checking side to side, then inched his way out. The instant his shoes disappeared the firing started. There was a hail of bullets from the roof, echoing through the snow-covered woods.

Now Yakoff was on his own again, surrounded by strangers. He poked the man standing next to him, one he'd given a loaf of bread to, and told him he wanted a lift.

"A what?"

"A boost, Help me to the window."

"I won't! You're gonna' get us all killed. The guards..."

Yakoff poked the man again, this time harder, stopping him in midsentence. "I need a lift 'cause I can't get to the window on my own.' You're gonna' help me or I'll guarantee you one thing." He'd captured the man's attention. "Wherever this train stops you won't be alive to get off..."

The man pondered his options for a second then lifted the believable youngster to the edge of the narrow opening. Yakoff pulled, straining every muscle in his arms, struggling for his very life. The night was black, at least one thing was on his side. Crawling through the window was comparable to edging his way across a bottomless pit filled with deadly snakes. For all he knew there was a Nazi on the roof with a rifle pointed down, waiting for the right moment to blow his brains out.

He gripped the edge of the boxcar with trembling fingertips, waiting for the exact instant to push off so as to avoid the fate of the first man through. His timing must be accurate or it would be all over. A telephone pole whizzed by and he pushed away with all his might. There was a giant flash of light from the roof of the car before he even hit the ground. The constant, repeating noises of the machine guns filled the night air.

A snowdrift broke his fall and inertia rolled him over several times. Puffs of white danced around his body as the bullets splattered the snow. Deadly thuds put deep holes into the surrounding trees, shaking them violently. The night was not silent.

Yakoff laid still, motionless, afraid to move. The train kept crawling into the darkness. After what seemed a very long time, the silence returned. Slowly, carefully, he stood up, examining every inch of his body to see if he'd been hit. It was another miracle he hadn't. Secure in the fact he was still alive he started back down the train track, the direction he'd come from, faithfully following his original plan of heading northeast toward the front.

He stayed within cover of the trees and stopped every fifty yards to call out Yosel's name as well as the other man's who'd jumped first. The night remained silent and he didn't find either body.

Hunger became a factor and he knew he had to find some food. There was a tiny light in the distance, far ahead and to his left. It was a farmhouse. Caution was exercised for he had no way of knowing who might be staying there. From a safe distance Yakoff saw two mangy dogs in the front yard, an obstacle he could deal with. Then there was something worse. The house had a large antenna on the roof.

It wasn't worth the gamble so he kept moving. A mile and a half down the road was another house, this one without dogs but still sporting a tall, shortwave antenna. He continued on, afraid to run the risk of finding either Germans or German supporters who could instantly report his whereabouts.

The sun was beginning to rise as Yakoff passed the crest of a rolling hill and spotted the third house, this one antenna-free. Smoke was rising from the chimney and a light shone through one of the windows. From his vantage point it appeared to be safe.

He was tired, bone-tired, exhausted. There was a barn, a shelter from the relentless wind which refused to stop blowing. A shadow slowly crept across the farmyard and silently opened the large wooden door. Inside was one milk cow and little else. Yakoff climbed into the hay and rested for the first time in several days. But it wasn't for long.

The creaking door awoke the youngster and his eyes popped open, instantly alert. It was a woman, probably in her mid-thirties, who had a thick, woolen scarf wrapped tightly around her head. He watched in silence as she milked the cow, wondering who she was as well as how many others remained in the house. Each spray of fresh milk into the tin bucket sounded like a meal in and of itself. When she finished a few minutes later she patted the cow on the rump and thanked her out loud, by name, for the milk.

Yakoff didn't knock. He opened the front door and walked inside. The milking woman was seated at a kitchen table with a man, probably her husband. Neither moved nor said anything. Nor was there any noticeable reaction to the red stripes covering their intruder's suit of clothes.

First Yakoff apologized, explaining he meant them no harm. He said he was lost, frightened and hungry.

"We're here alone," the man said. "There's no one else around." He was Polish and Yakoff could hear the fear in his trembling voice.

Having been lied to before, Yakoff checked the bedroom. It was empty. The woman heated the milk she'd just obtained and it was heartily consumed along with freshly baked bread and cheese. The couple was polite but probably out of circumstance, having no idea if the escaped prisoner in their home was armed or not.

Before he left, Yakoff put on a pair of the man's trousers over his own, more to cover the red stripes than for warmth. He also took a long, grey wool overcoat hanging in the corner. He filled the pockets with bread and the man, anxious to rid himself of the unexpected visitor, offered directions toward the nearest major highway.

There were many travelers on the road, along with several horse-drawn wagons and carts. Not wishing to attract attention he fell in line with four Italians walking towards a nearby town. The plan proved to be advantageous. Only moments after he'd joined them they passed a road crossing where a Gestapo was standing guard. Had Yakoff been alone he most certainly would have been stopped and questioned. Papers and identification would have been asked for. Instead, the Italians with Yakoff following suit, waved a friendly hello to the black-coated German and walked past without being bothered.

The town was filled with military personnel. There were soldiers and heavy equipment everywhere. It was a place Yakoff could little afford to be. Discovery and re-incarceration was waiting under a skull and crossboned helmet on every street corner. Smiles and friendly nods could not protect him forever.

A small group of local townspeople were walking away from the center of the village so Yakoff joined them, exchanging idle chitchat as they moved through the Germans. Man by man the villagers disappeared down various roads, into different houses, until once again he was alone in the countryside on the far edge of town.

After a short but cursory examination he knocked at the front door of a small, well-kept farmhouse. Over coffee, real coffee, Yakoff explained to the elderly couple inside the story about his factory being bombed-out in Warsaw and how he was trying to return to his home in

Krakow. The embellishment, laced with charm and innocence, was bought completely. They agreed to let Yakoff stay in their shed outside in exchange for much needed help with the chores.

He slept warm, ate well and worked hard, earning the trust of his new acquaintances. The man even gave Yakoff a used flannel shirt and a pair of pants to wear. Late one night, after the couple was safely asleep, he left the shed and crept into the nearby woods where he buried the red striped suit.

The timing of the burial was fortunate. The next morning they were all awakened by a German patrol. The officer in charge questioned Yakoff, wanting to know who he was and why he didn't have papers. Once again the youngster used the factory story and told them his papers had been stolen. He hastily added he was the elderly couple's son.

The officer turned to the man and woman, asking for confirmation. They replied in Polish they didn't speak or understand German. Yakoff, fluent in both languages, was told to interpret. It was all he could do to suppress a smile. He asked them if he'd been a hard worker over the last few days.

They nodded eagerly, smiling warmly, repeating, "Oh, yes. Oh, yes," in Polish. It worked. The Germans accepted it. They told Yakoff and his "parents" about a large meeting to be held later that afternoon on the outskirts of town. Attendance, they clearly explained, was required.

Most of the Polish residents of the area had refused to learn the German language, so the first order of the day was to find and select someone who could function as an unofficial liaison as well as interpreter between the soldiers and townspeople. Based on his early morning encounter with the patrol, Yakoff was the logical selection. It was an instant promotion to a position of prominence. He played his part well, feigning ignorance, innocence, and naivete in a carefully blended roll.

The entire population of the town was being mobilized as a labor force for construction purposes. No one was to be excluded. Men, women, and children would all work side by side. The German plan called for digging great, large ditches to supposedly stop the oncoming Russian tanks. The locals were more than surprised when Yakoff interpreted the proposal. A ditch, to accomplish what the Nazis wanted, would be at least twenty feet wide, six feet deep and stretch for miles across the countryside.

There was no argument or complaint. No one even offered any logical or realistic advice. If the Germans ordered that's the way it was going to be, then that's the way it was. The fact the exercise made absolutely no sense and was a worthless endeavor was totally irrelevant. Early the next morning everyone showed up with shovels and other assorted tools. During the night, the majority of the German contingency evacuated the town and retreated to the west. A skeleton patrol was all that remained to oversee the construction. The obvious lack of military personnel was the main topic of conversation for the entire day.

Yakoff, in essence, was totally in charge of the workers. In addition to interpreting, he was also responsible for motivating the force to work as hard and as fast as possible. He also ordered punishment for those who didn't. Shades of Auschwitz. He was now the main kapo. No one knew he was a Jew, and the opportunity for sweet and severe revenge against the Polish gentiles was tempting. However, he also realized the Russians were on their way and it was only a matter of time before the rest of the Germans left. Then he'd be on his own again and still in the hands of hostile forces.

Compassion made more sense, so he befriended the workers and made their task as easy as possible. He misinterpreted orders, creating an arena of organized confusion. The only time people actually worked was when the German patrol was virtually standing guard over them. Yakoff defended the workers and was responsible for preventing much punishment and anguish.

It was the end of the first, full day's work when they all heard it. The sound was a low-pitched thud followed by a short, hollow echo. It came from the east. The front was again within hearing distance. The Russians were pounding the once mighty Nazis, driving them back, driving them to oblivion.

Each succeeding day the sounds grew louder and after a week they could feel the ground quiver as the big shells exploded. Large convoys of Germans rolled through the quasi-construction area. Yakoff felt a realistic sense of satisfaction down deep inside each time the wounded came by. Some of those men, undoubtedly, had been guards at Birkenau and Auschwitz. They were paid, mindless assassins of women and children and now justice was finally prevailing. He was glad to see blood-stained bandages and the faces filled with anguish and pain.

The front line soldiers, marching with broken bones and bodies, started to come through. The satisfaction was replaced by the all too vivid memory of the death march from Auschwitz. Yakoff watched the slow moving column with his eyes, but his mind saw only thousands of fellow prisoners in striped uniforms, starving, dying, filling the ditches by the sides of the road. He pressed his eyes tightly together, trying to erase the horrible vision but it wouldn't go away. Every detail remained, every hollow-eyed face wrenched with agony and pain was there--just like they were only days before.

Even the SS deserted the town, leaving a lowly German sergeant in charge of the operation. It was the sergeant who privately told Yakoff how stupid the digging was. Even they knew that. But they were following orders, doing only what the high command asked. Plus, he added, their options were slim. If they weren't left in charge of this fruitless endeavor, they'd most certainly be transferred to the front.

The parallel viewpoint between the sergeant and the concentration camp guards was both clear and obscene. The guards proved their merit and necessity by blatant cruelty as well as an abundance of disregard for human life. The merit was sickly rewarded by allowing them to remain at the camp, continuing their destruction rather than transferring them to action. The bottom line was, the supposedly brave guards were actually cowards, afraid to go into the war itself and defend their precious fatherland.

On the tenth morning of the digging, Yakoff and the workers arrived at the site only to find it deserted. The Germans were gone, even the roads were empty. The heavy shelling had stopped and only random, occasional rifle fire could be heard in the distance. The Polish people were so well-conditioned by the Germans that even now they were willing to continue the work which had been ordered.

After several tries and much emotion Yakoff finally convinced them that some time during the night the Germans had pulled back, the front had moved somewhere to the other side of their town, they were now a liberated area. Even so, some still refused to understand.

"Free!" Yakoff screamed. "We're free!" The news was followed by a deafening quiet, almost a disbelief. There was no public celebration or rejoicing cries. People looked at one another, still unsure as to what exactly they were supposed to do. Some still held their shovels at the ready.

"Go home," the youngster pleaded. "Go home and be with your families." Tears began to well in his eyes and his voice started to crack. "Go home and be with your loved ones and be thankful you're finally free!"

The crowd slowly disbanded, each going their separate directions, leaving Yakoff alone. A farmer, an old man who Yakoff had saved from a beating, approached somewhat cautiously, inviting him to his place for dinner.

A medium-sized pig was killed, sliced and cooked. Potatoes were boiled in the blood of the pig and several loaves of fresh black bread were heaped on the table. The feast was conducted in silence and after, the farmer gave Yakoff a seven pound slab of fat to take home with him for the lady of the house to cook as she wanted.

Understandably, upon Yakoff's bountiful return, she was thrilled with the gift. The three discussed how different life was going to be without Germans constantly controlling their every move. Actually, they were in the middle of emotionally explaining how this had been the first day in years that Nazi soldiers weren't running their town when there was an unexpected knock at the front door.

It was three German soldiers, an officer and two others. They said they were the last fighting men to leave the front. They were exhausted, ready to drop with their next step and needed a place to rest. They assured Yakoff and his friends no one was going to be hurt. They were just going to sleep for awhile and in the morning they'd take some food and be peacefully on their way.

They placed their rifles in a nearby comer and took over the bed in the main room, all sleeping crosswise with their feet propped up on chairs. Within seconds it sounded as if all three were snoring, but it was impossible to be sure. If Yakoff made a run for the rifles and one of them was still awake they most assuredly would kill all three of them. Germans lied, all the time, so in whispers, Yakoff and the elderly couple decided to remain quiet and see what the morning would bring.

He was looking out the front window, toward the east, when he saw a nondescript shadow dash across the farmyard and disappear behind the barn. Then there was another. Then another. Too big to be animals, they had to be men. More Germans? That was the last thing they needed.

The half moon created streams of light which shone through the low hanging clouds. When a fourth figure ran to the cover of the barn Yakoff could see what was happening. The shadow was wearing a hat, a helmet. On its side he could make out an insignia of a hammer and sickle. They were Russians.

Slowly, without making a sound, he opened the door and walked outside, holding his hands high above his head. He had to get their attention without waking the Germans. It was a calculated risk that needed to be taken. If the Russians found the Germans on their own, they might feel Yakoff and the elderly couple were hiding them. Those consequences could prove to be irreversible. Plus, there was always the possibility of a gun fight with the old people caught in the middle.

As he rounded the corner of the barn the moonlight reflected off one of the rifle barrels. He froze in his tracks as he felt himself in the presence of others. There was a long exhale, then, "Tavarisch..."

It was unanswered.

"Tavarisch..." It was Russian for comrade, or friend, and spoken with a gut level sincerity that had been suppressed for a long time. The men appeared from the shadows, three soldiers and an officer, surrounding Yakoff with their guns trained on him. He lowered his arms and stared gratefully at the officer's face. "Thank God," he whispered. "Thank God you're finally here." Yakoff's fluent Russian was perfect, right down to the dialect, also learned from other prisoners at Auschwitz.

He told the officer who he was, that he wasn't a German and that he'd escaped from a concentration camp. The reason for risking his own life, he added, was there were three Germans asleep inside the house and he didn't want the people, his friends, to get hurt.

When the Russians acknowledged their belief by lowering their guns and thanking him for the information he walked directly to the officer, put his arms around the burly, bearded man and hugged him with all his might. The Russian, completely aware of the Nazi concentration camps and what it took to escape from one, hugged back. It was a moment of joy. Yakoff was finally, actually, free.

The youngster was given the honor of waking the Germans up by screaming "Auchstein!" at the top of his voice. Their surprise was understandable as they opened their eyes to four large Russian carbines. The moment brought great pleasure. And even more.

While the Germans' hands were being tied behind their backs, the Russian officer asked, "Is there anything at all we can do for you?" Yakoff smiled and nodded. Within a matter of moments he exchanged his own tattered, hole-filled shoes for the shiny, black leather boots the German officer was wearing.

There was more information to impart. A large bridge several miles away and spanning a wide ravine provided the easiest access to the east. The bridge was wired with heavy explosives and a patrol of German soldiers was waiting on the other side. Waiting for the bridge to be crawling with Russian tanks before they blew them and their occupants to kingdom come.

Once the Germans were secure they left one man as a guard and Yakoff led the other three Russians through the forest. He knew a place on the far side of the bridge where the water was shallow enough to cross. After they'd scaled the hill on the other side they silently made their way back toward their objective, crawling the last hundred yards and finding the Germans without any problems.

The surprise attack was effective; a short firefight followed by the German surrender. A demolition team was summoned the next day to successfully disarm the explosives. Yakoff's accurate information came from the German sergeant, the one left behind to finish the digging project. Several drinks on the last afternoon of their occupation had loosened his usually protective tongue.

Then came the Russians: troops and tanks and heavy artillery, trucks and transports and wagons filled with ammunition. Their spirits were high. They were beating the hell out of the Nazis and wore their pleasure proudly on the outside of their uniforms. A command post was established in the middle of town and was sorely in need of just one thing to communicate with the locals: an interpreter.

Chapter XVIII

Major Gorolof was his name. He was gruff and stocky, even by Russian standards. A long, thick, well-trimmed mustache covered his upper lip and trailed its way across both cheeks. He didn't believe Yakoff's story at all. Not even after two, full hours of interrogation.

"Would I do this to my own arm?" Yakoff pleaded, pointing to his tattoo.

"We found lots of Germans who tattooed themselves," he countered, "in order to escape prosecution. It's not uncommon."

"I'm a Jew. Why can't you believe that?"

"Recite the Kaddush," he said, a traditional Jewish prayer of mourning, usually said in synagogue.

Yakoff blinked in confusion, troubled for a moment with the literal translation. Then he switched from Russian to Yiddish and recited the prayer verbatim, both the mourner's part and the congregation's response.

Still Gorolof wasn't impressed or convinced. "Most German spies are forced to learn multiple languages," he growled. It was another test and Yakoff was taken by surprise. Gorolof was speaking in fluent Yiddish, the language they used to continue the conversation.

"Where did you learn to speak that?" Yakoff asked hesitantly.

The response was hard, "I'll ask the questions!" And he did. For another hour and a half. The Major was convinced, mostly because of the fluency in several different languages, Yakoff was a spy. With his ultimate and final determination he could order him shot, but for some unknown reason the interrogation continued to drag on. Apparently and thankfully, Gorolof wasn't quite convinced.

Yakoff pleaded, citing examples and atrocities from the camp, the march, his two escapes. Gorolof was not moved. He'd heard it before from Nazis attempting the same ploy. Germans, he said, even wore striped prisoner uniforms and turned themselves in to the Russians, begging for their lives. "You're all cowards," he said, pounding his thick, calloused fist on the table. "Worthless, sniveling cowards!"

All was lost. Yakoff could sense the end drawing near. To come this far, be liberated for one full day, and then executed by the very people who saved your life was the greatest atrocity of all.

Without ceremony or explanation Yakoff lifted his hands from his sides to his belt buckle. Slowly, with reserve, embarrassment, and a sense of strained futility, he lowered his trousers to the middle of his thighs.

The Major looked down in disbelief. It was something never before seen or even heard of. His eyes opened wide and an emotion bordering shock covered his face. There was a painful look of remorse as he closed his eyes and nodded, indicating for Yakoff to return his pants to their normal position.

Gorolof's eyes remained closed as he slid back his chair and stood to his full height. He slowly walked around the large desk, straight to the front of the violated youngster, looking deeply and compassionately into his very soul. A mist covered the Major's eyes, an understanding, a sorrow. He embraced Yakoff, holding him tightly to his chest, much as a father would his own son.

"I speak Yiddish," he whispered, "...because I too am a Jew. A Russian Jew."

Yakoff returned the embrace and the two held on to one another for a very long time. At last he'd found a friend. At last he was free.

Gorolof sent an underling out for food to eat and vodka to drink. During the hearty meal he was candid with Yakoff, expressing not only his innermost feelings but also the ramifications which would exist during the postwar period. He said he'd promised his parents in Russia if he found any Jews still alive he'd do whatever he could to help them. To date, he sadly reported, Yakoff was the first person he'd found who fell into that category. There was a long, reflective pause after the comment passed his lips.

He felt concern for Yakoff's safety, due to the mentality as well as attitude of the Polish people. His chances for survival here, should it be known he was Jewish, weren't much better than they were in Auschwitz. Anti-Semitism had grown to unheard of proportions since the war broke out. The rocks the gentiles threw at Yakoff and his friends while they were growing up were now much more deadly. The motivation behind this bizarre and inbred hate was still uncertain and undefined.

To travel or move throughout the countryside without proper identification would have been difficult at best, deadly at worst. The Major eliminated that particular obstacle by providing Yakoff with a card which he prepared himself. It was pink and written in Russian. Gorolof made it official by adding his own sweeping signature and a seal which he kept in his desk drawer. With this, he explained, Yakoff would be able to travel anywhere at anytime.

When Yakoff hugged the Major goodbye he felt much the same as he did when he left his father in Sierpc for his class trip to Warsaw. This time however, there were no classmates or friends. This time there were no guides or teachers. This time there was no set destination or planned travel arrangements. This time, like so many times before, he was on his own.

He left with "good luck, Godspeed" and his pockets stuffed with food. The first major intersection he came to was a flurry of activity, trucks going every which way. A uniformed female in the center of the crossroads directed traffic with a flourish comparable to an orchestra conductor. After several tries Yakoff finally caught her attention and she momentarily stopped traffic so he could join her.

"Could you possibly help me get a ride?" The question was posed with a humble sincerity which did little to soften her heavily preoccupied mood.

"Who are you and where are you going?" Short. Curt. Not very helpful or assisting.

Yakoff showed her the pink card and a new world opened up. She smiled, became instantly polite, and referred to him as sir.

"Which way are you going?"

That was a good question, one he hadn't honestly considered. Sierpc and Warsaw flashed quickly through his mind but he knew where he had to go first. He had to return to Auschwitz and see if anyone else was still alive. There was a long pause before he finally replied. "Southeast."

Without hesitation the woman stopped the next truck headed that direction. She spoke briefly but sternly with the driver and then pointed to an open spot in the rear where Yakoff could ride.

Dust swirled up from the road creating tiny whirlwinds as the truck roared out of town. Free, Yakoff thought to himself. Finally free. He repeated the phrase over and over, even saying it out loud, but still found it hard to honestly believe. He studied the pink card printed in Russian. He could speak the language but having never seen it written couldn't guess what it said. However, realizing its value he tucked it safely away.

The truck passed mile after mile of stark, grey, leafless trees, waiting patiently for the arrival of spring and the rebirth of life. Yakoff pondered the discussion he'd had with the Major, the one about not finding any other Jews alive. The thought was preposterous until the stark reality settled in that he, to his own personal knowledge, was the last living Jew in Europe. The concept gripped his throat like a noose, tightening with each turn of the wheel. It was air tight and he had to return to Auschwitz to find out for himself.

The large truck lumbered to a stop at a crossroad in a small town. The driver politely told Yakoff he was turning north so the youngster jumped out, thanking the Russian for the lift. It was nearly dark and the few dirt covered streets were mostly deserted except for three soldiers standing across the way.

Like the female traffic cop, their mood and reception changed considerably when Yakoff showed them the pink card. They were only about five miles from Auschwitz but the soldiers reported it was unsafe to travel alone at night.

"Wait till tomorrow," they said. "Come have a drink with us."

The local pub was filled to capacity with Russians, mostly soldiers. One, after hearing Yakoff was on his way to Auschwitz approached his table. "Were you in the camp?" he asked in his native tongue.

Yakoff nodded, hoisting another vodka his new friends had just purchased for him.

"There's some people here in town you might know," the soldier said.

It was a boarding house of sorts and the room was on the second floor. Yakoff's knock was tentative. He was in a strange place with strange people. It's probably some cruel joke, he thought to himself. The Russians are probably sitting in the bar right now laughing their heads off.

"Who is it?" The voice was soft, high-pitched and as tentative as the knock had been.

"Yakoff Skurnik," he answered in Polish, trying to sound brave. "From the camp."

A dead bolt lock was opened and the door slowly pulled back. The soldiers were telling the truth. There were two women, actually girls in their late teens, standing protectively inside the room. Their hair was no more than a half-inch long and they were both rail-thin. The numbers on their arms were in the high hundred and twenty thousands. Yakoff stared speechlessly and the girls stared back. They each had triangles under their tattoos. They were Jewish. He was not alone.

Over a cheap bottle of vodka, a gift from one of the soldiers, the three shared their camp experiences until early in the morning. The girls also escaped during the great march. One of their guards, for no apparent reason, opened up his submachine gun at the group they were marching with. Limp, lifeless bodies fell to the ground without warning, blood was everywhere, screaming and panic filled the air. Through it all, they related painfully, was the heinous laughter of the German soldiers. Mina, the younger of the two, and her friend Miriam, fell to the ground with the rest of them, somehow managing to escape the barrage of bullets. When the trailing column of prisoners caught up with them, the dead bodies were heaped on the side of the road. Through tears they explained how they were dragged with the others and left for dead, surrounded on both sides and on top, with corpses oozing blood, until the last of the prisoners was out of sight.

After awhile the conversation turned to thoughts concerning their newfound freedom, things they'd missed, things they were going to do. Both girls, thin as they were and with virtually no hair, were still attractive. They spoke candidly about men and with the assistance of vodka the talk turned to sex. Within a short time the discussion was blatant, beyond the usage or necessity of innuendo.

Both girls had lost their virginity prior to their capture and were, eager to relive the experience. Yakoff was embarrassed at the frankness of their suggestions. He'd heard about the things they referred to but only from other prisoners in the camp. Clothing was partially removed in an at tempt to arouse as well as seduce him. For most, the opportunity would have classically been referred to as golden. For Yakoff, he felt nothing. He tried concentrating, contemplating the unlimited possibilities. Still he felt nothing, absolutely nothing.

The girls had decided much earlier they were going to return to the camp with him. This provided the opportunity–the out–Yakoff needed. He faked a large yawn and stretching announced, "We've got a long walk ahead of us tomorrow so we'd all better get some rest." With that he curled up in an easy chair in the corner, closed his eyes and pretended to fall fast asleep.

The girls were dumfounded, not really believing what was happening. They doused the light and both climbed into bed. Believing Yakoff was asleep, they openly discussed what just transpired with a sense of pure amazement. Had they not just invited this attractive young man, who'd been locked up and kept away from sexual pleasures, even longer than they, to share the same bed with them? Had they not been more than clear in explaining feelings they had missed and wanted to renew this very night? Was it them? Could it be he found them both so unattractive and unappealing "Maybe he doesn't like girls," one said, quite out loud. The implication was remarkably clear. The pain that shot through Yakoff's body was comparable to the worst beating administered by Olschevsky and his lethal whip. He reached down, between his legs, wanting to react, wanting to respond, wanting to be hard. But the normal male human function had been sliced away by Doering and a dull scalpel. He felt nothing.

The girls talked awhile longer, arousing themselves with the pleasures they were going to receive the following night, pleasures from a real man who would offer satisfaction. Yakoff listened until their conversation ceased and the room was quiet. Then he listened to the silence for the remainder of the evening.

He was still young, not yet twenty-one, and faced an ominous responsibility he could not fulfill. The majority of the Jewish population, as far as he knew, had been annihilated. He was one of a handful, at best, of survivors left to perpetuate the race and he couldn't even do that. He questioned from deep in his heart the reason for his existence. Why was he spared when so many others had perished? What now, was he supposed to do with his life? Would he forever be fenced both mentally and psychologically within the singing wires of Auschwitz with pure, animalistic survival as his only goal?

His last conscious thought before he slept for a half-hour was the stinging memory of the comment Mina had made earlier: "Maybe he doesn't like girls' " A comment he was destined to carry with him for the rest of his life.

They walked in silence, following the railroad track back toward the dreaded place. Each step created more of a certainty they were the only survivors. For most of the trip, Mina and Miriam walked in front with Yakoff trailing by a few yards. The conversation and even worse, the realization from the previous night, established an inner need for him to be alone.

Their unspoken yet burning mental questions were in unison. What if the camp was empty, no one left, no one at all? Where would they go? Their hometowns had certainly been destroyed. What would they do? When the occupying armies left Poland, as they eventually would, their lives as Jews would be relatively worthless. They'd have to remain on the run, hiding, denying their religious faith and beliefs.

He wanted desperately to believe his father was still alive but try as he might the thought wouldn't come. When the Nazis blew-up their own 235 crematoriums, their demented logic of protecting their secrets would definitely remain still and lifeless, buried in the rubble. He reflected back to the night of their arrival and the first thing he heard about the special squad. No one on the Sonderkommando, the older prisoner told him, ever leaves the squad alive. That moment could have been yesterday. It was all so vividly clear, more indelibly implanted on his brain cells than the blue ink on his left forearm.

They reached the crest of a small incline and could see it all in the far-off distance. Birkenau on their left, huge, invincible. He'd never seen it from this perspective and had no idea or mental concept of its true size. The giant killer at last had been laid to rest. For the first time, through Yakoff's eyes, the chimneys weren't belching black smoke into the low hanging fog and mist.

Auschwitz, the main camp, was on their right. From here it looked like a well-kept university campus or a closely clustered group of apartment buildings. Russian artillery and heavy equipment was highly visible around both encampments. There was no feeling of homecoming, only painfilled memories. Their pace slowed and their steps were heavy but they had to be taken. They had to know. Yakoff could hear both girls crying up ahead.

As they grew closer an incredible sight appeared. There were people, other people, also returning to the camp. Prisoners like themselves, most still dressed in the tattered striped uniforms with nowhere else to go. They were starved, sick, alone, without friends or relatives, seeking only food to stay alive and warm shelter. They were survivors. Yakoff and the two girls were not the only ones left. Even so, the feeling of joy one might have expected was nowhere to be found. The Nazis had permanently stripped that emotion long ago.

Just ahead was the "Work Makes Freedom" sign. There was little sound other than the shuffling of feet toward the entrance. Today there was no orchestra with their silly German marching tunes, just the walking cadavers, desperate for a meal. Trucks rolled through the gate, filled with escapees too emaciated to walk. The war was over and these were the remains.

Several men were standing around the main gate, greeting their returning comrades and explaining procedures now in effect. Yakoff blinked, refocusing, he couldn't believe his eyes. It was Yossel Engel, his good friend from the bricklayers' school. He'd made it. He was alive. The two noticed each other at the same time and Yossel's mouth fell wide open. He too was stunned.

"I thought you were dead," Yossel said, eyes welling with tears. I heard you were shot trying to escape."

"I'm here Yossel! It's me! And you're alive too!" They embraced, confirming by touch what their eyes found so difficult to believe. "Are there others? Did anyone else make it?"

Yossel nodded. Several had already returned and they'd received word others were on their way. After introductions came the checking-in process, only this time the guards at the gate were Russian. He discovered a physical examination had to be taken before any food would be disbursed. This regulation came as a result of people with malnutrition eating too much solid food and subsequently dying. It had happened hundreds of times and the Russians were taking great precautions to prevent any further occurrence.

After Mina and Miriam were settled in and taken care of, Yakoff reported to the doctor in charge. It was a simple thing, no longer than five minutes, only for the purpose of determining if he was capable of eating solid food. The physician was shocked as well as embarrassed for Yakoff when he discovered the butcherous surgery which had been performed. He asked the youngster to return after he'd eaten and issued a pass for the mess hall.

Even though ravished with hunger, Yakoff first went out of his way to visit block 28, the hospital. He was looking for Harry Foreman, his friend who'd chosen to risk staying behind rather than endure the march. Questions were posed to every orderly, attendant, and patient in sight. No one knew or had heard anything. The memories of his own time spent in that building and the newly discovered profound effects which would alter the rest of his entire life became too much for him. Sweat broke out at his temples and in his palms. He felt boxed in, trapped again. Breathing was short, hard to get. He had to escape, had to be outside.

He sucked the fresh air deeply, quick gulps, a momentary gasping. Even though the Nazis had deserted this place nearly three weeks ago, they left in their cowardly retreat a lingering and repulsive aroma of death. Yakoff couldn't guess why but he doubted the smell would ever go away.

The camp was wide-open, without official sleeping assignments so he stayed in block 7, the old bricklayers' school, where past acquaintances were renewed. More than once he woke up in the middle of the night in a cold sweat and couldn't return to sleep until he'd walked all the way to the front of the camp in order to assure himself the main gate was still open. It was hard adjusting, after so long, to the unrestricted freedom of movement.

A percentage of the returning prisoners found staying within the camp impossible. In small menacing groups they'd enter the actual town of Auschwitz and force local German residents out of their homes and into the streets to fend for themselves. The action was viewed as reciprocal and there was never any remorse attached. The prisoners felt, with much justification, it was their right.

Yakoff revisited the physician and was turned over to a political commissar. He questioned the youngster twice a day with a stenographer present and took slides from all angles of the Nazi handiwork. Yakoff painfully retold the dreadful experience of the castration over and over. Where it happened, how, when, by whom. He determined the information along with the photographs were probably going to be used as some form of propaganda. At the time it mattered little.

The commissar explained if Yakoff was interested in attending the University of Moscow, it could be arranged. For a moment the thought was interesting, even intriguing, but he finally declined, saying he felt a responsibility to return to Sierpc and see if there were any other survivors. The commissar understood and the subject was never mentioned again.

There were two boys who had been miraculously spared, one ten and one twelve. This was unusual because virtually all children in that age group had been instantly taken to the gas chambers for destruction. Yakoff befriended and protected the newly orphaned children, making sure they got enough to eat and stayed with them to insure their food wasn't stolen away by someone older or stronger. In many instances the laws of the jungle still prevailed.

Within a week restlessness set in. There were rumors that refugees as well as residents of nearby towns were paying ridiculously inflated prices for nearly anything they could get their hands on. Clothing was high on the list of priorities. Yakoff, sensing yet another opportunity, solicited Yossel's assistance and together they broke into the Canada warehouse. Having worked there and knowing his way around made it a relatively simple task.

In their haste to evacuate, the Germans left the building nearly full of everything imaginable. Since clothing was what people wanted, clothing was what they took. They filled two large bags with shoes, coats, pants, dresses, everything they could stuff inside and still manage to carry.

The nearest major city was Krakow, a full day's walk away. So, when the sun rose the following morning it found Yakoff and Yossel walking briskly down the railroad tracks, headed due east, loaded with marketable merchandise and ready to do business.

About halfway there they switched over from the railroad tracks, which were icy and provided treacherous footing, to a nearby road heading the same direction. Then an unusual thing began to happen. People, total strangers, would hail the two of them to stop and offer to purchase the sacks.

"What's in the sacks?" they'd shout.

"Clothes," they'd answer.

"We'll buy them both," came the reply.

Then the strangers would make offers, sight unseen. Yakoff and Yossel would look at one another, shrug, politely refuse the offer and continue on their way. This happened several times and each time the price went up as they neared the city.

By the time they reached the outskirts of town they were being stopped every hundred yards or so. Small groups of people would form and actually bid blindly for items they'd never seen. The currency at the time was zlotys, each one having the equivalent of an American penny. When the price finally skyrocketed to three-thousand zlotys per bag, or thirty American dollars, they happily exchanged their burden for the much easier to carry folding money.

They were rich and anxious to enjoy the fruits of their labor. Krakow was a good-sized city and could provide any form of entertainment desired. A heavy population of Russian military personnel remained in the town and a wide-open, anything goes attitude prevailed. They were still celebrating the liberation and a party atmosphere was in abundance.

Yakoff found it unusually strange to not see German soldiers every which way he looked. For the first time in six years he didn't have to tip his cap, offer an insincere greeting, and step off the sidewalk into the street at the mere sighting of a uniform. After so long it was difficult to conceive, deep down, the war was really over and freedom was theirs.

The first order of the day? Food! They found a well-decorated and delightfully expensive restaurant near the center of the city. Being the worst-dressed of all the patrons inside mattered little. They had the funds to do whatever they wanted.

A middle-aged waiter with white hair haughtily approached their table. "Yes..." he asked, lifting his nose slightly at the unlikely customers.

"Food," Yakoff replied. He looked at Yossel and they both smiled and nodded. "We'd like some food."

The waiter made a grunting little noise and arrogantly handed them each a menu. Yakoff didn't notice the attitude, his mind was consumed with the foreign objects on the table in front of him. He'd never see a fork before and had no idea what its purpose might be. The only eating utensil he'd ever used was a spoon and he was even more confused because there were two of those.

Assuming the most expensive item would provide the most amount of food they each ordered the largest steak on the menu which was precede by a bottle of wine. The vintage grape helped loosen their attitude of uneasiness and soon they were having the time of their lives. There were plans to make, things to be done, lives to be lived. Women, Yossel added. Yakoff nodded noncommittally.

The arrival of the food brought another great surprise. Neither of the had ever seen a piece of meat this large and were quite uncertain as to exactly what to do with it. The potatoes alongside provided no problem but the steak was an entirely different matter. Not wishing to make total fools of themselves, they watched nearby patrons to see how they handled the situation. They all seemed to be using the long handled device with the prongs on the end.

Why not they deduced, and proceeded to mimic those sitting around them. First they tried to cut the steak with the fork. Ineffective. Then they speared the meat with their forks and tried to cut it with their spoons. Even worse. Yakoff had never used a knife at a table before and that added to the confusion. The waiter stood in the doorway by the kitchen, shaking his head, justifying his arrogance.

Finally, out of a combination of frustration and hunger, Yakoff said "the hell with it" and picked up the slab of meat with both hands. People seated nearby expressed shock and then amusement as the youngsters devoured the meal. Without trying or even being aware of it, their antics provided the entertainment for the rest of the diners.

Their plates were left spotless. Deprivation of food for so long created a genuine attitude that it was a sin to leave anything on your plate. That was something that just wasn't done. Ever.

They left the restaurant with their stomachs satisfied and their pockets still lined with money. The night and the streets were filled with excitement at every turn. Yossel made the suggestion they find some girls, an easy task, and then go have another drink.

At first the idea sounded wonderful. Girls, fun, someone to be with.

Then Yakoff remembered the sleepless night with Mina and Miriam and his inability to perform, to satisfy, to even react. The memory was clear and painful. They hadn't rejected him; quite the contrary. He had rejected himself. His own body had refused the greatest stimulation known to man. And, he sadly concluded, the likelihood of repetition was probable. It was an indefinable depth of anguish he didn't want to feel or experience again.

"No," he said, looking straight ahead. "It's been a long day already and we've got another one coming up. Let's just find a room and get some rest."

Yossel looked at him, clearly not understanding but chose not to question or challenge. "Is it Marsha?" he finally asked, with complete honesty and sincerity.

Marsha, Yakoff thought. Marsha. She was probably dead by now. And even if miraculously she might still be alive, there was no possible way of ever finding her. He wished in the instant before he answered Yossel's question, he'd told her about his operation. It was too late now.

"Yes," he finally said concealing the truth, "it's Marsha."

Chapter XIX

"What!? Where!?"

"Over in 7. By your bunk."

Yakoff ran the full-width of the camp as fast as possible. The news was something he'd never expected to hear. He honestly couldn't believe it was true. Through the door. Up the stairs, three at a time. Around the corner. There they were.

Leon, his cousin, and Heim Berkovich, another graduate of the brick-layers' school, sprang from the bunk greeting Yakoff with open arms and massive hugs. They were alive! They'd survived!

Like Yakoff they escaped during the march, waited in hiding for the Russian front to pass, and then worked their way back to Bielsko, a town thirty miles southwest of Auschwitz. Without background or experience they'd both obtained jobs as local policemen. Somehow word had gotten to them Yakoff was still alive and had returned to the camp, so here they were, to take him away to the easy life they'd discovered on the outside.

At last. A place to go, something to do, a sense of direction. Yakoff made another quick visit to the Canada warehouse to load up with some more clothing to sell. Leon and Heim laughed hysterically when they saw him toting the two large sacks, one over each shoulder. "You won't need that stuff, " they said. "We're living like kings."

Their description was accurate. The apartment was beautiful. It was originally occupied and furnished by Polish people, displaced by the Germans who evacuated less than a month ago leaving everything intact, right down to the exquisite paintings on the walls. It was large with three full sized bedrooms, a formal dining room and a parlor over-looking the train station on the other side of the street.

Leon and Heim had a third male roommate, also a policeman and three young girls lived with them. The girls, all attractive, did the cooking and cleaning and provided the nucleus for the nightly parties which usually lasted till dawn. Then couples would pair off and sleeping arrangements were rather indiscriminate with no one really much caring who slept with whom.

It was a wild time with most everyone grasping at any imaginable thrill and trying to jam excitement into every possible moment. The girls had several friends who regularly frequented the parties and made both themselves and their favors available to Yakoff. The first couple of nights he used the excuse he was too tired. Then he'd drink, using the overacted ploy of drunkenness to avoid their crystal-clear advances. Finally he started to stay out at night, drinking with friendly Russian soldiers in neighborhood bars until either the party was over or everyone had fallen asleep.

Leon and the others, especially the girls, often wondered why Yakoff avoided the open and casual sexual atmosphere. Fortunately no one ever asked and Yakoff never offered. His feelings of inadequacy and worthlessness as a man grew inside him like a raging cancer, destroying his mind and logic. Watching his friends having fun and enjoying themselves only served to deepen his own personal sorrow.

After a week and a half he knew he had to get away. There were places to go and questions he had to try to find answers for. Heim, his closest friend from the camp, felt the same burning emptiness and want for information. Together they set out on a journey they hoped would be filled with discovery.

The train, as well as the station, was jammed with people all trying to get somewhere else. Military personnel had priority over civilians and travel arrangements were difficult to make. Heim returned from the ticket counter and sadly informed Yakoff the train heading north was sold out, there were no available seats.

"We're going north," Yakoff said, grabbing his friend's sleeve, dragging him on the overcrowded train. They shuffled through people blocking the aisles until they found a compartment, first class no less, with two empty seats. When the conductor arrived, Yakoff handed him the pink card with the Russian written all over it. The man, also a Russian, read it carefully, returned it and then bowed politely wishing the traveler and his companion a good trip and a safe journey.

The once beautiful countryside was potted and pockmarked from bombs and massive ground battles. Small towns along the way had been virtually destroyed, some burned to the ground by the Germans as they fled. Refugees and displaced persons lined the tracks begging for anything, mostly food. Each mile made it more apparent the entire country was not in the midst of celebration.

On and on the train rolled, stopping frequently, picking up a few, letting off a few. It took two days to cover the two hundred and fifty miles. Heim was nodding, nearly asleep, but Yakoff's eyes were wide open and filled with anticipation when the conductor's voice bellowed through the hallway, "Next stop ... Sierpc."

The station was the same as Yakoff remembered, light blue with white gingerbread trim. Where usually his father had the only horse-drawn carriage there were now three or four, along with some motor-cars. Memories were bittersweet.

The moonless sky provided a much needed cover for the rest of their journey. It was a combination of childhood reflection as well as reliable rumors which led them through the back roads and away from the street lights. Jewish people, once terribly unpopular, were now openly hated and resented. It wasn't safe to be on the street at night and not much better during the day. Jews tried to hide their identity and avoided any contact with gentiles whenever possible.

They walked without speaking around the lake where older children used to throw rocks at Yakoff. In the distance he could see the hospital. The bombed-out wing had not been replaced. The public school was on their left, a building Jewish children never went near. Never. They passed the drugstore where Yakoff first functioned as an interpreter during the initial wave of German soldiers. All was quiet now.

Across the bridge, up the hill he'd climbed every day as a child, past the huge greystone apartment building and there it was–his old house, smaller than it seemed six years ago; more weather-beaten but still standing. There were no lights and it appeared to be empty but the risk of going inside was too great. He just wanted to see the place again.

The Germans had created a ghetto just up the hill and they decided to enter through the rear gate, probably the safest path to take. Yakoff's heart was saddened when he saw the synagogue where he was barmitzvahed, now boarded up, empty, never used. And across the street was the still-empty lot where once the largest synagogue in town held services. He could still see the ashes, a result of the Nazi and Gestapo torches.

They were shocked when they crawled over the rear fence of the ghetto. It was virtually deserted. They searched from house to empty house until they finally found a family of four, huddled in a second-story apartment.

They were fearful for their lives, fearful that Yakoff and his friend were the dreaded Polish underground, coming to torture and kill them.

Six years ago nearly twelve thousand Jews lived on this side of the river. Now there were less than one hundred. They were all gone. Most probably dead.

Yakoff didn't know the people so he asked for directions to find some of the others in hiding. He had to find out if any of his friends had survived.

The next apartment they went to was dark so they muffled their knock at the door. There was no answer.

"I'm Yakoff Skurnik," he whispered. "I grew up here in Sierpc and..."

The door opened before he could speak another word. Both Yakoff and the man standing in the doorway were speechless. Then...

"I didn't think you made it," the man said.

"I didn't think you did either," Yakoff replied. They hugged, their faces filled with disbelief. Then Yakoff introduced him to Heim. It was Yosel Reicholz, the man he'd escaped from the German train with, the second man through the window.

Of the few remaining Jews in Sierpc, no one could provide any information about friends or distant relatives. They did explain the Polish underground, the A. K., had pacted among themselves to execute as many Russians, Communists and Jews as possible. Travel was dangerous, discovery was lethal. They had to be careful.

Heim's hometown was forty miles to the northwest. The results of that visit were much the same as it was in Sierpc. The handful of Jews still alive could offer none of the assistance or information Heim was seeking. They were both fed well, shelter was provided, and early the following morning their journey continued.

Again the train was supposedly filled to capacity and again the pink card from the Russian Major provided free and unquestioned passage. This was a short trip, a half day, only seventy-five miles. On approaching their final destination the entire assemblage of passengers grew incredibly silent. The sight through the soot-stained windows was awesome, breathtaking in the most negative sense imaginable.

The city of Warsaw, as far as the naked eye could see, was flat. Countless Allied bombing raids, the ghetto uprising, followed by weeks of heavy German shelling and self-destruction by the Jews held captive within the infamous Warsaw wall, had virtually leveled every single building which formerly made up the huge inner city. It was absolute rubble, total destruction.

They'd heard about the uprising, when a small but incredibly brave contingency of Jews finally decided to fight back. Their hearts swelled with pride at the scattered, piecemeal bits of news about others like themselves, historically passive people who finally decided they'd had enough and were going to die fighting, rather than just die. They'd even heard reports of great destruction within the city, but nothing like this. The city didn't exist anymore. It was gone.

Yakoff was intimately familiar with the streets of Warsaw, he knew them like the back of his hand. This came as a result of spending nearly two years there in the ghetto. Two years of hunger, two years of forced labor at the hands of the Germans without pay of any kind. This was before Auschwitz and provided the education in survival that helped him stay alive.

But now, even the streets weren't discernible. There was nothing except a huge, endless, flat pile of brick and stone. Nothing moved. There was no life or even a sign of it. A slight breeze through the rubble created an eerie, misty cloud which hovered just off the ground and waved ever so slightly, announcing to the silent passengers that the earth below was one giant unmarked grave.

The city of Praga, actually a suburb of Warsaw, was due east of the river Wista, the same peaceful waterway which brought Yakoff and his classmates here so many years ago. The wide channel once teeming with industry and travel was quiet and practically deserted. The crystal-clear blue water Yakoff remembered had turned mournfully into a dull and murky reddish-grey, the tragic result of the winter rains washing lingering dust through streets and over the banks. Yakoff momentarily questioned the reddish hue. Was it really a by-product of bombed and broken bricks or was it actually the blood of tens of thousands of fellow Jews?

The visit to Praga was necessitated because the town had a Jewish community center. Its primary function was to provide information services for survivors looking for relatives or friends. It was seldom a happy place.

"I'm Yakoff Skurnik," he finally said after waiting in line nearly two hours. "Has anyone inquired about me?"

The elderly woman behind the well-worn desk began to flip through pages of a large ledger. The size of the journal was optimistically deceptive. The few sheets it contained were only partially filled.

"No," she said. "No one yet." Her eyes were filled with compassion and understanding, even after delivering this same depressing message hundreds of times. The volunteer's empathy was understandable. She too was the sole survivor from her own large family.

"I have two sisters who stayed behind after our transport left. Maybe they..."

The kind-eyed lady nodded, she knew the rest of the sentence.

"What are their names?"

"Also Skurnik. Henia and Mania."

She repeated the searching process and once again looked up sadly into Yakoff's hopeful eyes.

"I'm sorry," was all she could offer. She recorded Yakoff's name as well as where and how anyone could get in touch with him. He thanked her for her time and also for trying, then quietly exited the building.

The last time he'd seen his two older sisters was the night his family was forced at gunpoint into the transport. Henia and Mania were strong minded and refused to leave, choosing instead to stay behind, take their chances and fend for themselves in the ghetto. When the Nazis came pounding on the door, the two girls were safely hidden.

Yakoff imagined they'd probably been alive until the very last. That's the kind of people they were. They were fighters and more than likely stayed alive and actually participated in the uprising. But when the German artillery began their heavy shelling and leveled the city, there was only a handful of survivors left to relate the truth about what happened.

Hope was a primary motivation which superseded logic. Faith was believing in something you couldn't see. Trust was a fading glimmer that there was still some justice left in the world. And the realistic probability of either one of them still being alive was unlikely.

Telephone service and mail delivery were nonexistent. Messages and letters were transported by people traveling both to and from various and assorted destinations. It was a crude system but seemed to work. Its efficiency was predicated on a bond between the survivors. People who had shared and experienced the worst mass tragedy of mankind would reach out to others, asking nothing in return and do anything they possibly could to help.

They'd seen all there was to see and done all they could do in Warsaw. It was time to move on. Their discovery-seeking mission had provided little insight. It mostly served to clarify a grim and bleak portrait as to how desperate things really were.

The two day train ride back to Bielsko was silent, reflective. Both Yakoff and Heim anticipated being in the presence of friends again. They each felt a strange psychological dependence on being around and with others who understood and shared what they'd experienced and managed to live through. The prospect of seeing even a few recognizable faces gave the return trip a homecoming feeling.

That sensation, like so many previous feelings, was short-lived. The train station was still packed with people desperate for a chance to leave. The milling throng spilled outside to the front of the station and then into the street, making their exit slow and hazardous. It was while they were weaving through the crowd Yakoff noticed it. At first he thought it was a welcoming sign, then it occurred to him it was actually quite the opposite. Two of the girls who lived in the apartment were standing in the parlor window waving their arms wildly. Yakoff grabbed Heim's sleeve and they both stopped dead in their tracks.

Through the crowd and across the street they could see three men waiting at the main entrance of the apartment. Yakoff had seen many men like these before and experience in this regard provided a lesson well learned and long remembered. The men were plain-clothes Polish policemen and it was unlikely they were passing out civic awards.

It was more probable someone had discovered or suspected Jews were living in the building and the police were there to arrest first and question later. The girls' frantic waving prevented them from walking into the middle of a trap.

Without hesitation or discussion they turned around and reentered the train station. "What'll we do now?" Heim whispered, a clear resonance of panic in his voice.

"We have no choice but to leave." With Yakoff it was matter-of-fact. When in doubt ... flee. His freedom was a precious commodity, the only one he had left, and he wasn't about to jeopardize it for something as insignificant as idle curiosity.

Heim, with few other options, stayed with Yakoff as he reentered the next available train which happened to be heading north toward Katovitz. The magic pink card and Yakoff's bravado provided all that was necessary for their passage. It was a short ride so instant decisions had to be made. Yakoff, not knowing a soul, said he was going to remain in Katovitz for awhile. Heim chose to stay on the train and head north with no particular destination in mind.

The two parted, vowing somehow to meet again. Where, when, or how, at this moment in time, was impossible to determine. Yakoff waited, watching until the train faded in the distance. The station was not unlike the one in Bielsko. There were people everywhere, pushing, shoving, moving about. Even in this wall-to-wall mass of humanity the same thing occurred again. The same thoughts, the same feelings, the same everything. Yakoff was alone, completely alone.

The town had a large concentration of Jews, most of them underground or in hiding, wisely refusing to publicly acknowledge their religious beliefs. The Polish animosity and nighttime retribution created a fine line on which the Jews had to walk. The situation was tense. As a precaution, Yakoff obtained some Russian clothing, an overcoat, shirt and pants from a friendly soldier in Bielsko. These along with his black leather boots and his fluency in Russian provided a highly workable cover. It was generally safe for him to walk the streets.

There were three in the group standing on the street corner. They looked safe enough, but it was unwise as well as dangerous to blindly trust anyone. Yakoff approached the trio with a confident spring in his walk and stopped barely three feet in front of them.

"Amchu..." he said. The delivery was bland, flat, without emotion. It was a Hebrew word, widely used as a signal among and between Jewish people, much the same as the Christian sign of the fish in earlier days of persecution.

The three stared back at Yakoff without acknowledging his disguised message of friendship. It was quiet on the street. He repeated the word and still received no response. It was as if they were deaf-mutes, not understanding or comprehending his ovation.

He shrugged and was about to walk away when he noticed their faces for the first time. They were each covered with an aura of fear. Subtle but certainly there, even in the dim light of the street lamp. Without speaking they began to move in the opposite direction, away from Yakoff.

Finally it came to him and he ran until he caught up. "I'm not Russian," he said. "Or Polish. I got these clothes as a disguise." There was still no response. Finally, "I'm a Jew..." It was a rather brave announcement to be making to total strangers but Yakoff was playing a strong hunch. The consequence of being wrong could have been fatal. They still offered no comment.

"What's the matter with you guys? Talk to me."

Nothing.

"Are you afraid to tell the truth or ashamed to be Jewish or what?"

They stopped in their tracks and the smallest of the three finally spoke.

"How do we know you're telling the truth?" The voice was cold, untrusting and the emphasis was on the word, "you're."

Slowly, making sure they could all see, Yakoff raised the left sleeve of his overcoat to his elbow. Once they saw the number on his forearm, no further words were necessary. But the smaller man offered one, just one. "Amchu."

Over coffee and vodka in an all-night restaurant, the four shared stories and got to know one another. Hershel Prengler and his younger brother Israel, had been in hiding for more than two years. They'd lived in basements and brickyards, only coming out at night to find scraps of food or steal fresh vegetables from nearby farms. Completely surrounded by the German army for the entire duration, they watched helplessly as tens of thousands of fellow Jews were carted away to their destruction. Miraculously they'd managed to avoid capture. Sunlight, after not seeing it for so long, was a much appreciated treat.

Their companion, strangely enough, was a Polish gentile who'd been traveling with them since the Russian army pushed the Germans back. Yakoff found their friend to be understanding toward their cause as well as their constant state of peril, but still couldn't force himself to trust the man completely. Too many gentiles had turned too many Jews over to too many Germans. It somehow never quite made sense.

There were two others in their group, Hershel reported, who were waiting at a room in a boarding house down the street. A major meeting between all six followed and the first determination was that Katovitz was not a safe place to be. The Russians were pulling out, leaving the Poles in charge again and their attitude was considerably less than receptive. The second determination concerned where they might possibly go without being constantly challenged or questioned.

"I had a long, detailed talk with a Russian Major," Yakoff said. "He told me Stalin had literally opened the doors of the Russian prisons and told the inmates if they could make it to Berlin they could have the city." The intense fear and paranoia felt toward the Russians was perpetrated much more by these convicted and released prisoners than by the regular army. Their ferocity both on and off the battle field was a sight never before seen.

"The point is," Yakoff continued, "if we follow the Russians from a reasonably safe distance, by the time we get to Berlin the city should be wide-open and we can do whatever we want. Those guys will run both the Germans and the Poles out of town and we should have free reign." The plan made sense and was agreed to unanimously. The only remaining question was how to get there. Yakoff pacified their uncertainty with two words, "Trust me."

The train station, like all the others, was filled to capacity. "Stay close," Yakoff said. "And just look like you know where you're going." It was easier said than done. The five friends were following a complete stranger and in the middle of a potentially volatile situation. They were all, with the exception of Yakoff, extremely uncomfortable with both where they were and what they were doing.

He led them onto the train and settled into a private compartment. Hushed whispers and guarded reservations grew to outlandish proportion with, "You're out of your mind," and "You're gonna' get us all killed." A wave of his hand and a "Don't worry about it," did little to relieve their anxiety.

The conductor opened the door and five of the six felt with a certainty they were on their way to prison. There was an abundance of sweat within the small room. Like he did it everyday, Yakoff handed the pink card to the conductor and added, "These men are traveling with me." The ticket taker nodded, smiled politely and wished them all a good trip.

Yakoff's new friends were speechless as well as highly impressed. They all examined the card but of course none could read Russian so its true meaning and impact wasn't understood. It'd done the job and that's all that mattered. Before the train reached full-speed their door opened again and a young Russian officer stood blocking the way. He stared at Yakoff and the others with a " you're in my seat" kind of look which was accompanied by a low menacing growl. Five pairs of eyes looked at the floor, expecting the worst. Yakoff stood, faced the man and handed him the card.

Without hesitation the officer excused himself, but not before apologizing for the interruption and inconvenience. Smiles filled the room for the duration of the trip.

After a hundred miles the pattern of the engine began to change. They were slowing down in the middle of nowhere. There was nothing but open fields in all directions. A few minutes later the conductor entered, telling them the bridge up ahead had been bombed out. They were going to have to walk several miles, crossing a suspended foot-bridge in the process, to get to the next town.

This was not an uncommon situation. It had happened on many previous trips and complaint about anything this insignificant would have proven to be a worthless and futile endeavor. The passengers quietly and orderly exited the train and began their trek through the chilly, late winter air.

Their first real sighting in the far-off distance was a greyish-black, low cloud covering. It hung to the ground like a protective blanket, both sides clearly defined. Others more experienced with the terrain and territory explained the thick mist up ahead was lingering over the city of Breslau.

The city was large from a comparative standpoint with a population of over two-hundred and fifty-thousand. But that was before the war. The Jews, which accounted for nearly a third of the total, were all gone. Trains, trucks and forced marches took them to various concentration camps within the newly occupied Poland where virtually all of them perished under Nazi rule.

As they approached the once mighty and vital city they could see the black hanging cloud was actually smoke. The Russians had moved through only days before and the town was still smouldering and burning. Tall buildings, even entire sections had been leveled, but nothing like Warsaw. Nothing could compare to that. The conquering army had attacked faster than expected and forced the Germans to flee before they could execute their mindless acts of destruction. The result, thankfully, was the majority of the city was left standing and intact.

There was a general atmosphere of confusion. The remaining German civilians were in hiding or at least staying well out of the way. The Poles acted and moved like sheep at the sight of a military uniform and Russians were everywhere. They could be seen on nearly every street corner, celebrating their recent victory, downing glass after glass of vodka. The rumors preceding the arrival of the Russians had a vast sweeping effect in keeping the women and children off the streets.

Yakoff, Hershel and the others determined quickly the place had a good feel. It exhibited all the wide-open characteristics they were expecting to find in Berlin. "Why not..." was their combined attitude and they decided to stay for a few days and see what, if anything, they could put together.

Living accommodations were beyond what any of them had ever dreamed. They walked into the downtown section of the city to the corner of Rossentraus and Thirty-sixth Street where they found a delightfully preserved apartment building. It was six stories high with two apartments per floor, each exquisitely decorated and totally deserted. The previous occupants left in such a hurry all of the refrigerators still contained an abundance of fresh food. One of the residences even had a meal fully prepared and waiting on an antique dining room table.

One-half of the ground floor level housed a bakery that had been closed for awhile. There was a thick layer of dust on the inside of the large picture window. Even so, as the group squinted to see through, it appeared all the equipment was intact.

Their timing happened to be exact and all but the doors on the first floor were unlocked. After a brief discussion concerning their good fortune, each of the six selected their own huge apartment, carefully secured the doors behind themselves and retired for the night.

The next morning on their way to find some breakfast they discovered the building was not theirs alone. A German couple and several relatives quietly occupied the first floor apartment. Yakoff, dressed and looking like a Russian, stood in the background with his arms folded across his chest, an authoritative position. Hershel, not fluent but at least partially conversant, interrogated the man and his wife in their native tongue.

They discovered the man owned the bakery. Yakoff pulled Hershel aside and a plan was quickly devised. Yakoff would pretend to be a Russian, Hershel would interpret in German and they would officially commandeer the building, the bakery, and force the German to run it for them.

That was fine with the German, he'd be thrilled to get back to work. The problem he explained, and the reason the bakery was closed, was he had no supplies. It was impossible for him to obtain necessary ingredients like flour and sugar.

Yakoff made a comment in Russian.

"What?" Hershel said not understanding.

With his arms still folded across his chest and without changing expression Yakoff switched to Yiddish, "Tell him it's alright. Tell him we'll provide the supplies."

Hershel gave him a look, a mixture of despair and confusion. "Tell him," Yakoff repeated. So he did.

The German's face filled with joy and he excitedly pumped everyone's hand, being most appreciative as well as cautious with Yakoff, whom he believed was now his captor.

Later when the group questioned Yakoff about how he intended to find and then obtain the baker's ingredients, he casually replied, "I don't know but they're around here somewhere and we'll find them." The group shook their heads in disbelief, chorusing the impossibility of such a task. It was attitude as far as Yakoff was concerned. He knew it could be done, he just didn't quite know how. Plus, his new friends hadn't had the opportunity to watch the Gypsy at work. They fortunately had missed seeing Yakoff procure items of equal impossibility within the singing wires of Auschwitz.

Two doors down from their building, was a sign openly proclaiming its occupant: The Temporary Office of the Russian Counterintelligence Agency. Their function, now that the German army had been run out, was to discover, interrogate and imprison any Nazis or Third Reich members who remained in hiding. Their tactics were callous, their methods brutal, and they were effective in getting the job done.

Yakoff came to know the captain in charge of the office in a rather oblique manner. Girls, both German and Polish, were constantly seeking safe haven at night. Finding six young men alone in a large, well-furnished apartment building proved to be a gold mine in security for countless young women. With their arrival came the nightly parties and Yakoff again found himself psychologically forced back into the streets and bars.

He drank with the Russians, talked with the Russians, got to know them and vice-versa. One night when Yakoff confided to a nearly inebriated sergeant that he had escaped from Auschwitz, the sergeant took him to the office and introduced him to his captain.

After a brief but explicitly detailed conversation about his experiences in the camp..." So you hate the Nazis, huh?"

The question was redundant. Yakoff merely stared at the older man.

"Ever feel a desire to get back at them? To get even?"

The stare continued over thoughts of his family and friends, innocent victims of an unnecessary and perverse insanity, lives wasted and more. There was no possible way to get even Yakoff thought. None. A boiling began down deep in his stomach. The anger, which sometimes rested but never went away, was returning in full force. Visions of their apartment building filled with attractive young women eager to experience the ways of the world flashed through his mind. And while those other normal young men enjoyed life to the fullest, Yakoff found himself drinking with Russian soldiers, embarrassed, despondent, unable to satisfy a woman in the slightest degree. The stare was cold and hard. He nodded "yes" in reply to the captain's questions.

Yakoff was given special identification papers confirming he was working for the Russian Counterintelligence Agency, a nine-shot pistol and a permit to carry it. He was in business–a Nazi hunter. In addition to providing a deep sense of satisfaction, it also established the perfect reason, alibi, and excuse to spend his nights on the street and away from their apartment.

Sexual desire and motivation was still in abundance. That's a matter of the mind and even the heart. It was the lack of ability to transfer the mental to the physical which was so devastating. He tried once with a beautiful young girl, Polish, probably no more than eighteen. His mind was on fire, a passion he'd never felt before. The girl was equally ready and willing.

This time it went so far as bed. But even lying in the arms of a beautiful, naked young woman, and mentally trying as hard as he could, the arousal he so desperately desired would not occur. Crushed again, embarrassed, depressed, he excused himself saying he had work that was bothering him and had to be done.

He dressed and silently left her alone in his room. That night, as he followed up Russian leads and awoke people to question them about names and addresses of Third Reich members, he wasn't only looking for Nazis; he was looking for Doctor Doering, the man responsible for keeping him awake this night and all the others.

Chapter XX

The German baker was growing politely impatient for something to do, so Yakoff visited the Russian motor pool and asked to see the officer in charge. After sharing his highly impressive credentials he quietly proposed an off-the-record transaction. "Let me use one of your trucks and we'll give you a percentage of the profits."

Not only did the officer agree, he also threw in a driver and an armed guard. The next day, with Yakoff providing directions, they arrived at a warehouse which was taken over by the Russians. The same deal was proposed, accepted, and the truck was filled to capacity with flour and sugar.

That night the baker and his family worked the ovens as fast and as much as possible. Before dawn word spread and a line of customers trailed its way completely around the side of the building. The bonanza and instant success was clearly a result of the fact that this bakery, the one Yakoff and the others now owned, was the only working business of its kind in Breslau.

No one could figure out how they were doing it or where they were getting their supplies. Concern from others was irrelevant, the reality remained that fresh bread was being produced on a twenty-four hour a day basis and record profits were being accrued. Even so, the demand far outweighed the supply. Ingredients were being stockpiled and the major problem facing the group was how to increase their productivity.

Expansion was the simple and economic solution so they took over two more bakeries in different parts of the city. They were both, understandably, instant successes. The members of the group were entrepreneurs, they were successful, they had more money than they could possibly spend. Banks were nonexistent so paper bags stuffed full of cash were kept in the apartment building. Their new-found wealth created an even larger abundance of women.

The businesses, provided they had the necessary supplies, literally ran themselves. All Yakoff and the others had to do was deliver the flour and pick up the money. The Germans running the bakeries wouldn't have considered cheating or holding back income from their new owners. They each felt their lives would be placed in jeopardy if they ever did such a thing. Their feelings and concerns were probably accurate, but fortunately for all of the involved parties, were never put to question or a true test.

Yakoff grew bored and began to spend more and more of his time with the counterintelligence people. It got to the point where it became an obsession. And why not, he argued, why the hell not? What else did he have to do?

"You're gonna' like this one." The captain's voice was serious, not a trace of humor. He straightened a ribboned hammer and sickle medal over the left breast pocket of his jacket. "We got an eyewitness who was a prisoner at the camp where she worked. Said she was one mean bitch."

"SS officer?" Yakoff asked, showing no emotion or feeling one way or the other.

The captain nodded. "Been holed up here about two weeks. Only leaves her apartment to get food."

This time Yakoff nodded and turned to leave the office. "Yakoff," the captain said, "the fact she's a woman don't mean shit. She's a killer. Mostly women and children. And she's sure as hell not above killing you to escape again."

"She got a gun?"

"Probably." There was a long pause. "Be careful."

Yakoff took two uniformed Russian privates with him. They were on permanent assignment and Yakoff, by action and edict was the group leader.

The second floor hallway was dark and empty. It was also very quiet. When they silently turned the door knob of the woman's apartment it was locked. Yakoff held his forefinger to his lips and pressed his ear against the door. After a long moment of silence he whispered to the others, "Someone's in there. I heard something move." He stood away from the door and drew his pistol.

One of the stocky Russians lifted his leg and with a mighty thrust kicked the door down. The three rushed in with weapons drawn and caught the startled woman sitting alone on her couch. She jumped to her feet and looked desperately around the room, trying to find a path of escape.

"Don't move," Yakoff shouted. The woman was surrounded. There was panic in her face. Yakoff spoke in German, loud and very clearly.

"We've been informed you're an officer in the SS..."

"And a coward," one of the Russians added.

Yakoff silenced the man with a wave of his hand. "We're taking you to the office for interrogation."

The woman had heard about the tactics used during interrogation sessions and knew their results firsthand from those she'd conducted herself.

"No!" she screamed. "I'm not! I wasn't! I didn't!" Her eyes glazed with a fiery rage and her cheeks became scarlet. The panic and fear turned instantly to hate which had festered like an unattended sore for the entirety of her lifetime. She made a sudden lunge toward Yakoff and was stopped instantly as the butt from one of the Russian rifles met her squarely in the face. Blood exploded from her nose and gums as her teeth were loosened and her brain rattled. Both knees buckled and she slumped to the wooden floor. It was very different for her to be on the receiving end of pain.

They took her to the office, to a small room which contained three straight-backed chairs, and questioned her for more than two hours. She was strong, that was for sure, and persisted in her denial of any involvement with the SS. She had no papers or identification and was caught several times in the web of her own lies. She was not informed of her rights–she didn't have any.

The Russians wanted to assist in the process, little things like breaking one finger at a time, or fire applied directly to the soles of her feet, but Yakoff held them back with a classic good guy—bad guy routine. The uniformed soldiers wanted her to talk, to confess, so they could chalk one more off their list and ship her away. Yakoff wanted more than that. Much more.

Her hands were tied behind her back and she was taken downstairs into the basement. It was dark and dingy with a sickening aroma left behind by previous prisoners. Yakoff got a musty, slimy feeling all over each time he descended the creaky wooden stairs. The decision not to eradicate the rat population was on purpose.

They led her past several empty cells to the far wall and a four-by-four windowless room, amounting to little more than a stark, barren closet. The bench and walls were damp and slippery to the touch. When the Russians untied the woman, Yakoff was careful to remove the belt from her dress and her scarf. Captured Nazis had a tendency of killing themselves and he didn't want this one to get away. Then they locked the door behind her, leaving her completely alone as they returned to the first floor to wait.

A deck of cards and a bottle of vodka were produced and the trio started to work on both of them, drinking steadily, dealing slowly, taking their time. They had nothing better to do and the lady downstairs wasn't going anywhere.

Yakoff laid the three of diamonds on top of the pile and thought about his prisoner. She was probably in her mid-forties, not much older than his own mother would have been if...

"Play the card Yakoff, it's your turn." The Russian to his left brought him back to the reality of who the woman really was. She probably had a husband somewhere, more than likely children, regular visits to church with accompanying beliefs were also likely. None of that mattered. She was a trained killer, disciplined in the ways of delivering pain, misery and prolonged agony. She had both the mentality and ability to pat her own children on the head, kiss them on the cheek and send them off to school. Then, moments later, she could abuse Jewish children with anything from kicks in the face to white-hot branding irons on their frail little bodies. Then she'd march them, while she laughed, to the showers. That's who she really was.

She couldn't see the rats but she could hear them. Chirping noises behind the wall and scurrying, scratching sounds on the floor in front of her feet. They were used to human beings and mostly went about their business as if the closet was still unoccupied. In the dark she hadn't seen as one of the soldiers reached into his pocket and left a handful of bread crumbs on the floor, specifically designed to draw the well-fed rodents to this area.

One of them brushed past her leg. It was wet and slimy. She screamed and the three men at the card table smiled. Things were going well. Another rat, larger and braver, took a nip out of the woman's ankle and she screamed again, this time much louder. More smiles.

They left her alone for three hours; time to think, time to reflect. She felt a great sense of relief when she heard footsteps coming down the stairs and the slimy creatures disappeared back into the walls.

The soldiers intimidated, threatening the worst kinds of torture and extensive sexual abuse, but the woman through a floodgate of tears, continued her denial. Finally Yakoff, again playing the good guy, stepped in and asked the Russians to leave, but not before one of them restocked the rodent food supply in the corner.

"Look," Yakoff said softly. "I can't hold these guys off much longer.

They just want to kill you and have it over."

"But I ..."

"You know about the Russians. They don't care what they do to you. The woman continued to sob and Yakoff pretended to be sympathetic toward her plight.

"There might be one thing..." He toyed with the words as if they were spoken for the first time. He was teasing her, playing with her mind and her life.

"Yes..." she whispered, drawing out the word. "What is it?"

"They know you're SS but it's not really you they want." She listened. He'd struck an attentive chord. "If you'll give them the names..."

"No!" she screamed. "I can't. I don't know any!"

Yakoff turned to leave. "Fine," he said, like it was no big deal to him. "It's your life."

With one foot out the door, "Wait..." He turned back around. "I can't help you but ... what's your proposition?" She was taking the bait. Now it was only a matter of time.

"They want the names of ten SS officers and where they can find them. If you help and this can be accomplished, I promise you'll be set free and no one will bother you again."

He could hear her breathing pattern increase. It was a gasping which lasted for over a minute. Finally she whispered in the darkness, "I can't..."

He closed the door, locked it and before he reached the top of the stairs the rats had returned along with the screaming.

The shorter of the two Russians won the bet as to how long it'd be before she finally broke. It was two ticks shy of half an hour. In her quest to obtain freedom, she went beyond the required number of names and provided the whereabouts of twelve Nazis in hiding.

Before the sun rose the following morning all twelve had been arrested and filled the cells in the basement of the office. The criteria for their correctness in determining Nazi war criminals, was whether or not those captured would lead them to others in exchange for their freedom.

Once the dozen were safely incarcerated and each refused to cooperate or talk, the woman was released from the closet. The accused were now facing their accuser and the female Nazi was in a most uncomfortable position. She turned to Yakoff and whispered, "You promised..."

Yakoff said nothing. He stared at the twelve killers in the cage. Their bravado and stature was totally stripped along with the black uniforms they once so proudly wore.

"You promised," she repeated, this time with a frenzy in her voice. Still silent, Yakoff opened the door to the main cell and pushed the woman inside. He felt no remorse or sympathy for the woman's predicament. If they killed her, they killed her. It didn't matter to him one way or the other. His plan had worked. Instead of beating or torturing one confession of involvement from one individual he'd devised a method of entrapment which proved itself over and over. He kept the cells filled with Nazis eager to trade names and locations for their own freedom.

Their freedom was never granted. At least not by Yakoff. The captives who'd turned informant were marched to a gathering camp on the outskirts of town and held there until enough were accumulated to fill a well-guarded train.

Sometimes Yakoff would drive the horse and buggy which kept pace for the Nazi prisoners marching in front. The buggy was for those too sick or disabled to walk. It didn't matter. They all went to the camp and waited for the next available train to transport them to Siberia.

The captain in charge was more than pleased with Yakoff's performance as well as results. One day he even acknowledged Yakoff had done more for Russia than most Russians had. The compliment, while politely received, didn't mean anything. Nothing at all. Yakoff was doing what he was doing for a lot of different reasons, but Russia certainly wasn't one of them.

He helped track and capture the killer Nazis for his persecuted ancestors over the last two-thousand years. The loss of his family was a primary motivating factor. A reason to avoid the continual burning pain of being around seductive women added to his relentless drive. But mostly, he risked his life every time he arrested one of the murderers who used to wear the skull and crossbones because it felt good. There was an absolute sense of satisfaction each time one of them turned coward and exposed others in order to save their own lives.

He was efficient and competent at what he was doing. He was looked up to and respected. He was cold, calculating and successful. Personally responsible for capturing over two-hundred Germans hiding in basements and attics. The same Germans who'd rousted innocent Jews from their homes and marched them to the ovens.

But more than any of this came a feeling virtually nonexistent in his life. One he vaguely remembered from his early childhood. One he'd almost given up any hope for. Yakoff felt and experienced that vague mental concept known as freedom. Real, unrestricted, unqualified, unconditional freedom. That was the best part of it all.

It went on like this for nearly four months, night and day. The supply routes for flour and sugar remained open and all three bakeries continued to be incredibly successful, creating enormous profits. Other bakers in nearby cities bought their extra ingredients for even more sacks full of cash. The closets in their apartment building looked more like vaults in a bank.

Yakoff's antics and activities became widely known and many acquaintances from Auschwitz found their way to the Gypsy and his newfound life of luxury. It was common to find at least one of the ex-prisoners in the apartment at all times.

Nearly all the survivors were traveling from one place to another and completely uncertain about their future. Breslau, for awhile, was a safe place to be. They received shelter, in most cases the finest shelter they'd ever known, food in both volume and quality, and no one ever left without their pockets first being stuffed with money. Yakoff was overly generous in that regard and went out of his way to help those less fortunate than he.

The apartment building became a haven for wandering Jews. And the parties as well as the abundance of women was a highly unexpected plus. The travelers, even though most of them knew about Yakoff's operation in the camp, still wondered why he refused to participate in the nightlong festivities. They were aware of the operation itself but none were cognizant of the permanent effect on their host. It was a secret and a burden Yakoff chose to keep to himself. Still, to the man, they respected what he was doing with the counterintelligence agency and never openly questioned his selection of activities.

Yakoff returned to the apartment after spending all night at the gathering camp. He'd purposely waited until midmorning so most of the girls would be gone. The letter was left in the middle of his bed where he couldn't possibly miss it. He had to read it three times before he could truly comprehend or believe its contents.

Isaac, his friend from the Auschwitz laundry, sent the letter via a traveler who was passing through Breslau. There were the standard greetings and of course all about the things Isaac was doing, but the last paragraph was the one he read over and over. Not only did it clearly explain Marsha was alive and well, but it also listed her address in Lodz, a town barely seventy-five miles away.

He blinked at the news. His heart raced. She's alive and nearby. He screamed the news to the others in the building as he hastily packed a valise. Within fifteen minutes he was also carrying nearly fifty letters to be delivered to others; friends and relatives who were known to be in or around Lodz. His excitement was contagious; the rest of the group had heard the stories about Marsha many times and were thrilled at their friend's good news.

When the good-byes and good lucks were finished at the train station, the last thing Yakoff did was carefully check his pistol, making sure it was loaded. He showed his pink card to the conductor but by now the identification in his possession assured passage both whenever and wherever he wanted to go.

The ride was slow with several stops at smaller towns along the way. He vividly recalled every time they'd seen each other and every word they'd spoken in their hushed whispers. He wondered if she still remembered their quiet exchange during the momentary meeting alone, the phrase about "Out of this dough, bread will come." He wished now he'd told her about Doering and the operation. His thoughts carried him quietly into the blackness of the night.

It was late when he finally arrived and the station was nearly deserted, only a few tattered souls sleeping on the cement, waiting for the morning train. The streets outside were much the same except for an occasional Russian soldier drinking on the sidewalk. In time Yakoff found the directions he needed.

The address was a large three-sided complex with a courtyard in the middle and a padlocked iron gate to keep potential intruders out. After double checking the address in Isaac's letter he removed his pistol from the holster and shot the lock to oblivion. It was interesting, not one single light in the entire complex came on to see what the commotion was.

Once inside, finding the correct apartment number was an easy task. He took a deep breath, expanding his chest and could feel the perspiration forming in his armpits. Then with a mix of anxiety, confidence, uncertainty and excitement, he knocked on the door.

It was Marsha who answered and she looked wonderful. Her eyes were sparkling and her dark brown hair, now two inches long, was mostly covered by the white lace scarf Yakoff had given her. They stared for a moment then both began to smile, neither quite believing what they were seeing. Yakoff walked across the threshold with his arms extended and she returned the gesture. Tears flowed from her eyes as they hugged one another for only the second time in their lives. This time without a cautious ear listening for a warning cough. There was an unconscious refusal to let go as she kissed his neck and cheeks, over and over.

Finally satisfied the encounter was reality rather than a continuation of fantasies, she released her grasp but still held tightly to his hand. Another man was in the room and Marsha introduced him as an old and dear friend who looked out for and was taking care of her.

Her description of old was certainly apropos. The man appeared to be in his mid-fifties. He was pleasant and seemed genuinely concerned with Marsha's best interests. The three talked for hours explaining what they'd been doing for the last several months but Yakoff was reserved. He didn't say anything about the intelligence work he was doing or the fact the bakeries and other endeavors had made him virtually a rich man. He explained he lived in a nice apartment and had a business providing a comfortable living. This deletion of the real facts came after much forethought. He knew what he had to tell her before any decision of permanence could be made, and he also didn't want to affect that decision with his current life-styles, situation or circumstance.

Marsha would have to take him at face value, for what he was, not what he had. What he was, was unable to perform sexually or father children.

Finally all three retired with Yakoff sleeping on a cot in the kitchen. Sleep came slowly as he tossed and turned, trying to find the right sequence of words to properly explain the operation and his permanent situation to the girl he loved. Even after all he'd been through, tomorrow would be the roughest day of his life. The sun was starting to rise as he drifted off to sleep.

It seemed only a few moments later when a great commotion rattled him wideawake again. It was Marsha, dancing happily around the tiny kitchen preparing breakfast, making as much noise as possible, doing whatever she could to wake up her handsome prince.

When she saw the body twisting and the eyes open she ran to the side of the cot, knelt down and continued the hugging and kissing from the previous night. Yakoff was thrilled with the gesture as well as the outpouring of emotion. He passionately returned the embrace, finally feeling wanted, finally feeling loved. At that moment he would have been blissfully happy if time would stop completely, freezing them forever in each other's arms.

Breakfast was uncomfortable. It was long and tedious, filled with more idle conversation from Marsha's older friend. Yakoff pushed his food from side to side, wanting only to be alone, to talk and somehow explain his horrible secret. Marsha continued to express her happiness, alluding several times to how wonderful everything was going to be when the two of them returned to Breslau, got married and began a family. Yakoff forced a polite smile.

The sky was a crystal-clear pale blue, the picture postcard kind. It was uncommonly warm, even for the middle of July. As they walked down the busy street, other pedestrians would stare at Yakoff, wondering why on earth he was wearing a thick Russian overcoat, but of course no one had the nerve to actually stop and ask him. It was just as well. The overcoat, uncomfortable as it was, was warn solely to conceal the pistol on his hip.

They turned into a small, well-kept park and found a deserted bench near its middle. As they walked they held hands, each thinking and imagining they'd never let go. Occasionally they'd smile at one another without speaking, as if each was able to read the other's mind.

"Let's stop here," Yakoff said, pointing. It was peaceful and quiet, away from the sounds of the city. The trees and bushes were lush with a dark, velvet green. Miraculously this was a special place, somehow untouched by a war which ended only months ago. "We have to talk..."

Marsha smiled, sure the conversation was going to be about their future, filled with delightful plans for a lifetime of happiness.

"There's something you need to know which is important' " The serious tone in his voice erased her smile. Concern filled her face and she squinted her eyes.

Yakoff gulped silently and stared at the ground. He spoke very slowly, just above a whisper. "Please ... please don't talk or say anything until I've told you the whole story."

She studied the young man's grief-filled face and nodded. Yakoff let go of her hand, rubbed his eyes, took a deep breath and   began. He spoke clearly and in a monotone for nearly fifteen minutes. He explained from the beginning and in graphic detail, exactly what Doering had done to him. The only part he left out was the actual pain from and during the operation. He continued to look straight ahead rather than into her fragile and drawn face.

He didn't have to. He could hear her breathing grow irregular and could feel her body trembling beside him. He continued to stare at the ground and watched for a moment as her tears gently splashed on the pavement below. A tiny hand, motivated by deep compassion, reached out and tenderly touched his leg.

Well, he thought, the big part of the story's done. Now comes the worst part, the resultive part, the irreversible part. The part which hurts the most and won't ever go away.

"Sexually," he said, choking out the words, "I can't ever be any good to you." She didn't respond. She didn't have to. She understood. "I can't perform..." He wanted to finish the sentence but couldn't. Marsha nodded. She understood. And her tears hit the ground with an increasing regularity. "I can't produce children..." he was fighting for emotional control. "I can never be a father..."

That was it. It was out. He'd told her everything. They sat in silence for a long time, only their breathing echoed quietly across the green grass carpet. He wanted her to talk, to say something, anything. He'd talked for fifteen minutes, she could at least respond. She could nod or pat his hand or say "It's alright," or something. But there was nothing.

"Marsha, " he finally whispered. "You're the first and only woman I've ever loved in my life. I want you to think over what I've just told you before you decide what you want to do about us. Take your time. Day. Two. Whatever you need."

As they walked back to her apartment, Yakoff told her he'd stay away and give her time to think, only returning at night to sleep on the cot in the kitchen. She didn't speak another word the entire way.

He walked the streets alone, occasionally stopping for a drink with a Russian soldier. He was confused and frightened, thrilled Marsha was alive but deathly afraid of her eventual response. Relieved he'd finally told her the horrible truth but concerned about having shared his life-long pain with the woman he loved. All he could do was hope. That's all he had left.

It was dark when he returned, darker than the night before. He wanted to safely wait until their dinner was over so he wouldn't have to politely sit through more idle, worthless chitchat. Right now that was the last thing he needed. He needed his aloneness, as did Marsha.

The older man had already retired and Marsha was waiting-up alone. She wasn't wearing the scarf Yakoff had given her. He noticed but didn't say anything as she motioned for him to sit on a nearby couch. It was apparent her crying had continued throughout most of the day. Her eyes were red and her cheeks blotchy.

This time she was going to verbalize her response, and asked just as Yakoff had earlier, that he wait until she finished before he said anything. There were no hugs, kisses or embraces, only two young people too hurt and embarrassed to even look into each other's eyes.

Emotion crept in and out of her voice but she tried to remain mechanical in her delivery. What she had to say was difficult enough

266

and Yakoff didn't fault her attempt at maintaining composure. As he listened he could feel his fingers, hands and entire body begin to quiver and tremble. I am the man, he told himself over and over. I have to be strong.

She explained that the gentleman she was staying with was actually functioning as her mentor. He was helpful in her readjustment to freedom and provided much valuable advice and counsel. They'd talked all day she said, about the situation Yakoff had introduced that morning and the long term results marrying him would have on her life.

"He likes you," she said. "He really does. And he couldn't be more sympathetic about what happened..."

Yakoff felt a flash of anger and betrayal. What he'd told Marsha this morning, no one knew. No one. Now she'd shared the whole rotten thing and all its sordid details with a stranger. It was difficult but he took a deep breath and held his temper.

"But," she slowly continued, "there's more." Now Yakoff looked up at her and the look was unreturned. She explained her friend and quasi guardian had a nephew in Russia who was going to be visiting Lodz in the near future. He'd suggested Marsha wait until she met the other young man before she made a final and lasting decision about Yakoff.

Sure, Yakoff thought, weighing the overbalanced irony, wait until you can meet a real man, one who can satisfy you and make you feel like a real woman. He captured the thoughts and held them closely within.

Marsha saved her personal and innermost feelings for the last. Yakoff could feel her hurt as the words drifted slowly from her mouth. It was difficult and painful but it had to be verbalized. She had to be equally honest with the man she loved.

"There aren't." she quietly said, "many of us left...you know... Jews." Yakoff knew. "It's important..." the words came out slow with difficulty, "for Jewish children to be born, for families to be raised who can raise other families..." Her words trailed off but that was unimportant. Yakoff clearly knew in his heart what she was saying. Further explanation was unnecessary.

He rose, looking down at her and slowly nodded agreement. She was right and there was no logic in the world which could dispute her feelings or words. Without speaking he walked to the kitchen and quietly repacked his valise.

She was standing when Yakoff returned to the living room, tears streaming down both cheeks. There was bewilderment, confusion and hurt in her eyes. And worst of all, there was no possible way he could remove or diminish any trace or degree of it. They held each other for only a moment, each truly knowing it would be their last embrace. Then Yakoff forced a small smile, whispered goodbye and walked silently out of her life.

Chapter XXI

The high-energy party stopped dead in its tracks when Yakoff appeared at the front door. The entire group was near shock for they all expected to be meeting Marsha, the girl they'd heard so much about. Several asked the obvious question but Yakoff shook his head and finally silenced them all with, "It didn't work out."

There were a few sincere "That's too bads" but mostly blank, disbelieving stares. They didn't know the extenuating circumstances and Yakoff felt further explanation was unnecessary. It was a long uncomfortable moment before someone cheerily suggested, "Well, let's get this boy back on track with a little action." Two attractive German girls moved toward Yakoff, one on each side, ready to chase away his blues and depression, ready to help him forget.

A cursory stare froze them both where they stood. Now it was very quiet. "I have work to do," was all he said as he dropped his valise, turned and left the apartment.

He wanted to cry but tears wouldn't come because he knew in his heart Marsha was right. He respected her feelings as well as honesty but that didn't take away the pain. He was alone and would continue to be alone. Worthless as a lover, worthless as a man. His self-esteem and self-respect diminished to the point of virtual nonexistence. Instead of passion or lust, he felt anger and frustration each time he saw or met an available female.

He buried himself in the counterintelligence work, transferring his self-disdain and frustration into nonstop activity as a Nazi hunter. His success continued and his tactics altered. He grew vicious and ruthless using methods of interrogation he'd learned from the Nazis themselves, methods previously used on himself. The Nazis were good teachers, he'd callously remind himself each time he forced a confession.

The rest of the group, his friends, began to openly criticize his lack of assistance with the bakeries. No one could figure out his renewed passion in helping the Russians. But that didn't matter either. Nothing did. He didn't need friends, he didn't need anyone. He was alone and that's the way it was going to be.

The drinking increased, which was an obvious side-effect. The soldiers would play accordions and sing and dance among themselves and Yakoff joined in with their merriment. There wasn't anything else for him to do. He couldn't sleep, he couldn't eat, he just tracked and interrogated Germans and then drank with the Russians until he passed out. He was drinking away Marsha, drinking away his condition, trying to forget it all. After what I've been through he concluded, this is my destiny. What a life.

Completely by accident, while standing on a street corner drinking vodka from a barrel with several soldiers, he met a young girl and her brother. They were lost and in need of directions which were mechanically given. When Yakoff looked at the girl, a spark of some sort danced between their eyes. He shrugged it off as he watched them walk away.

The two returned the following evening to thank him for helping them. The spark occurred again, this time even stronger. They talked and then the three went for some coffee. The girl was attractive and it was obvious she liked Yakoff. Why shouldn't she? He was good looking, well versed in several languages and cultures, traveled, and had a lot of money.

Yakoff enjoyed the attention being heaped upon him but his logic and common sense challenged every heartbeat. He told himself not to get involved and avoided ever being alone with her. But his emotions were taking control. He was mixed. He wanted to but knew he couldn't.

Hilda was her name, petite, gleaming black eyes and hair, attractive to the point men always looked twice whenever she walked by. Yakoff felt a sense of pride when they were together but the pride was always tempered by the same burning frustration which would not, could not go away. The knowledge he couldn't do for her what any other man could, ate at his insides like a raging cancer.

He tried not seeing her, tried being impolite, tried avoiding her and even refused to talk whenever she and her brother came around. None of it worked. She was too magnetic, too appealing, the spark refused to go away. He wanted her desperately, and each time the feeling surfaced, it was like a long dull butcher knife twisting slowly in his heart.

The Russians, the streets, and the vodka were his only temporal relief, drinking himself to oblivion and the point of believing some miracle might somehow occur and magically return his manhood. The numbness, just before he passed out, was the best and easiest time of the day.

Yakoff awoke that particular morning in a strange bed, a strange place. Nothing was familiar except the hangover pounding like a twelve pound sledge hammer at both temples. He was confused, disoriented, wearing strange bed clothing, certainly not his own. He focused slowly and looked around the room searching for his own clothes and more importantly his pistol. He had absolutely no idea where he was. Not a clue. Then he heard a familiar voice from the other room.

It was Hilda, speaking with her brother in whispers. Probably being polite, Yakoff thought, so they won't wake me up. He felt odd and out of place in someone else's pajamas but wasn't quite sure what to do. Then, for the first time it occurred to him: how in the hell did I get here? He tried but couldn't get a handle on an answer.

"Hilda," he called in a voice a little louder than normal, wreaking havoc with his brain cells. He was rubbing his eyes and holding his head when they both entered. He greeted them with a sheepish grin.

"Good morning," he said, testing the water.

They returned the greeting without smiles.

"Are you alright?" Hilda cautiously asked.

"Other than a little confused." There was a long, dry pause and another grin. "Could someone possibly explain how I got here?"

"We found you last night," Hilda's brother said. "Passed out in the gutter. We were afraid you'd get run over or something so we brought you up here."

Yakoff nodded, indicating thanks for their concern and trouble. The mood was solemn, actually grim. He was going to apologize but chose instead to show his appreciation later by taking them both out for dinner, possibly even some small gift.

He was a little embarrassed with his next sentence. "Uh, what about my clothes? I mean, how did I get into these things?"

Hilda's brother cleared his throat. "The second we laid you down in bed you started to throw up." Yakoff grimaced and closed his eyes. He felt like an idiot. "All over everything. The bed, yourself, everything..." Now he felt even worse. "We had to prop you up in a chair while we changed the sheets and had to get you out of what you were wearing."

"You're good friends," Yakoff said. "Really good friends. I appreciate your help." But the mind was questioning who actually changed his clothes. He wasn't wearing any underwear, so one or perhaps both of them had discovered his secret. He started to speak but fear held his tongue.

"We washed your clothes and hung them by the stove in the kitchen. They're dry now."

With that as a cue, Hilda left the room and returned seconds later carrying his clothing. She still hadn't spoken more than three words. Then, just as coldly, they both left him alone to get dressed.

As Yakoff left the apartment, he told them he'd be back later that evening and they'd all go out for dinner. Their response was less than enthusiastic but he was confident he could make it all up to them. They were, after all, good friends.

His confidence waned throughout the day as he questioned over and over if Hilda had been in the room while he was naked. He became nervous and tense at its probability. She was the only one who could honestly answer or put him anywhere near being at ease. Painfully, he deduced he had to tell them both the whole story. They'd understand, they were friends. Even if she hadn't seen, he was going to tell her anyway.

He bought fresh flowers on the way over. A peace offering. His last conscious thought as he knocked on their front door was the question plaguing him all day: was Hilda in the room? Did she see?

There was no answer. That's odd, he thought. So he knocked again, this time louder. Still no answer. When he turned the doorknob it was unlocked and the door creaked as he pushed it open.

The apartment was empty. Their clothing and personal belongings had all been removed, only the furniture remained. There was no note, no nothing. He stood in the emptiness knowing his bothersome question had just been answered.

The majority of the Russian military started to evacuate, heading west, cleaning up towns along the way that they'd conquered. Only a skeleton of the main force remained to act as little more than policemen while the Poles reorganized. At first there was little noticeable change, life went on much as it had since the Russians arrived. Then two rather dramatic events occurred.

"We're pulling out, Yakoff. Leaving day after tomorrow." The captain was all military. He never showed any emotion, the epitome of a well-trained soldier.

"But why? I mean..."

"Our work is done here. We got the majority of the Nazis and it's time to move on."

Military decisions were something he had learned to accept so

Yakoff merely nodded. He didn't agree completely because he felt there were still SS people in hiding. But any further discussion or conversation would have only proven to be moot.

Then an interesting thing happened. The captain let down his military guard and spoke with Yakoff as if he were a friend rather than a volunteer. He thanked him for his assistance, dedication and perseverance over the past four months and assured him if there were medals or citations to hand out, Yakoff would certainly be the first recipient.

A feeling of pride and accomplishment followed the rare and humanistic display. And true to his word, two days later, the sign on the front of the building which read "Counterintelligence Office" was missing. The office, stark to begin with, was now completely bare, as if it never existed.

The second event concerned the Polish citizenry. With the Russians, from a command position out of the picture, the Poles began to quickly exercise muscles which had been bound for a very long time. Once they were back in power their first order of the day was to insist, forcibly in some cases, that everyone within the city register by name, address, occupation and citizenship.

The plan was not well received but as the police force was considerably enlarged it was somewhat adhered to universally. The scene was comparable to a cattle drive with long lines of people waiting to get the seemingly worthless ordeal out of the way.

"Name?..."

"Yakoff Skurnik."

"Address?..."

He told him.

"Occupation?..."

"Baker."

"Citizenship?..."

"Stateless."

The clerk looked up. He was new on the job and hadn't heard that one before. He rubbed his lower lip with the eraser of his pencil and raised one eyebrow.

"I beg your pardon?..."

"Stateless. I have no country."

The man with the pencil hesitated for another second and Yakoff slightly increased the volume of his voice, "Write it down." So the man did.

Yakoff wasn't the first and certainly not the last to claim stateless citizenship. Many Jews felt no kinship, allegiance or loyalty whatsoever to Poland. The majority of the survivors had no remaining family, real hometown, so to speak, or friends to return to. Poland, historically, was bathed in anti-Semitism. Yakoff grew up with it as did virtually every other Jew still alive.

With the war over and the country in a rebuilding process, there were new places to go and lives to start anew. It was a simple and rather obvious decision. The Jews were tired of being persecuted and were going to go somewhere, anywhere else. They were individually in search of a country where freedom was substantive and meaningful, where it meant more than something you gave hollow lip-service to.

Most Poles traditionally, over and above their inbred anti-Semitism, were willing to assist the Nazis in finding and pointing out Jewish citizens. Many had openly betrayed their own supposed countrymen, not all to save their own lives either. An alarming percentage of Poles exposed Jews in hiding or trying to pass as gentiles in order to stay alive because they believed in the Nazi mentality, perverse as it was, of Arian supremacy.

Yakoff and many like himself felt allegiance to Poland as a country, a government, or the individuals who remained, was wrong. It was wrong from a moral, ethical and religious standpoint. How could he ever believe in or be supportive of a nation of people who'd opened basement doors so Nazi machine guns could viciously murder innocent women and children? He couldn't. And he wasn't alone in his feelings. He was a stateless citizen, a man without a country.

On the other hand, he was most certainly a man in search of a country. The priorities he'd established over the years and the criterias he was searching for began with freedom: freedom to worship, act and be as he wished. Mostly perhaps, it was freedom from unjustified persecution. He dreamed of a land of opportunity; where ability and talent, hard work and perseverance were rewarded. He longed for a country where peace prevailed, where rocks weren't thrown and bullets weren't fired.

Poland was not that country or place and he honestly felt down deep in his heart it never would be. The faraway lands most often spoken of were America, Canada, Australia and Israel, the newly established home-land and country of the Jews. Their wandering had ceased. The state of Palestine had finally earned the status of country. Jews throughout the world, after thousands of years, at last had a place they could refer to as home.

With a struggling Polish government back in power, the Jews

instantly reverted to their second-class citizenship. Yakoff, virtually without any authority in the absence of the Russians and their unchallenged military, returned to work in the bakeries where he spent most of his time. It was time he was biding, for he knew soon it would be necessary to leave Breslau and find his way to another country. That was the underlying thought on nearly everyone's mind.

Edith was Jewish. She came into the bakery to buy a loaf of bread one day and somehow never quite managed to leave. She and Yakoff went through the ritual of dating for awhile and then the announcement to friends of a semiformal engagement, but she virtually moved bag and baggage into Yakoff's apartment only days after their first meeting.

It was an interesting relationship which grew and developed over the months they were together. She was young and attractive, like Marsha and Hilda, but it was different. She was attractive in a foreign way, aloof from most, a little removed. Yakoff had been badly burned twice and refused to allow any pretense to come between them.

The first night they slept together he told her about the operation and his condition. In the dark she said she understood but he fully expected, as he drifted off to sleep, to find her side of the bed empty in the morning. He was right.

He felt remorse but silently accepted the finality of what was. Yes, the pain returned and no, he couldn't fault her decision or hate her for her actions. Then he heard a noise from the kitchen. Seconds later he was standing in the doorway watching Edith prepare a gigantic break-fast for both of them. She'd stayed. She hadn't crept off in the middle of the night after all. Maybe she did understand. Maybe she cared enough that she really could deal with Doering's butchery and love him unconditionally.

Sometimes honesty has a tendency of begetting other honesty. Not always, just sometimes. Such was the case with Edith. Eventually she told Yakoff, plain and straightforward, she was interested in leaving the country and Europe if possible. She knew Yakoff would be leaving in the not too distant future and set her sights on going with him. The trade didn't bother Yakoff, it didn't even offend him.

As for their getting married and leaving the country together, well, that was a long way down the road. It was the proverbial bridge which would one day have to be crossed. Nothing to worry about for awhile. For the time being, they'd enjoy life and continue to make money with the bakeries.

But the money and profits began to slowly dwindle. Supplies were still available but in the absence of the Russian army they had to be purchased.

The group wasn't working at a hundred percent profit margin anymore. The government, anxious to replenish their depleted treasury, levied taxes on all individuals and businesses. At first it was small, almost a token, perhaps to get people used to the idea. Then with quick and increasing regularity it became larger and larger, more and more. People grumbled and complained but the government was persistent to the point of assigning individuals to watch particular businesses. Money was collected on a weekly and sometimes daily basis. Even so, the bakeries continued to provide profits, just not as much as they had in the earlier days.

Wayward travelers, friends and strangers, continued to stay with Yakoff whenever they were passing through town. One such visitor was Heim Berkovich, Yakoff's closest friend from the bricklayers' school. Most reunions and finding someone alive who was believed dead, were causes for great celebrations and elaborate parties. When Heim showed up, the party went on for days.

It was also a time for reflection. So many people had perished that finding someone you knew from the camp always seemed to create a sense of awe and wonder. The fact any were still alive continued to be a miracle.

As prisoners in the camp, their conversations centered around their lives before they were captured and forced into the trains. They seldom if ever spoke about their future, for the probability of death was always just one short step away. Now, free at last and still alive, the future was the only thing they talked about. Where they were going, what they were going to do, so many plans to make and execute.

Heim proudly announced he was on his way to Israel, the promised land. The first stop he said was going to be Marburg, Germany, where he would stay until the completed arrangements were finalized.

What before had been a "one of these days" sort of thing, was now a crystal-clear reality. Yakoff's best and dearest friend was actually going to do it. He was going to leave Poland and start a new life in a free land. The thought and prospect which had been discussed so much and so often was happening, and Yakoff was excited about it.

Together they devised a plan where Heim would go on ahead by himself and set things up. He'd find an apartment for Yakoff and register him as a displaced person wishing to enter a foreign country with the respective consulate. That could be done before Yakoff's arrival and much time could be saved.

"Which one?" Heim asked.

"Which one what?" Yakoff asked back.

"Which country do you want me to register you for?"

That was a good question. Yakoff knew he was going to leave but seriously hadn't decided where he wanted to go. He pondered for a fraction of a moment, trying to keep all his options open. Then, "Israel, Canada and the United States."

"All three?"

"Uh huh."

Heim could tell he was serious. "But which one do you really want?"

"I'll go to whichever one opens up first."

They smiled broadly and embraced, each patting the other vigorously on the back. Yakoff was finally going to do it. Two days later he handed Heim the equivalent of five-thousand American dollars and waved excitedly as the train slowly chugged its way out of the station.

He had trouble sleeping that night. He laid in bed, eyes open, mind racing with sugarplum visions of his future, his new life. The uncertainty of where he was going created a tingling sensation mixed with excitement over the unknown. He felt good, happy, positive. Positive about everything except the young woman with him. No big deal he thought. We'll work it out when the time comes.

The time was coming sooner than he expected. Within three weeks a message arrived from Heim explaining everything was set up and the wheels were in motion. He read the letter several times, momentarily overtaken with joy. There was no particular need or reason for him to be in Marburg during the required waiting period so he decided to continue to live his relative life of luxury until he absolutely had to leave.

At least that was the plan until the man wearing the Polish army uniform came into the bakery. He was young and obviously proud of his brand-new clothing. He strutted around, making sure every customer took careful notice of both him and his stature of importance. When he made the announcement, "Yakoff Skurnik," his voice cracked and betrayed his adolescence. Smiles filled the room but laughter was suppressed.

Anxious to leave this most uncomfortable situation the soldier presented Yakoff with a sealed envelope looking very official. Then he hastily made his exit. The crowd on the other side of the display counters murmured impatiently. The majority of them were regular customers, knew Yakoff reasonably well and were more than curious about this rather unusual happening.

Yakoff broke the seal, removed the contents, studied it for a moment and then looked at the waiting audience with an expression bordering near shock.

"I've been drafted by the Polish army."

This was a by-product of the forced registration. The government was drafting every young male resident for service in the military. Yakoff had one week before he was to report for active duty.

Before the week was up they sold the bakeries to three Polish men who'd somehow managed to hide and retain some money during the German occupation. None of the three had a glimmer of an idea how a business should be run and their chances of success were remote. That wasn't a consideration in the transaction. Their money was good and that's all that mattered.

The day of his scheduled induction, Yakoff was packed on a train heading due west with a suitcase full of money and Edith.

Chapter XXII

Marburg was a reasonably isolated community with Frankfurt one hundred and fifty miles to the south and Bonn and Cologne about a hundred and seventy-five to the west. It was a melting pot of Europeans, all anxiously waiting to leave behind unmarked graves and sleepless, fear-filled nights. Military presence was also a force with a large contingency of American soldiers in control of the town. It was bustling, filled with activity, filled with people consumed and engulfed with dreams of a better life.

The communication from Heim was entirely accurate. He found an apartment for Yakoff that was perfect. It contained everything either a bachelor or a young engaged couple could possibly want. During his stay, Heim found something else–Sara–a young Jewish girl who was also a survivor from one of the camps. He was in love, blissfully, happily in love. They were going to be married and go to Israel together. Yakoff couldn't have been happier for his friend.

When the excitement over their upcoming journeys and Heim's announced engagement subsided, Yakoff inquired about the five thousand dollars. The expression on his face didn't change in the slightest when Heim told him, with considerable embarrassment, the money had been stolen. The subject was dropped and never broached again. It wasn't that important.

Rounds of visits and interviews with various consulates began. It wasn't at all what Yakoff had expected. Their interrogations, without the physical of course, almost bordered on the same level of intensity as the Germans or Russians. The Americans were the worst of the three. They wanted to know everything. Then they wanted to know it again.

The interviewer had a mustache which looked like it'd been drawn on, and equally thin eyebrows. One was permanently raised whenever Yakoff was in his office. His apparent primary concern, and the one he kept going over and over, was Yakoff's involvement with the Russians. He never quite said it out loud but persisted in intimating if Yakoff wasn't a Communist he must certainly be a Communist sympathizer. Volumes of contrary explanations didn't sway the man's opinion. His mind was set. He explained further investigation was necessary and continued to bury Yakoff's folder in the ever-growing pile. Also, to enter America you had to have a job waiting which was guaranteed upon your arrival. This was an undisputed prerequisite.

The two surviving relatives Yakoff had were an uncle and his grand-mother on his father's side. They were both in the United States living in New York and Yakoff wrote them asking for advice and assistance. Mail service was slow and the return letter seemed forever in coming.

The Canadian consulate, on the other hand, was eagerly accepting applicants. They brushed over Yakoff's involvement with the Russians as well as his activities as a Nazi hunter as if it were nothing. They did, however, have a rather unusual stipulation that seemed to concern itself with personal appearance more than anything else: you had to have all your own teeth or comparable replacements.

The Nazis and the Auschwitz experience had viciously removed several of Yakoff's teeth, at least a half dozen, and the practice of dentistry during the war years and immediately following was virtually nonexistent. The interviewer explained that the reasons for and the continuation thereof had no impact on their current regulations. Rules were rules. He was nice enough about it and said whenever the missing teeth were replaced to come back and admittance would be virtually automatic.

Yakoff shook his head in bewilderment as he walked away from the office. Who could believe such a thing? Imagine, teeth as a requirement to enter a country. It never did make sense to him and he wondered throughout the entire ordeal with the Canadians if there might have been some other unspoken reason for their hard-line attitude. He never knew.

The representative from Israel was an entirely different matter. Hebrew and Yiddish were spoken. There was a feeling of being at home. It was a new country starting virtually from scratch and opening their arms to anyone who would help the nation grow and thrive.

Going to Israel wasn't the problem; getting there was. Stories causing great concern had drifted back as far as Marburg itself. Exact quotas had been established for the numbers of people as well as the time-frame in which they would be allowed to enter. Yakoff could never figure that out nor could any of his friends, but that didn't alter the reality of the situation.

There were far more people anxious and wanting to go to Israel than the restrictive quota called for. So ships like the "Exodus" tried to circumvent the regulations and deliver these freedom-seeking passengers. The majority of the unauthorized vessels were stopped on the high seas by the British. The ship's inhabitants, mostly Jewish, were taken to the island of Cyprus to await final clearance for entry.

Cyprus, so the stories told, was certainly not in the same category as the concentration camps but call it whatever you wanted, the people on that island were still being detained against their will. That, as a possibility, was not appealing.

So the various interviews just dragged on and on. A large Jewish Community Center had been established and was helpful in providing assistance of various kinds to those who impatiently waited to get out. Within a few weeks Yakoff realized he was probably going to be spending more time in Marburg than was originally anticipated. He knew if America was going to be his final destination he'd have to have some sort of skill or trade which would guarantee his employment.

The help the center made available was invaluable. They enrolled him at the University of Marburg and paid the full tuition. At last he had something else to do with his time in addition to the rounds and rounds of seemingly pointless interviews.

School was interesting enough. There were about thirty other people in his class, all there for the specific purpose of learning to be film projectionists. They were instructed in thirty-five millimeter equipment operation, repair and film splicing. It was all new to Yakoff and carried a certain sense of intrigue, since he'd never seen equipment like this. The challenge of taking something apart, putting it back together and making it work again was fascinating and the young man seemed to possess an innate ability to accomplish the assignments successfully.

A package finally arrived from the United States. Understandably his uncle and grandmother were thrilled to learn he was still alive. The carefully wrapped box also contained an assortment of different foods, all of which were eagerly consumed by Yakoff and some close friends.

He immediately wrote back to them explaining about the university and the education he was receiving. Perhaps with this information his uncle might have an easier time in securing the necessary letter which would guarantee his employment. Then another thought began to take hold. His grandmother was getting along in years and had clearly expressed in her letter she'd like to see Yakoff before she died.

He really didn't have any idea how old she was, that was something he'd lost track of completely. Denying her request would certainly have been difficult for she was his only surviving blood relative. The more he thought about it the more he realized he wanted to see and be with her, perhaps as much as she did with him. There was an inner need to capture some of the past and place it in a timeless state where it could be fondly remembered and carefully guarded. She was the only person alive who could help him do that.

There was a short block in the downtown district which had several cafes and coffee houses. Each seemed to have its own ethnic origin and functioned as meeting places for friends, old and new. Individual languages were spoken at these places and heated conversations would sometimes last until early in the morning.

Yakoff was with Edith and a few other friends when he saw a familiar figure walking down the sidewalk on the other side of the street. He strained, trying to make him out, but he was too far away to see. Still there was something–the walk, the carriage-something. He drifted out of his own conversation, studying the other side of the road.

The man went into a sidewalk cafe and from his gestures and mannerisms, it was apparent he was looking for someone. After a brief conversation with a waiter the man turned and looked back across the street. In the light Yakoff could see the face. He could see it, he just couldn't believe it.

He stood, pushing his chair back, and began to walk away from the table. Edith and the others watched speechlessly, having no earthly idea what was going on. When he reached the sidewalk, the man on the other side of the street finally recognized him and they both stopped for a second, as if visually examining one another.

The man was David Levin, Yakoff's friend from Auschwitz; one of the men who had undergone the same terrible sterilization and butcherous castration.

They walked slowly, like gunslingers, to the middle of the street where they looked at each other for one more second and then embraced. They whispered as if trying to protect the secret they shared from the rest of the world.

"I heard you were alive and I had to find you." David's voice was strong, filled with understandable emotion.

"Where have you been? How did you get away?" Then holding David's shoulders, "How are you?"

"Time for that later. I had to find you because I have good news for both of us ." Yakoff instantly recognized the seriousness in his friend's voice and listened intently. "I have heard about a doctor, in Paris, who has great sympathy for men like you and me..."

Yakoff knew what he was saying, "Yes..."

"He performed an operation on a man like us who was also castrated and it was successful. It helped the man, Yakoff. It helped."

Paris was beautiful. It was fall and the leaves were changing. The fact they were traveling without papers or authorization mattered little. It was a trip which had to be taken regardless of the cost or risk. The twisting agony resulting from the loss of his manhood was a constant thing, as obvious to Yakoff as the loss of an arm or a leg. The difference was, there were no replacement parts, nothing could compensate for the deficiency. Nor were there any pills available to stifle or still the wants and desires in his mind and heart.

Doctor Dubois was much younger than they'd expected. He looked to be in his early thirties and had dark blue eyes with a piercing quality nearly as effective as his scalpel. Outwardly he displayed the normal qualities of a surgeon: cool, distant, incredibly professional. But as he listened to their story, they could feel his sense of compassion and caring.

Dubois confirmed the story David Levin had heard. He had indeed performed the surgical procedure on another castration victim.

"There are no guarantees," he said.

"We understand," Levin replied.

"What else can we do?" Yakoff added. "You are our only hope."

"And," Dubois continued, "even if the operation's a success, it could still be only temporary." Their quizzical looks explained their lack of comprehension. "It might not work all the time..."

"You mean the erection?"

Dubois nodded. "And we don't know how long it'll last."

Nothing he could say would alter their feelings or change their minds. Yakoff had captured it completely with his "last hope" statement.

They were admitted that afternoon for tests and more tests. Some were just a pain in the neck, others hurt elsewhere. When they broached the subject of cost Dubois insisted that since it was considered to be experimental surgery it would be performed without any fees.

Testing went on for a week, the same ones over and over. It didn't make any sense to either of them but they weren't going to question anything the good doctor said or did. For all practical purposes they were placing their futures in the hands of a total stranger.

But the "stranger" concept had disappeared by the day of the operation. During countless visits they'd grown to know the man well and trusted him completely. It was obvious to both David and Yakoff that Dubois wanted permanent and lasting success from this endeavor as much as they did. The last thing Yakoff remembered before the anesthesia took over was the three of them shaking hands and all wishing each other good luck.

Edith was lovely. Her pure white skin was silhouetted by three candles flickering on the nightstand. As she moved toward the bed her nakedness became more clearly defined and an excitement raged through Yakoff. It was surging, wavelike, a new feeling, unusual and quite wonderful.

Even though he'd slept with her for more than a hundred nights it was the first time he'd really noticed her perfectly formed body. When she slowly removed two ivory combs her soft brown hair fell slowly to the middle of her chest and back. It acted as a frame, erotic, incredibly exciting, dangling temptingly on either side of her firm, inviting breasts. Her nipples were erect, a dark, passionate shade of red, nearly as red as her moist waiting lips.

With his eyes, he traced her untouched skin slowly down to her pubic area. It was fascinating and he stared, for he knew this was the first time he could offer satisfaction to her virgin treasure.

There was a swelling in his groin, foreign but discernible. A slight smile edged its way onto the corners of his mouth. He wanted to look, to see the miracle himself, but Edith's eyes reflected all he needed to know.

They opened wide and her smile matched his own. She moved her tongue from side to side across her upper lip and it glistened in the candle-light. Her breasts enlarged with a deep inhale and small gurgling sounds of exploding passion escaped from her throat. A clear drop of fluid began to slowly crawl down her inner thigh as she stood by the side of the bed and leaned forward, reaching with her silk-soft hand for Yakoff's erection.

Everything was a slow moving cloud of white, like a sheet of swirl-ing, steaming milk. He could hear voices but couldn't understand what was being said. He tried to shake his head, to clear the cobwebs, to get some focus but it wouldn't move. He remembered shaking hands with David and Doctor Dubois...

That was it. Doctor Dubois. The strange voices he was hearing were French. Moments later, the doctor entered the recovery room. "There was no pain," Yakoff said, and both of them were pleased with that news.

Dubois told him the hormonal implant, just under the skin and inserted in his lower left stomach wall, had gone smoothly. Determining the success of the procedure was now a matter of time.

The recovery period lasted nearly a month and by the end of it Yakoff had mastered another language. His mind was incessantly on Edith and how things were going to be when he returned to Marburg, when the pleasant and nearly continual dream would become a reality.

When Yakoff and Edith separated, they mutually and maturely decided their future would be dealt with and determined upon his return. It wasn't really spoken but they both knew if the operation was successful they'd remain together. Based on all early indications, that was certainly the case. He missed her and was anxious, more anxious than ever to see her.

Edith was staying with a sister and a brother-in-law at a displaced persons' camp about twenty-five miles from Marburg. They felt that would be much safer than remaining in the apartment by herself. Yakoff met them on several occasions and was comforted she was with friends and not sitting at home alone and becoming bored.

As each day ticked slowly by he missed her more and more. The scenario for their reunion was replayed in his mind a thousand times. That was during the day. At night the dream repeated itself, growing more vivid with each recurrence. He was ready.

When the month was finally over David Levin decided to remain in Paris. After listening to Yakoff go on and on about Edith, he didn't even bother to ask if he wanted to stay with him.

"I can't thank you enough Doctor." There was no question about his sincerity. "You've changed my life. You've given me..."

Dubois held up his hand, stopping Yakoff in midsentence. The accolades were fine and certainly appreciated, but the real test was yet to come.

"Hold your thanks until after you've been with Edith he said, smiling. Then for the hundredth time, he explained the uncertainty of the efficiency of the implant. It was iffy at best. "No one knows..."

This time Yakoff interrupted him. "I'll be fine, Doc. I'll come see you again when it stops working."

Dubois walked him to the front door of the hospital. There wasn't much left for either of them to say. Six weeks and circumstance had drawn them close to one another, almost like a team or a partnership which now had to split up in order to gauge its effectiveness. The parting was quick; it was best that way.

Edith was lovely, just like the dream. She had on a white dress that looked like it was made of gauze and her hair reflected the bouncing sunlight. Her open arms were a welcome sight but when they embraced and pressed their bodies together Yakoff felt a distance, an unexplainable and undefinable space between them. He didn't say anything in front of her relatives and his confused silence continued all the way back to their own apartment.

She was beautiful, even more so than he remembered. A fragrance of some spring flower was on her neck and it only served to further ignite his already peaking desire. It was a challenge to keep his hands off her in the course of the twenty-five mile journey. Yet the smile was disturbing, haunting, like she knew something he didn't. Perhaps it was a secret of some sort. Yes, that's it. A secret. Good news. He decided to go along with her little game and let her tell him what it was in her own good time. After all, what else could it be?

The late fall German wind was brisk and chilled them as they fumbled with the key to the apartment door. Yakoff was internally pleased with his assessment of the situation. He smiled to himself as he pulled his jacket collar a little closer to his neck.

A drink. That's it. He'd suggest a drink to warm them as well as offer her an opportunity to talk and explain her secret before they went to bed and made love. He poured, mulling over the decision he'd made to postpone the passion. He wanted her desperately but was overcome with fright. He was nervous to the point of trembling, so much so, the neck of the vodka bottle was tapping out a steady beat on the edge of the glass. It was embarrassing and he held the bottle with both hands. It didn't help.

He smiled, still nervous, as he handed Edith her glass. "To us,' he said, lifting his own.

She lowered hers and stared at the floor. "We need to talk about us." Her voice was slow and flat. She enunciated clearly, making sure Yakoff completely understood every word.

He turned his back, downed his drink and cleared his throat. "I guess there's something you want to tell me..."

He didn't have to turn around to know she was shaking her head yes, He filled his glass and listened quietly while she spoke.

At first she danced with the subject, saying how long he'd been away, how lonely she'd been, things like that, insignificant trivia as a preface to the crux of the conversation. He knew what was coming and fixed another tall drink.

Two more after that and she finally got to it. There's this man, she said, who lived near her sister's house and was friends with her brother-in-law. Well, anyway, one night he came over for dinner and since she was so lonely, this nice man offered to talk with her and provide some moral support. Support turned into lunches, then dinners, then movies and long walks with intimate conversations in the moonlight.

"He's the captain of a soccer team..." then she stopped. Evidently that was the end of her story, her secret.

"Do you love him?" It was difficult, but he got the words out without choking on them.

"Yes."

Edith slept in the bed, alone. Yakoff spent the night in the living room. Again and again he reflected over the last six weeks of his life. The changes, the conversations, the operation, the waiting, hoping and dreaming. He dwelled particularly over one of the last things Doctor Dubois had said, the line about holding his thanks until after he'd been with Edith.

Through the unfair irony of it all he wanted to smile but the pain wouldn't allow it. She tried to continue the discussion in the morning but he couldn't. There wasn't anything left to say. When he dropped her off at her sister's apartment there were no tearful good-byes. Actually, there were no words spoken. Life would go on. At the moment he had no idea how, but he knew somehow it would.

The weeks turned into months and the months into years. Permission was granted to enter Israel but because of his grandmother he'd decided to go to the United States. That decision was turning into a nightmarish eternity of red tape, stalls and delays. The boring wait had a slow, grating effect, like a dentist grinding down a tooth without novocaine. Fewer and fewer people remained. There was little if anything to do. The town was dull and listless.

Yakoff had been in Marburg for nearly three tortuous years, waiting for any one of several people to make a positive decision in his favor. Several friends had come through and all were gone. Harry Foreman was there for awhile and he was now in America. Heim and Sara got married and made it safely to Israel. He was the only one left.

287

The displaced persons camps remained but their populations dwindled considerably. Even the country was returning to relative normalcy, at least as much as a postwar country could. The prospect of spending the rest of his life in Germany was unappealing, depressing, and something he couldn't do, not after what Germany had done to him.

There was yet another change at the American consulate, a new head man was coming. After three more weeks of waiting, Yakoff was finally granted an appointment. He'd been through it before, countless times, and had no real reason to believe this time would be any different.

Yakoff was polite, as usual. The man was distinguished with greying temples and an expensive three-piece suit. He nodded as he shuffled through the thick file and listened to the story. They spoke in German.

Yakoff was frustrated, in a corner with no way out. Under his breath and to himself he whispered, "It just doesn't make any sense..." the difference was, the words were muttered in Yiddish.

"What did you say?" the man asked.

"Nothing." There was resolve in his voice.

The man smiled and repeated the question, only this time also in Yiddish. Yakoff was stunned, taken aback. "Tell you what," the man said, "let me look into your case and you meet me here tomorrow at noon."

After extensive thanks and a sleepless night Yakoff returned to the office. The man, continuing his smile, said it looked like something might be arranged. There was a large bulletin board in the main hall of the building where names of people who'd been granted permission to travel were posted. "Check the board," the man said and shook Yakoff's hand warmly.

The next morning he was there when the list was posted. Nothing, followed by intense grief and more depression. He'd been tricked, lied to, he wanted to choke the man till the buttons on his vest popped off. Not a particularly wise plan of action.

The second morning he returned because he didn't have anything else to do. The corridor was empty and the daily list had already been posted. The walk was slow and mechanical, without expectation. He had to read it three times before his mind would accept and believe his name was actually there.

The rest of the afternoon was spent standing in lines in the administrative office on the first floor of the building. He'd spent over three years around and with people who were on their way to a new life and at last he was one of them.

"Yes?" the kind-faced lady behind the counter asked.

"My name is Yakoff Skurnik..." The announcement was proud, a volume the entire room could hear. The message, while simplistic in its five short words, was destined to alter and affect the lives of countless individuals throughout the passage of time. In his heart, young Yakoff knew, that someday his brutal wounds, contracted during the greatest atrocity known to mankind, would heal enough that the tragic story could finally be told.

"..and I'm going to America."

Epilogue

Yakoff Skurnik arrived in New York on October fifth, 1949, the day he still considers to be his official birthday. Less than two weeks prior to his departure his grandmother died.

Later that year, while washing dishes for three dollars a day and completely by accident, he ran into Hershel Prengler on the lower east side of the city. Hershel was the friend Yakoff met in Katovitz, traveled to Breslau with, and started the bakery business with.

Hershel, a resident of Dallas, was visiting New York for a wedding. He invited Yakoff to come to Texas and start another business together. The off-the-cuff but serious proposal was more than intriguing and within the month Yakoff boarded a train and ventured into the deep west.

He arrived in Dallas possessing a dollar and thirteen cents, a deep-seated will to survive and a burning passion for freedom and success.

They opened a dry goods store with borrowed merchandise, lived in a ten dollar a month, one-room apartment and Yakoff taught himself to speak English by listening to local radio stations.

With hard work and nonstop, backbreaking hours the business flourished and they became respected pillars in the community. Eventually, Yakoff sold his half of the enterprise and traveled to California where he proudly became a U.S. citizen in the fall of 1954 and legally changed his name to Jack Oran.

Missing Dallas and many friends he returned to Texas still possessing the entrepreneurial spirit. After many careful months of searching he opened the Lone Star Bicycle Repair Shop. Sales and services expanded to lawn mowers and even motor scooters. The business grew steadily.

In October of 1964 he added a line of Yamaha motorcycles and eventually phased out all the other facets and merchandise. Today, Lone Star Cycle, in Dallas, Texas, is one of the leading motorcycle dealerships in the United States. Jack further expanded this thriving business in 1971 by adding Oran Imports, a major firm which provides parts and accessories to motorcycle dealers throughout America.

Jack Oran, by his dedication, deeds and actions, has triumphed and overcome personal loss and hardships that few people can even begin to comprehend. His story and his life, while tragic at the onset, is living, breathing proof that with persistence, faith and belief, the American Dream exists and lives on.

About the Author

Gene Church has previously had published: *The Pit* (E.P. Dutton/ Simon & Schuster) and *No Man's Blood* (Great Western Publishing Company). He has also written multiple episodes of *Quincy* for network television as well as a documentary on the life of Ernest Hemingway. Church has written and worked on several motion picture screenplays. *Circle of Power* based on his book *The Pit* was executive produced by Anthony Quinn and he recently completed *Shadows* for Columbia Pictures, Inc.